Sunset

BULBS

BY PHILIP EDINGER, SUSAN LANG, AND THE EDITORS OF SUNSET BOOKS

SUNSET BOOKS INC. • MENLO PARK, CALIFORNIA

AGE-OLD FAVORITES

Bulbs have a history stretching back thousands of years. Nomadic tribes gathered them for food; ancient agrarian societies cultivated a variety of edible bulbs, among them onions, garlic, taro, lilies, ginger—and even daylilies, which were grown for their blossoms. As food crops, all these plants offered the twin virtues of durability (a long shelf-life, to put it in modern terms) and portability.

Beyond their utilitarian value, of course, many bulbs offer floral beauty—a quality that cannot have been lost on the earliest civilizations. If such plants could be grown for food, why not for beauty, too? Today, the thriving commercial production of numerous bulbs purely for garden decoration attests to the allure of their flowers and foliage.

This volume offers ample proof of the charms of the varied plants we call "bulbs." As you'll discover, their culture involves no great mysteries; there truly are easy-to-grow bulbs for all climates and conditions. Turn the page—and begin your exploration.

SUNSET BOOKS INC.

Director, Sales and Marketing: Richard A. Smeby
Editorial Director: Bob Doyle
Production Director: Lory Day
Art Director: Vasken Guiragossian

Staff for this book:

Managing Editor: Suzanne Normand Eyre
Copy Editor and Indexer: Rebecca LaBrum
Photo Researcher: Tishana Peebles
Production Coordinator: Patricia S. Williams
Proofreader: Marianne Lipanovich

Art Director: Alice Rogers
Map Design and Cartography: Reineck & Reineck, San Francisco
Computer Production: Fog Press

Cover: *Hyacinthoides non-scripta.* Photography by VISIONS-Holland.
Border photograph (*Convallaria majalis*) by Saxon Holt.

PHOTOGRAPHERS:

Scott Atkinson: 41 bottom; **Max E. Badgley:** 18 bottom left-1, middle right-2, bottom right-1; **R. S. Byther:** 18 bottom left-2, bottom left-3, bottom right-3; **Marion Brenner:** 101 top; **Richard L. Carlton/Visuals Unlimited:** 18 top right-2; **David Cavagnaro:** 7 top right, middle right, bottom right, 18 top right-1, 45 bottom right, 61 top right, 68 top, 73 top, 77 top, 82 top, 97 left; **Peter Christiansen:** 9 bottom; **R. Cowles:** 18 top right-3; **Charles Cresson:** 22 bottom, 107 bottom; **Claire Curran:** 81 top, 83 top; **R. Todd Davis:** 6 top, 15 top right, 67 bottom left, 87 bottom; **Dr. Auguste DeHertogh:** 70 top; **Ken Druse:** 35 top right, 38 bottom, 47 left, 89 left, 94 bottom, 99 right; **Derek Fell:** 3 top, 3 middle bottom, 4, 6 middle, 7 top left, 18 middle right-3, 24, 33 top, 42 bottom, 49 right, 61 bottom right, 67 top right, 69, 72 bottom, 78 bottom left, 96 bottom, 102 right, back cover top right; **William E. Ferguson:** 14 bottom; **David Goldberg:** 18 bottom right-2, 77 bottom; **William Grenfell/Visuals Unlimited:** 18 middle right-1; **Thomas Hallstein:** 41 top; **Lynne Harrison:** 7 bottom left, 40 top, 47 bottom right, 53 left, 54 top, 56 top, 60 top, 65 top, 66 top, 71 middle right, 85 top, 88 top, 104 top left; **Saxon Holt:** 6 bottom left, 14 top, middle, 17 bottom, 21 middle right, 23 top, 26 top right, 27 top, 28 left, 32 top, 34, 35 left, 35 bottom right, 36, 37 bottom, 44, 45 top right, 46, 53 bottom right, 56 bottom, 65 bottom, 84 right, 98, 103 bottom right, back cover bottom; **Horticultural Photography:** 57 bottom; **David McDonald/PhotoGarden:** 29 middle, 42 top; **Kevin Miller:** 76 top; **N. and P. Mioulane/M.A.P.:** 3 bottom, 30, back cover top left; **Netherlands Flowers:** 101 bottom; **Don Normark:** 43 top; **Hugh Palmer:** 15 top right, 63, 78 top left, 100 right; **Park Seed Co.:** 84 left; **Jerry Pavia:** 6 bottom right, 15 top left, 60 bottom, 62, 64 bottom, 68 bottom, 75 bottom right, 81 bottom, 82 bottom, 87 top, 91 top, 92 right, 99 left, 104 bottom right, 107 top; **Joanne Pavia:** 7 middle left, 59 bottom, 70 bottom, 79 bottom; **Pamela K. Peirce:** 23 bottom, 72 top, 105 right; **Norman A. Plate:** 1, 2, 8, 9 top, 13 bottom, 16 top and bottom left, 17 top, 20, 21 top, bottom left, bottom center, bottom right, 26 bottom left, 32 bottom, 52 bottom, 71 bottom right, 73 bottom, 74 left, 75 top right, 85 bottom, 86, 92 left, 105 left, 106 left; **Susan Roth:** 40 bottom, 67 bottom right, 71 left, 100 bottom left; **Eric Tankesley-Clark:** 74 right, 76 bottom; **Michael S. Thompson:** 13 top, 26 bottom right, 27 bottom, 28 right, 29 bottom, 37 top, 38 top, 39, 45 left, 47 top right, 48 top, 49 left, 50 top, 52 top, 53 top right, 54 bottom, 58, 66 bottom, 71 top right, 75 bottom left, 78 top right, 80, 90, 93, 94 top, 95, 96 top, middle, 102 left, 103 top right, 106 right; **VISIONS-Holland:** 3 middle top, 10, 22 top, 29 top, 43 bottom, 48 bottom, 50 bottom, 51, 55, 59 top, 64 top, 79 top, 88 bottom, 97 right; **Darrow M. Watt:** 57 top, 83 bottom; **Wayside Gardens:** 91 bottom; **Peter O. Whiteley:** 16 top right, 87 middle, 103 top left; **Tom Woodward:** 33 bottom, 61 bottom left, 100 top left; **Tom Wyatt:** 12, 89 right.

Contents

The beauty of bulbs touches us in varied ways. The experience may be grand and overpowering—the breathtaking sight of a sweep of tulips in a public planting, for example—or as simple and intimate as encountering a single blooming snowdrop or crocus where only unbroken snow

HERE COME THE
BULBS

had been the day before. Sometimes, we expect to find bulbs' bounty: what is a summer wedding without arrangements of gladiolus, or a springtime brunch without pots of daffodils?

Visualize several popular bulbs—iris, hyacinth, tulip, daffodil, and lily—and you'll realize how greatly the plants we call "bulbs" can differ in appearance. They are so varied, in fact, that they raise an obvious question: what is the common thread drawing these seemingly unrelated plants together? The answer lies beneath the soil. All so-called bulbs grow from structures that serve as storage organs, depots where the plants accumulate nutrients to supply energy for growth and bloom in the year to come. Botanists draw firm distinctions between true bulbs and other structures with a similar function, but generations of gardeners have used "bulb" as a generic term both for true bulbs and for the plants that grow from bulblike organs: corms, tubers, rhizomes, and tuberous roots.

A sea of flowering bulbs proclaims that spring has come. Yellow narcissus and peach pink hyacinths *(Hyacinthus)* provide a splashy foreground for an imposing clump of orange-red crown imperial *(Fritillaria imperialis)*.

5

WHERE IN THE WORLD...?

TOP: *Crocus* and *Chionodoxa*
BOTTOM: *Sparaxis tricolor*

The bulbs in our gardens come from almost everywhere but Antarctica; their native lands represent virtually the complete range of habitable climates and encompass every combination of wet and dry, cold and hot. A look at these diverse climates explains the presence of bulbs in each: equipped with storage organs, the plants are well able to survive periods of less than hospitable weather. Knowing something of a particular bulb's native environment also makes it easier to understand that plant's needs in your garden.

DRY SUMMER, WET WINTER. The cradle of the world's bulb population is a broad latitudinal strip that extends from Spain and North Africa through the Mediterranean region, eastward through the Near East, Turkey, and Iran, and on into western China. Nearly all parts of this vast expanse experience winter precipitation (rain or snow) and hot, dry summers. In some areas (particularly the lands from central Asia into western China), winters are fairly cold, but much of this bulb-rich territory has the classic mild-winter Mediterranean climate. The same sort of climate reigns in California, parts of Chile, and South Africa's Cape Province; not surprisingly, these areas too are home to large bulb populations. Glory-of-the-snow *(Chionodoxa)*, crocus, freesia, ixia, and harlequin flower *(Sparaxis)* are just a few of the many bulbs native to dry-summer, wet-winter regions.

In such climates, bulbous plants grow during the cooler, moister period of autumn through early spring. As spring days grow longer and warmer, they begin to flower, sometimes seeming to rush into bloom while conditions are still favorable for setting seed. Then, as flowers fade and seeds mature, the bulbs accumulate nutrient supplies that will sustain them, in a dormant state, after summer heat and dryness have withered foliage and put an end to the annual growing period.

WET SUMMER, DRY MILD WINTER. A smaller group of bulbs, most notably the summer-flowering African natives such as glory lily *(Gloriosa rothschildiana)* and common calla *(Zantedeschia aethiopica)*, hail from regions where rainy weather comes during the hot summer months, while winters are cooler and drier. Growth occurs during the warm-season rainy period; plants go dormant or grow more slowly when rain ceases and weather cools.

Zantedeschia aethiopica

Fritillaria meleagris

WET SUMMER, COLD WINTER. The wet-summer, cold-winter climate is a widespread one, found in northern and central Europe, in parts of China and the Himalayan foothills, and in much of the United States, Canada, Japan, and Russia. Technically, precipitation comes in varying amounts throughout the year—but in winter, that precipitation is likely to be snow, and even if snow is absent, winter temperatures are too low to encourage growth. Bulbs are dormant through the cold season, then reawaken when soil starts to warm; many flower in late spring or summer, retaining foliage until shorter days and cooler temperatures trigger dieback in late summer to midautumn. Numerous lily species, the better-known species of *Erythronium,* and some fritillaries (such as *Fritillaria meleagris*) are native to this sort of climate.

Zephyranthes atamasco

INTERMITTENT RAIN. A few bulbs, such as habranthus and fairy lily *(Zephyranthes),* come from regions where moist and dry periods alternate irregularly. In this climate, the advantages of a bulb are obvious: the plant always has stored energy to carry it through unpredictable dry episodes. Bulbs native to these climates may flower more than once a year, whenever they receive enough rainfall (or watering) to stimulate another growth cycle.

YEAR-ROUND RAINFALL. In an area where rain falls all year, why would a plant need any kind of bulb? Even in these benign, typically subtropical to tropical climates, there's often a distinct difference between moister times of year and drier periods—and bulbous plants can get by on less water during the drier season, which is nevertheless still warm enough to keep leaves green. Some true bulbs from these regions—such as crinum and pineapple flower *(Eucomis)*—belong to plant

Eucomis comosa

families rich in bulbous plants. Such individuals may represent not so much the development of a bulb in response to climate as the adaptation of a bulbous plant to a tropical environment.

Crinum × powellii

FAMILY CONNECTIONS

As a look through "An Encyclopedia of Favorite Bulbs" (pages 31–107) reveals, most popular bulbous plants belong to a relatively small number of plant families. In fact, 63 of the 83 entries in the encyclopedia fall into just the three families listed below.

Leucojum

AMARYLLIDACEAE

Agapanthus	**Leucojum**
Amaryllis	**Lycoris**
Clivia	**Narcissus**
Crinum	**Nerine**
Cyrtanthus	**Pancratium**
Eucharis	**Scadoxus**
Galanthus	**Sprekelia**
Habranthus	**Sternbergia**
Hippeastrum	**Tulbaghia**
Hymenocallis	**Zephyranthes**
Ixiolirion	

Gladiolus

IRIDACEAE

Babiana	**Iris**
Belamcanda	**Ixia**
Crocosmia	**Schizostylis**
Crocus	**Sparaxis**
Dietes	**Tigridia**
Freesia	**Tritonia**
Gladiolus	**Watsonia**
Homeria	

Allium

LILIACEAE

Allium	**Fritillaria**
Alstroemeria	**Galtonia**
Brodiaea	**Gloriosa**
(and	**Hemerocallis**
Dichelostemma,	**Hyacinthoides**
Triteleia)	**Hyacinthus**
Calochortus	**Ipheion**
Camassia	**Lachenalia**
Cardiocrinum	**Lilium**
Chionodoxa	**Muscari**
Colchicum	**Ornithogalum**
Convallaria	**Puschkinia**
Eremurus	**Scilla**
Erythronium	**Tulipa**
Eucomis	**Veltheimia**

Bulb Types

To a botanist, the word "bulb" refers only to true bulbs. Horticulturists and the general public, however, use the word as a generic term for plants that grow from five distinct types of underground structures: true bulbs, corms, tubers, rhizomes, and tuberous roots. Despite the technical differences, all serve the same function—they are storage organs, holding reserves of food that can keep the plant alive (often in a dormant or semidormant state) from one growing season to the next, through drought, heat, cold, or other climatic vagaries.

The characteristics of each bulb type are summarized here. The bulbs described in the encyclopedia (pages 31–107) are grouped by type on the facing page.

TRUE BULB

A true bulb is an underground stem base containing an embryonic plant complete with leaves, stems, and flower buds, ready to grow when conditions are right. Surrounding this embryonic plant are *scales*—modified leaves that overlap each other in a scalelike manner, giving the bulb as a whole a swollen, often pear-shaped contour. The *basal plate*, at the base of the bulb, holds the scales together and produces roots.

Many bulbs—narcissus and tulip *(Tulipa)* are familiar examples—are sheathed in a papery skin called a *tunic*, which protects against both injury and dehydration. Some bulbs, such as lily *(Lilium)*, lack a tunic; they need extra care in handling, and they cannot remain exposed to the air for long before they begin to dry and shrivel.

An individual bulb may persist for many years, periodically producing new, smaller bulbs *(increases)* from its basal plate.

CORM

Like a true bulb, a corm contains a stem base, but in this case the tissue is solid—purely a swollen underground stem base—rather than a series of overlapping modified leaves. Roots grow from a basal plate at the corm's bottom; the principal growth point "sits" at the top of the corm. Gladiolus and crocus are two favorite plants that grow from corms.

Some corms are covered in a tunic. Though superficially similar to the tunic covering a bulb, a corm's tunic is formed from the dried bases of the previous season's leaves rather than from a specialized layer of modified leaves.

THE FIVE BASIC BULB TYPES

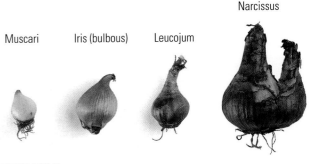

Muscari   Iris (bulbous)   Leucojum   Narcissus

TRUE BULB

Watsonia   Freesia   Crocus

CORM

Begonia   Cyclamen

TUBER

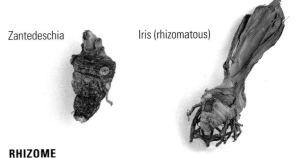

Zantedeschia   Iris (rhizomatous)

RHIZOME

Dahlia

TUBEROUS ROOT

Each corm lasts just one year, depleting its stored energies in the growth and bloom process. As it shrinks away, however, a new corm forms on top of it; numerous increases *(cormels)* may also be produced around the new corm's basal plate.

TUBER

Like corms, tubers are swollen stem bases. But whereas a corm has a fairly clearly organized structure, a tuber does not. There is no tunic of any kind, nor is there a basal plate; roots grow from the tuber's base and sides, and sometimes from the top as well. And instead of just one (or a few) growing points, a tuber has multiple growth points scattered over its upper surface; each one is really a scalelike leaf with a growth bud in its axil.

An individual tuber can last for many years. Those of some plants (cyclamen, for example) continually enlarge but never produce offsets. Other tuberous plants, such as caladium, form protuberances that can be removed and planted separately to become independent tubers.

RHIZOME

The best-known rhizomatous plant is doubtless the tall bearded iris; other familiar ones are calla lily *(Zantedeschia)* and canna. A rhizome is really a thickened stem that grows horizontally (in most cases), either partially or entirely underground. There is no basal plate; roots grow from the rhizome's underside. The primary growing point is at one end of the rhizome, encased (when dormant) in scalelike embryonic leaves. Additional growing points form along the rhizome's sides or on the upper surface.

Because growth proceeds in a straight line (usually horizontally) and because the increases give rise to full-fledged new plants, a planting that starts with a single rhizome can become more numerous and occupy more space as the years pass and the increases move into the soil around the point of the original planting.

TUBEROUS ROOT

Of the five bulb types, only the tuberous root is a true root, thickened to store nutrients, rather than a specialized stem. In a full-grown dahlia or daylily *(Hemerocallis),* to cite the best-known examples, roots grow in a cluster, with the swollen tuberous portion radiating out from a central point. The growth buds lie on the roots' *necks* (at the top), on bases of old stems, or in a *crown* (the point where all the roots come together). Normal fibrous roots, for uptake of water and nutrients, grow from the sides and tip of each tuberous root structure.

An individual tuberous root can give rise to a separate plant as long as it is severed from the cluster of tuberous roots with a growth bud attached to its neck (as in daylilies) or to the base of an old stem just above it (as in dahlias).

WHICH BULB IS WHICH?

Here are all the entries in "An Encyclopedia of Favorite Bulbs," grouped according to type.

Muscari

TRUE BULB
Allium
Amaryllis
Calochortus
Camassia
Cardiocrinum
Chionodoxa
Crinum
Cyrtanthus
Eucharis
Eucomis
Fritillaria
Galanthus
Galtonia
Habranthus
Hippeastrum
Hyacinthoides
Hyacinthus
Hymenocallis
Ipheion
Iris (some)
Ixiolirion
Lachenalia
Leucojum
Lilium
Lycoris
Muscari
Narcissus
Nerine
Ornithogalum
Oxalis (some)
Pancratium
Puschkinia

Scadoxus
Scilla
Sprekelia
Sternbergia
Tigridia
Tulipa
Veltheimia
Zephyranthes

CORM
Babiana
Brodiaea (and
   Dichelostemma,
   Triteleia)
Colchicum
Crocosmia
Crocus
Erythronium
Freesia
Gladiolus
Homeria
Ixia
Sparaxis
Tritonia
Watsonia

TUBER
Anemone
   (most)
Arisaema
Arum
Begonia
Caladium
Colocasia
Corydalis

Cyclmen
Eranthis
Gloriosa
Oxalis (some)
Sinningia

RHIZOME
Achimenes
Agapanthus
Anemone
   (some)
Belamcanda
Bletilla
Canna
Convallaria
Dietes
Iris (many)
Oxalis (some)
Polianthes
Rhodohypoxis
   (but see
   encyclopedia,
   page 94)
Schizostylis
Tulbaghia
Zantedeschia

TUBEROUS ROOT
Alstroemeria
Clivia
Dahlia
Eremurus
Hemerocallis
Liatris
Ranunculus

Tulipa (left) and *Hyacinthus* (right)

Bulbs are easy to grow. That's a truth thousands of gardeners learn each year, as they admire the enchanting crocuses, tulips, irises, and lilies that looked like nothing more than lifeless lumps and bumps when they were planted months before. Pay conscientious attention to their few simple needs,

GROWING BULBS
OUTDOORS

and the bulbs in your garden will reward you with beauty for a long time to come.

One cardinal rule to keep in mind is this: next year's performance is determined by this year's care. Bulbs purchased from nurseries or catalogs have been grown under optimum conditions to ensure a good initial display in your garden—though you will need to give them the overall climate, watering regime, and exposure they prefer (see "An Encyclopedia of Favorite Bulbs," pages 31–107). If they're to stage an equally dazzling show the following year, however, you must also satisfy their requirements after the blooming season ends. The following 12 pages outline the basics of bulb culture.

With the flowering of naturalized winter aconite *(Eranthis hyemalis)* and snowdrops *(Galanthus),* a lightly wooded hillside turns to a tapestry in yellow and white.

Buying Bulbs

A bulb is a ready-made floral factory, complete with embryonic leaf and flower buds and a supply of nutrients (stored during the previous year's growing season) to fuel its next growth cycle. For beautiful results the first year, buy top-quality bulbs—those that have been grown, shipped, and stored under the best possible conditions.

HOW TO CHOOSE, WHEN TO PLANT

As you select your bulbs and decide when and where to plant them, keep three guidelines in mind: appearance, size, and timing.

APPEARANCE. The look and heft of a bulb are clues to its general health. In most cases, look for plump, firm bulbs that feel heavy for their size. A soft, squashy feel usually indicates some sort of rot; lightweight and/or visibly shriveled bulbs may have lost too much moisture to recover well. (Two conspicuous exceptions are anemone and ranunculus; these usually look unpromisingly wizened.)

SIZE. Big bulbs are likely to give the most impressive performance. The largest tulip *(Tulipa)* and hyacinth *(Hyacinthus)* bulbs, for example, produce larger flowers on taller, thicker stems; in the case of ranunculus, the largest roots will give you *more* flowers than will the smaller sizes. (If you're willing to give bulbs a year or two to build themselves up in your garden, though, you'll get fine results with smaller sizes—and their reduced cost makes them a good buy.)

Ready-to-plant bulbs beckon from nursery bins.

TIMING. Finally, it's usually best to plant bulbs when they are dormant and fresh (they should not be dehydrated). The only exceptions to this rule are evergreen types such as clivia, which can be set out from containers at any time. In most cases, totally dormant bulbs are devoid of leaves and roots; in a few instances—iris and daylily *(Hemerocallis)*, for example—the bulb will have leaves and roots but will be sold at the least active period in its growth cycle. Responsible growers dig their stock at the optimum times, and retail outlets offer the bulbs as soon as they are received. Early shopping secures the freshest bulbs for planting.

SOURCES FOR BULBS

Nurseries and mail-order catalogs offer a tantalizing array of bulbs. Neither source is categorically better than the other, but each has its pros and cons.

RETAIL NURSERIES. In early autumn, retail nurseries and garden centers abound with bins and boxes of spring-blooming bulbs; the scene is repeated in early spring, when summer-flowering kinds become available. At these "hands-on" sources, you can easily check out the quality of the stock (while being seduced by the alluring color photos that accompany the display), and you can take your purchases home immediately. The only drawback to retail purchase is the limited selection: retailers tend to stock only tried-and-true best-sellers.

MAIL-ORDER SUPPLIERS. Colorful catalogs can be just as enticing as retail nurseries, but when you buy by mail, there's always a wait between order and receipt. Mail-order suppliers fall into three categories: the ultra-specialist, offering just one or a few kinds of bulbs; the general specialist, offering a broad range of different bulbs; and the general nursery catalog, which includes some bulbs among its varied offerings.

Ultra-specialists may carry a great assortment of varieties within their specialty, with prices ranging from modest to stratospheric. These catalogs appeal to specialists in the particular plants, who are willing to pay high prices for scarce novelties. The general gardener will enjoy browsing through the lower-cost offerings, which typically present more choices than retail nurseries do, at comparable prices. Many ultra-specialists grow their own stock, assuring shipment of fresh bulbs at the proper planting time.

General specialists carry more bulb types than you're likely to find at retail nurseries, though the selection within each type is more limited than that offered by an ultra-specialist. These suppliers usually do not grow the stock they sell; they buy it from specialty growers and bulb brokers. The quality of stock depends on the firm's integrity. The best ones offer top-quality bulbs shipped at the proper planting times—subject, of course, to receipt of stock from their suppliers. Freshness is comparable to that of bulbs in good retail nurseries.

General nursery catalogs, which sell bulbs in addition to a variety of other plants, are something of a calculated risk. Check shipping times to be sure they correspond with the best planting times for the bulbs offered; always look for guarantees and conditions under which you can receive a refund if quality or performance is unsatisfactory.

One final note: in any catalog, beware the words "tremendous bargain sale—end-of-season special!!" Reputable suppliers may offer genuinely good deals, but unscrupulous ones may simply be trying to unload poor-quality stock.

Match each bulb to its preferred growing conditions. Here, moisture-loving yellow flag *(Iris pseudacorus)* luxuriates in boggy pondside soil.

PLANTING

Buying top-quality bulbs assures you of the best potential first-year performance, but three other factors also influence the outcome: location, soil, and proper planting. By addressing these points at the start, you'll enjoy good performance not only in the first year, but also in the seasons to come.

LOCATION

Each entry in the encyclopedia (pages 31–107) notes a preferred exposure and year-round watering regime. Choose planting locations where the conditions match up to these needs.

SOIL

Assess the quality and condition of the soil where you want the bulbs to go. Because so many bulbs need good drainage, this is the quality to determine first (see "Soil types," above right). Many garden soils will pass muster for the majority of bulbs; any soil that grows good annuals or vegetables should be satisfactory, with no more preparation than digging and, perhaps, fertilizing (see page 17). But if you have sticky clay soil and want to grow more than common calla *(Zantedeschia aethiopica)* and yel-

low flag *(Iris pseudacorus),* or if you have sievelike sand which would limit you to sea daffodil *(Pancratium maritimum)* or Oncocyclus irises, you'll need to make amends.

SOIL TYPES. Any soil is a dynamic combination of mineral particles, organic matter, air, and water. As water penetrates soil, it percolates through the pore spaces between particles; the air in these spaces is at first displaced, then restored as the water moves farther down or disappears through root uptake and evaporation. Poor drainage—too much water occupying the pores for too long—can drown roots and rot bulbs.

With their tiny, tightly packed particles, *clay soils* have greatly reduced pore space and, hence, poor drainage: the water-air exchange is slow, and these soils tend to remain too damp during and after rainfall or watering. *Sandy soils,* on the contrary, have good drainage in the extreme; their relatively large, loosely packed particles let water move through swiftly. Rot is seldom a problem; instead, roots can suffer from lack of moisture and nutrients unless watered and fertilized assiduously.

AMENDING THE SOIL. Both clay and sandy soils can be markedly improved with the addition of organic matter (compost, for example). In clay soils, organic materials literally force the soil structure apart; the tiny particles become grouped into larger aggregates, and water penetrates more easily. In sandy soils, organic materials become lodged in the relatively large pore spaces and function as sponges, slowing the passage of water and dissolved nutrients.

Remember that soil amendment isn't a one-time-only affair, since organic matter is always in the process of decomposition. In nature, this occurs fairly slowly: leaves and grasses, animal droppings and remains settle on the soil surface, then gradually rot away. In the artificial environment of gardens, though, we accelerate the process by intensive cultivation that involves watering and fertilizing. Thus, soil of any kind needs a periodic thorough amending, preferably done shortly before planting.

Well-composted organic matter is the champion soil amendment. Choices range from homemade compost to packaged products.

To speed up planting, use a bulb planter (TOP) or excavate the entire planting area to the correct depth (BOTTOM).

When soil is moist enough to be easily worked, dig it to a depth of 8 to 12 inches; then break up any large lumps and rake the surface smooth. Scatter fertilizer (see page 17) over the surface, then spread on a layer of organic matter. Be generous: use roughly 25 percent by volume of organic matter to soil, even more in problem soils. If you dig to a depth of 12 inches, for example, use a 3-inch-deep layer of organic material. Finally, dig or rotary-till the amendments into the soil and rake it smooth again. Ideally, let this prepared soil settle for a week before planting.

PLANTING TECHNIQUES

For each entry in the encyclopedia (pages 31–107), proper planting depth and spacing are specified under "Garden culture." With this information in your head and bulbs in hand, you're ready to plant.

For planting a small number of bulbs, nothing beats the familiar trowel. Simply dig the hole and set in the bulb so that it makes complete contact with soil at the bottom; then fill in, firming the soil around the bulb.

If you have quite a few bulbs to set out, though, planting by trowel requires too much time and effort: here, you're wiser to choose other devices and techniques. A bulb planter lets you remove plugs of soil easily: just insert, twist, and lift (and then drop in the bulb). When all bulbs are in place, rake the removed soil back into the holes. If you have a large area to plant, you may find it simpler to shovel out the soil to the proper planting depth, set out the bulbs in the arrangement you want, then cover them with the excavated soil. Follow the same plan to set out rows of bulbs: dig a trench to the correct depth, space the bulbs in it, and cover with soil.

After planting, water thoroughly to establish good contact between bulbs and soil and to provide enough moisture to initiate root growth. Subsequent watering depends on the particular bulb's needs; consult the encyclopedia.

FOILING THE SPOILERS

Underground animals can disturb bulb plantings—or even wipe them out altogether if the bulbs are especially tasty. Moles are notorious for pushing bulbs around; gophers and voles consider certain bulbs gourmet treats. In thwarting these pests, traps and poison baits have limited success. The most effective control is simply to keep the pests from reaching the bulbs—and the best way to do this is to plant your bulbs in wire baskets. A fairly small mesh (with ½-inch openings) will frustrate pillaging predators, yet easily allow bulb roots to penetrate the surrounding soil.

To make your baskets, you can use galvanized chicken wire or hardware cloth. Wire is easy to work with; hardware cloth is more difficult to cut and bend, but longer lasting. Cut a 12- by 36-inch strip of chicken wire or hardware cloth, form it into a cylinder (which will be about 12 inches in diameter), and twist or wire the ends together. To

make the bottom of the basket, cut a 12-inch square of wire or hardware cloth; attach it by folding the corners up over the sides of the cylinder and hooking them into the mesh.

Once the baskets are completed, dig holes in prepared soil and sink in the baskets. To discourage determined predators from gaining ground-level access, you can set baskets with their rims extending about 4 inches above the final soil level. Fill baskets with soil to the proper planting depth, firming the soil to prevent settling; then set in bulbs and fill in with soil the rest of the way.

Western pocket gopher

You can use the same idea to construct predator-proof raised beds. After you've built the bed, tack ½-inch hardware cloth onto the bottom, then set the bed in the soil; or position the bed first, then line the bottom with hardware cloth, folding the edges to extend about 3 inches up the bed's sides. Fill the bed with soil, water well—and you're ready to plant.

NATURALS FOR NATURALIZING

Allium (some)	*Homeria*
Anemone	*Hyacinthoides*
Brodiaea	*Hyacinthus* (some)
Calochortus	*Ipheion*
Camassia	*Ixia*
Chionodoxa	*Ixiolirion*
Colchicum	*Leucojum*
Convallaria	*Lilium* (some)
Crocosmia	*Muscari*
Crocus	*Narcissus*
Cyclamen	*Ornithogalum* (some)
Eranthis	*Puschkinia*
Erythronium	*Scilla*
Freesia	*Sparaxis*
Fritillaria	*Sternbergia*
Galanthus	*Tulipa* (some)
Habranthus	

Naturalizing Bulbs

Beds and rows of blooming bulbs are beautiful, but no less lovely are more casual plantings: a golden drift of daffodils across a grassy meadow, clumps of nodding bluebells in a woodsy clearing. If this sort of natural look is just what you want, follow the guidelines below.

CHOOSING WISELY

Not all bulbs are good naturalizers; the proven performers are listed on this page. To find out which ones will succeed for you, consult the encyclopedia (pages 31–107) for the climate each prefers. Then make sure you have an appropriate planting area—usually a sunny slope or meadow or a lightly shaded woodland, depending on the bulb. Finally, make sure the bulb's moisture needs are in sync with your region's natural rainfall (or with your ability to provide water when needed).

ACHIEVING THE EFFECT

The traditional naturalizing method is to broadcast a handful of bulbs over the desired planting area, then plant them where they fall. To achieve the most realistic effect, you may need to adjust the scatter pattern slightly: the drift should be denser at one end or toward the center, as if the bulbs began to grow in one spot, then gradually increased to colonize outlying territory. Wherever necessary, adjust spacing so bulbs will be able to grow and increase without immediate crowding.

Be sure to plant bulbs at their preferred depths, at the proper time of year. Thereafter, let nature take over. You can enhance performance, though, if you give plantings an annual application of fertilizer (see page 18).

After a number of years, you may notice a decrease in flower quantity and size. At this point, the planting is becoming overcrowded, and it's time to dig, divide, and replant. For more information on dividing, see pages 20–21.

Time-tested favorites for naturalizing include daffodil (*Narcissus;* TOP LEFT), crocus (TOP RIGHT), and hardy cyclamen (BOTTOM).

GENERAL CARE

Once your bulbs have been properly planted, they'll put down roots in preparation for their next round of growth and bloom. At this time, a little extra attention will bring rewards in the current season and build the bulbs up for a satisfying performance the year after that.

WATERING

From the moment it begins growing until some point after flowering has ceased, a bulb needs ample water. Its annual mission is to grow, flower, set seed (this step we gardeners thwart), and store nutrients for the next year. Depending on type, bulbs vary in the time over which they need water each year. Those native to areas with long, hot, dry summers typically need no water at all by summer, but many summer-flowering bulbs (native to summer-rainfall regions) need moisture until the plants shut down in autumn. Know the needs of the bulbs you grow, then tailor your supplemental watering schedule accordingly.

To do the greatest good, water must penetrate deeply. Think of a bulb—a daffodil *(Narcissus),* say—planted 6 inches deep. You can assume its roots extend at least 6 inches below that; therefore, each watering should moisten the soil to a depth of at least 1 foot. A casual sprinkling, whether provided by you or by rainfall, will not suffice.

In milder-winter regions, adequate deep watering may be furnished by rainfall in autumn, winter, and spring; in colder areas, snow melt followed by spring rains do the job. But whenever the natural supply is inadequate, be prepared to supplement it. As a general rule, *never let the root zone dry out during the growing and flowering period.*

For each bulb described on pages 31–107, you'll find information on water needs and timing. In general, *deciduous bulbs* start to enter dormancy a month or so after flowering; yellowing of foliage is a clue. At this point, you can usually reduce or withhold water (depending on the particular bulb's preference) until new root growth begins. For many spring-blooming bulbs, root growth resumes in autumn; for summer-flowering types, the next need for regular moisture usually comes the following spring.

Petite *Tulipa batalinii* 'Yellow Jewel' makes its appearance through a mulch of bark chips.

Evergreen bulbs have no true dormant period, so they can rarely go completely dry. No overall rule about water needs applies to all evergreen types, however, so be sure to consult individual encyclopedia descriptions for water requirements of the bulbs you grow.

One caution: when bulbs are in bloom, overhead watering can weigh down or topple stems of taller kinds. In rainy regions, it's wise to stake tall flowering stems; where rainfall is scant, you may want to devise an irrigation plan for use during the blooming season.

MULCHING

Mulches are nothing more than a layer of organic matter spread over the soil surface, but they bring numerous benefits. A mulch makes a planting look neat. It keeps the soil that lies beneath it cool; it conserves moisture by slowing evaporation. It helps suppress weeds by blocking the light their seeds need to germinate—and if any do sprout, they're easily pulled from the loose mulch. Finally, mulches decompose and, in the process, improve the condition of the soil.

Like many other plants, bulbs usually respond to mulching with improved performance. (Bearded irises are a notable exception; they will rot if mulched.)

The best mulches are loose or coarse enough for water to penetrate them easily, yet not so lightweight that wind can blow them away. Compost is a favorite choice; bark chips and wood chips are widely used. Pine needles are popular wherever they're available, and even thick-textured leaves (those from evergreen oaks, for example) can be satisfactory. In some areas, byproducts from regional agriculture are available as mulches: rice hulls, grape pomace (skins and crushed seeds), cotton burr compost.

FERTILIZING

Though bulbs will grow and bloom in most soils without the help of fertilizer, fertilized bulbs perform better: the plants are healthier and huskier.

FERTILIZER CHOICES. Two general forms of fertilizers are available: *dry (granular)* and *liquid*.

To apply *dry fertilizers,* you typically scatter them over the soil, then scratch them in (or dig them in, if you're preparing or reworking a planting area). If the fertilizer is the standard type, moisture quickly dissolves its granules, releasing the nutrients they contain. If the fertilizer is a timed-release sort, however, its soluble nutrients are contained in permeable synthetic pellets; a small amount of fertilizer dissolves with each watering, delivering the nutrient supply over a longer period of time. Such fertilizers are particularly convenient for container culture, since the necessary frequent waterings quickly leach nutrients from the soil.

Liquid fertilizers include both liquid and water-soluble dry concentrates. In either case, you dilute the concentrate in water, then apply the solution to the soil. Liquid fertilizers are most frequently used on container-grown bulbs, though they also give an instant boost to plants grown in the ground.

Whether dry or liquid, all fertilizers are either *complete* or *incomplete*. Complete fertilizers contain all three of the major nutrients essential for plant growth: nitrogen, phosphorus, and potassium. Incomplete types are lacking in one or two of these. For more information on the major nutrients, see "A Fertilizer Primer" (at right).

Fertilizers containing phosphorus and potassium have the greatest effect when dug into the soil before planting.

A FERTILIZER PRIMER

Most commercial fertilizers are *complete*, meaning that they contain the three major plant nutrients: nitrogen (N), phosphorus (P), and potassium (K). *Incomplete* fertilizers contain just one or two of these three; some of the so-called bulb foods, which contain only phosphorus and potassium, fall into this category, as do nitrogen-only fertilizers. The percentage of each element is stated as a number on the fertilizer label. The numbers 8-10-5, for example, identify a fertilizer that contains by volume 8 percent nitrogen, 10 percent phosphorus, and 5 percent potassium. A 10-0-0 formula contains by volume 10 percent nitrogen, but no phosphorus or potassium at all.

NITROGEN is the nutrient needed in greatest quantity for growth. It is also the element most likely to be deficient in garden soil, since it's water soluble and easily leached from soil by rain and watering. Nitrogen may be present in fertilizer in several forms, but it's usable by roots only in its nitrate form—so if you want quick results, buy a fertilizer containing nitrate nitrogen. Fertilizers containing nitrogen in organic or ammonium form (including nitrogen derived from urea or IBDU) provide a slower and more sustained release, since their nitrogen must be converted to the nitrate form in the soil before it can be assimilated.

PHOSPHORUS, the second of the three major nutrients, is expressed on fertilizer labels as phosphate (P_2O_5) and described there as "available phosphoric acid." Often billed as a bulb-builder, it is indeed important to the development of roots, bulbs, and seeds. Unlike nitrogen, it is not water soluble. Instead, the phosphoric acid binds chemically to soil particles in its immediate vicinity; from there, it is slowly released into the microscopic films of water surrounding those particles. Nearby roots can then absorb it. Thus, if phosphorus is applied to the soil surface, only roots in the top inch or two of soil will benefit.

POTASSIUM, the third major nutrient, is expressed on package labels as potash (K_2O) and described as "available" or "water-soluble" potash. In the soil, this water-soluble potash is quickly converted to insoluble *exchangeable potassium*, which roots can absorb by contact. Like phosphorus, therefore, potassium is least effective when applied to the soil surface. For greatest benefit, it must be applied near the root zone.

WHEN AND HOW TO FERTILIZE. There are three important times to fertilize bulbs: when you prepare a new planting or thoroughly rework an old one; when bulbs begin to grow each year; and after the year's bloom season has ended.

When you're preparing soil, simply scatter on dry fertilizer in the amount the package specifies, then dig or till it in. Use a high-phosphorus complete or incomplete fertilizer; so-called bulb foods are high-phosphorus types. Incorporating phosphorus and potassium into the soil gets these elements into the bulbs' root zone, where they can be assimilated. If you are planting bulbs individually, you can dig a bit of fertilizer into the bottom of each hole, then cover with 1 to 2 inches of soil before planting the bulb.

As bulbs begin to grow, they benefit from a feeding to enhance the quality of the current season's flowers. At this time, nitrogen is the needed element. Applied as a bulb is readying itself for bloom, it can increase the height of stems and the size of leaves and flowers. After flowering ends, make a second application: this will promote active root growth and improve assimilation of the other two major elements as bulbs stock up for the next year's growth.

For these second two applications—as growth begins and after bloom ends—use a dry nitrogen-only fertilizer with a modest amount of nitrogen, say 10-0-0. You also can use a complete fertilizer such as 10-10-5, but keep in mind that the phosphorus and potassium won't have much of an effect unless you can dig the fertilizer in (see below). Begin by watering the area so that soil and roots are moist; then scatter on fertilizer and water again to dissolve it. If you can lightly scratch or dig the fertilizer in, any phosphorus and potassium it contains will be more effective than they would be if applied only to the soil surface. If bulbs are planted in rows, it's easier to get these two largely immobile nutrients into the root zone: dig narrow, about 8-inch-deep trenches close to the plants (taking care not to damage roots); then scatter fertilizer in the trenches, cover it with soil, and water thoroughly.

For plantings of spring-blooming bulbs, you will apply fertilizer in early spring, then again in late spring or early summer; for summer-blooming types, the applications come in spring and again in late summer or early autumn. For autumn-flowering bulbs that grow during autumn, winter, and spring, fertilize once in autumn as foliage starts to grow, then perhaps again with a lighter application in early spring before leaves start to yellow.

Some evergreen bulbs may need fertilizing more than twice during the growing season, and perhaps at other times of year as well. For all bulbs (deciduous or evergreen) whose requirements differ from the general schedule above, specific instructions are noted in the encyclopedia (pages 31–107).

PESTS AND DISEASES

The truly trouble-free plant does not exist, but the presence of a predator doesn't always mean serious trouble. Some pests and diseases, however, can bother bulbs enough to warrant control; these are described on the facing page. Suggested controls for each pest are listed in order of increasing toxicity.

Be aware that new controls continue to be developed, while existing ones may be withdrawn from sale if research reveals that their use carries possible health or environmental hazards. For current recommendations, consult your Cooperative Extension agent or experienced nursery personnel.

Iris borer   Mealybugs   Mites

Narcissus bulb fly   Powdery mildew   Squirrel

Snail   Thrips   Virus

Aphids   Botrytis   Bulb rot

PROBLEM	DESCRIPTION	CONTROLS
Aphids	Soft-bodied, rounded insects, ranging from pinhead to matchhead size; green, gray, pink, reddish brown, or black. Clustered on new growth, they suck plant juices; heavy infestations distort growth (and aid the spread of viruses).	Hose off with water; spray with insecticidal soap, pyrethrum, diazinon, malathion.
Botrytis	This fungal disease attacks leaves and flowers, weakens plants. Look for gray or brown spots, fuzzy mold spreading over decaying tissue. Damp early-spring weather favors growth; wind and rain spread spores.	Destroy infected leaves and flowers; spray with chlorothalonil.
Bulb rots	Basal rot, soft rot, and crown rot are fungal diseases that cause bulb decay; they are particularly serious in damp soil.	Plant in well-drained soils; water judiciously. Discard infected bulbs. For crown rot (white webbing with seedlike dormant spores), soak bulbs and soil with PCNB.
Iris borer	Burrowing grub attacks iris rhizomes; found from Iowa to Atlantic, Canada to Tennessee. Drab moths lay eggs in early autumn. Larvae hatch in May and June; they eat leaf edges, enter rhizomes and hollow them out.	Clean up garden in autumn; hand-pick borers; spray weekly with dimethoate from early spring through June.
Mealybugs	White, ⅛-inch insects, round to oval, fuzzy looking; cluster at bases of leaves and stems to suck plant juices. Found where air circulation is poor, particularly on house plants and container plants.	Spray with insecticidal soap, horticultural oil, diazinon, malathion, acephate; use spreader-sticker.
Mites	Tiny, spiderlike insects found on leaf undersides (often with webbing); leaf surface is pale and stippled. You'll need a magnifying glass to see them. Infestations increase rapidly in hot weather. Mites can destroy bulbs in storage.	Spray with insecticidal soap, horticultural oil, dicofol; dust stored bulbs with diazinon.
Narcissus bulb fly	Burrowing grub attacks *Narcissus*, also *Galanthus, Hymenocallis, Leucojum*. Beelike flies lay eggs in spring at leaf bases; grubs infest bulbs and hollow them out. Infested bulbs are soft, squashy.	Check bulbs before planting and destroy any grubs; dust leaves and soil with diazinon as leaves emerge.
Powdery mildew	Fungal disease leaves a powdery, white to gray covering on leaves, stems, and flower buds. Heavy infestation debilitates plant. Favored by poor air circulation, shade, weather with warm, dry days and cool, moist nights.	Avoid planting in mildew-prone locations; spray infected plants with triforine.
Rodents	Gophers and voles eat bulbs growing in the ground; mice chiefly dine on stored bulbs; chipmunks and ground squirrels dig up planted bulbs.	For gophers and voles, see "Foiling the Spoilers" (page 14); for mice, securely cover or enclose boxes of stored bulbs with screening or wire mesh; for chipmunks and ground squirrels, cover planted beds with screening or wire mesh.
Slugs and snails	Night-feeding mollusks (snails have shells, slugs do not) feast on leaves, stems, and flowers, leaving telltale trails of silvery slime. They live in cool, damp, shady places and in garden litter.	Hand-pick and squash; deter with copper strips; bait with metaldehyde, methiocarb (keep away from pets).
Thrips	Microscopic tan, brown, or black insects feed on petals, causing brown discoloration; heavy infestations distort blooms. To check, tap a flower over piece of white paper and look for moving specks.	Spray with diazinon, malathion, acephate, dimethoate.
Viruses	Microscopic organisms live in plant tissue, usually causing reduced vigor, flower distortion, streaks on flowers or leaves. Sucking insects (aphids, mealybugs) can spread viruses.	Discard all plants showing virus infection; control sucking insects.

Off-Season Care

Bulbs require the most attention from the moment they begin growth until the last flowers fade—but you'll also need to provide some care beyond the bloom season. During this post-flowering phase, your tasks will involve three main areas: dividing, storage, and (in cold-winter regions) winter protection of certain in-ground bulbs.

DIVIDING: MANY FROM ONE

With the exception of most tubers, bulbs produce increases which can be detached to establish new plantings. In fact, you will need to dig and divide periodically to keep plantings from becoming too crowded for good growth and bloom. Bulbs differ in their rate of increase: some can remain in place for years before crowding takes a toll, while others proliferate so rapidly that only frequent division will maintain quality. In general, the best time to dig and divide bulbs is at the proper planting time for your region.

STORAGE

Not all bulbs require annual digging and storage, and some need to be stored in some climates but not in others (check the encyclopedia, pages 31–107, for details on specific bulbs). Usually, though, storage is indicated when a bulb left in the ground cannot survive one of two conditions: winter cold or summer water.

In the first case, some bulbs can be grown in regions beyond their hardiness range if you dig them, then store them over winter under cool but not freezing conditions (35° to 55°F/2° to 13°C). Container-grown bulbs can remain in their pots in a dark, dry place.

In the second case, spring-flowering bulbs that demand dry summer conditions may succeed in rainy-summer areas if they are dug when leaves die back, stored dry over summer, and replanted in autumn. If you grow these bulbs in containers, you can simply withhold all moisture during the dormant phase.

The two storage methods presented below cover the needs of all popular bulbs. One cautionary note applies to both: if mice seeking shelter find your bulb storeroom, they'll have a banquet. If you suspect that mice may be a problem, securely cover or enclose the stored bulbs with screening or wire mesh.

VENTILATED STORAGE. Bulbs that have a protective tunic—such as narcissus and gladiolus—can be stored in mesh bags or piled loosely in boxes or baskets. Exposure to air keeps them dry and discourages rot, while the protective skin helps prevent dehydration.

To prepare bulbs for ventilated storage, follow this sequence (any exceptions are noted in the encyclopedia entries for individual bulbs). When foliage has yellowed, dig bulbs from the ground or knock them from their containers. Remove leaves and soil; then spread the bulbs on newspapers in a shaded location and let them dry for several days. It's best not to separate bulbs before storage, since broken surfaces offer easy entry for disease organisms and increase the chance of dehydration. Store the dried bulbs in a cool, dry, dark place (35° to 55°F/2° to 13°C) until the proper planting time for your area.

DIVIDING BULBS

When a bulb planting has become crowded, or when you want to make additional plantings of a favorite bulb, it's time to dig and divide. Because each of the five bulb types—true bulb, corm, tuber, rhizome, tuberous root—produces its increases in a diferent fashion, the division technique you use will depend on the bulb you're working with. The illustrations at right give instructions for dividing each of the five types.

True bulbs form increases that remain attached to a common basal plate. To divide, carefully break apart connected bulbs at base. For lilies, remove outer scales from basal plate, dip base ends in rooting hormone, and plant.

Corms renew themselves each growing season: a new corm and small increases (cormels) form on top of the old corm, which becomes flattened, shriveled, and worn out. To divide, separate healthy new corms and any cormels from the old corms.

COVERED STORAGE. A number of bulbs (caladium and begonia, for example) lack a protective covering; if exposed to the air for long after digging, they'll begin to shrivel. If dehydration continues during storage, the bulb may die or become severely debilitated before replanting time.

Dig and dry these bulbs as directed for "Ventilated storage" (facing page). Then place them in a single layer in a box or clay pot, making sure they don't touch one another (should any bulb rot during storage, the separation lessens the chance of decay spreading from one bulb to another). Cover with dry sand, vermiculite, sawdust, perlite, or peat moss, using enough to cover bulbs by about ½ inch. Replant bulbs at the proper time for your area, dividing them at that time if needed. If any appear dry or shriveled, plump them up in moist sand before replanting.

WINTER PROTECTION FOR IN-GROUND BULBS

Some bulbs may successfully remain in the ground in regions a bit colder than their preferred zones if you give them above-ground winter protection. A layer of insulating material spread over the soil surface has two benefits. First, it keeps the soil temperature from dipping as low as that of unprotected earth. Second, it *moderates* temperature—a critical point in snowless winters or in any region where weather is likely to alternate between warm and bitter cold. During bursts of springlike temperatures, protected ground remains colder than unprotected ground, and the bulbs under cover remain inactive; they aren't tricked into producing growth which would then be killed by a return to subfreezing weather.

It's important to apply winter protection at the right time. After the first hard frost in autumn, spread a 4- to 6-inch layer of protective material over the soil. A variety of materials can be used. Regional favorites include conifer boughs; marsh, prairie, and salt hay; and ground corn cobs. Whatever you use, make sure that winter snows and rains won't pack it into an airtight mass.

Leave the protection in place until just before the start of the normal spring growing period; then rake it aside.

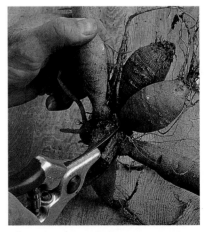

The kind of winter storage you provide for dormant bulbs depends on the particular bulb. Some need covered storage (TOP); others prefer ventilated storage (BOTTOM).

Tubers increase in size and number of growing points as they age, but most don't form discrete increases. To divide, cut a large tuber into two or more sections, making sure each section has one or more growing points.

Rhizomes produce new plants from growth points that form along their sides. To divide, break apart sections at the natural "waists" between them, making sure each division has at least one growing point.

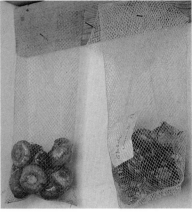

Tuberous roots form multiple growing points. Some, like daylily *(Hemerocallis),* form separate plants that can be pulled apart; others, like dahlia (above), do not. To divide the latter, cut apart so that each root has a growth bud.

Bulbs in Containers

Growing bulbs in containers entails no more effort than growing them in the ground. The few extra steps involved are balanced by reduced labor for soil preparation and planting. And since so many bulbs take well to container culture, you have a wide range of choices—though you may have some difficulty narrowing the field.

Planting bulbs with successive flowering times will let you enjoy months of uninterrupted bloom: as one colorful potful of flowers fades, bring on another that's just coming into blossom. This sort of portability also makes it easy to rearrange your garden—just move the pots to new locations.

CHOOSING CONTAINERS

Suitable containers for bulbs are so numerous that you should have no trouble finding the look you want. Six basic sorts are described at right.

Positioned atop a garden pedestal, delicate *Zephyranthes candida* stands out amid the surrounding foliage.

Potted springtime extravaganza features tulips *(Tulipa)* in red shades, daffodils *(Narcissus)* in both yellow and white with orange cups, and orange-red crown imperial *(Fritillaria imperialis)*.

Unglazed clay (terra-cotta) pots are the old stand-bys, available in a great assortment of sizes and shapes; some even have surface decoration. Because moisture evaporates through the pot as well as from the soil surface, plants in these pots need the closest attention to watering.

Glazed clay containers retain moisture much better than their unglazed counterparts. Choose color and decoration carefully—you don't want the pot to compete or clash with the flowers it displays.

Wooden containers offer a neutral, earthy-looking foil for plants of any sort. They retain moisture as well as glazed clay, and their thicker sides provide better insulation from extremes of temperature. Decay-resistant woods like cedar, cypress, and redwood make the longest-lasting containers.

Concrete and aggregate containers are heavier and costlier than other types, but their moisture retention is excellent and they provide the best insulation of any kind of container.

Plastic containers, ranging from purely utilitarian black or green nursery "cans" to red-brown imitations of unglazed clay pots, are as moisture retentive as glazed clay pots and usually less expensive than unglazed clay ones.

Paper pulp pots are lightweight and inexpensive; they come in earthy tones of tan to dark brown. They retain moisture better than unglazed clay, but not as well as other types. They last for about 3 years at best.

PLANTING

Some bulbs are nearly always grown in containers—achimenes and gloxinia *(Sinningia speciosa)*, for example. In these cases, you'll find detailed instructions for container culture in "An Encyclopedia of Favorite Bulbs" (pages 31–107). The majority of bulbs that may be grown in containers, however, fall into the three basic groups described below.

GROUP A. These are largely tropical and subtropical plants; many of them grow from tubers. All need a moisture-retentive but fast-draining soil mix. The following formula works well:

1 part peat moss
1 part compost or leaf mold
1 part perlite

Mix a complete fertilizer (approximately 5-10-5 formulation) into the potting mix, using the quantity the label specifies. Plant bulbs at the depth and spacing recommended in their encyclopedia entries.

GROUP B. Bulbs in this group fall into two subgroups, based on the duration of their container lifetime.

Subgroup 1. These bulbs perform well in a container for one season, but should be set out in the garden at their next proper planting time. Narcissus, tulip *(Tulipa),* and crocus are three familiar examples. Because these bulbs will be in a container for just one flowering season, you can space them closely and plant them with their tips just beneath the soil surface.

Subgroup 2. The many bulbs in this subgroup can succeed in containers for more than one year, provided they receive the dormant conditions they need. Alstroemeria, lily-of-the-valley *(Convallaria majalis),* and freesia are a few of these. Plant them a few inches apart, at the depth recommended in their encyclopedia descriptions. Divide and repot when flower quality and quantity decline.

For either subgroup of group B, you can choose from two potting mixes.

For a mix that drains rapidly, use:
1 part peat moss
1 part other organic material (compost, leaf mold,
  ground bark)
1 part builder's sand

For a more moisture-retentive mix, use:
1 part soil (loam to sandy loam—not clay)
1 part peat moss
1 part builder's sand

Mix a complete fertilizer (approximately 5-10-5 formulation) into either mix, using the quantity the label specifies.

GROUP C. These bulbs can remain in one container for several to many years. Agapanthus, clivia, amaryllis *(Hippeastrum),* and common calla *(Zantedeschia aethiopica)* are among the better-known individuals.

Because these plants will be contained for several years, be sure you choose fairly sizable containers—at least 8 inches across and 12 inches deep—to accommodate good root growth. Use either of the soil mixes suggested under group B; plant bulbs a few inches apart, at the depth recommended in their encyclopedia entries. Some of the bulbs in this group actually perform better when roots are crowded; they need repotting (and perhaps dividing) only when the containers are crowded almost to the bursting point.

WATERING

The water needs noted in the encyclopedia entry for each bulb apply to container-grown as well as in-ground bulbs. Remember, though, that container plants can dry out quickly, due to the limited amount of soil and the container's exposure. Be sure to keep soil moist during the growth and flowering period.

FERTILIZING

Bulbs in containers for just one flowering season (group B, subgroup 1) need no fertilizer beyond that which you add to the potting mix. Bulbs that will stay in containers for 2 years or more will appreciate further attention.

Liquid fertilizers and timed-release dry types (see page 17) are the fertilizers of choice. Liquids give plants an instant boost but have little staying power, since nutrients are quickly leached from the container with each watering. In general, apply them monthly during the

Parrot tulips spring from an equally flamboyant glazed clay container (TOP); strawberry pot houses a collection of crocus (BOTTOM).

growing season, diluted according to package directions; or apply every 2 weeks, diluted to half-strength. Always water the soil thoroughly before applying the fertilizer solution.

Timed-release fertilizers can be applied less often than liquids, since they release nutrients gradually over time (the period of effectiveness depends on the particular formulation). One application at the start of the growing season may be sufficient; for evergreen bulbs in group C, a second application about 4 months later is often beneficial.

GROWING BULBS
INDOORS

If you enjoy bringing pots of blooming bulbs indoors to brighten and decorate your living space, why not grow bulbous plants specifically for interior use? It's easy—and what's more, it's fun to watch from close quarters as those bare, drab seemingly lifeless chunks of stem or root are transformed into full-fledged plants with dazzling flowers or foliage.

For seasonal color indoors, you can "force" many bulbs: by manipulating temperature and light, you can fool them into growing and flowering earlier than they would in nature. This technique lets you enjoy blooms in winter rather than waiting for spring—a welcome prospect anywhere, but especially in regions where winters are cold. In those frosty climates, forced bulbs provide a living source of color while the outdoor garden rests. The following pages offer simple directions for forcing popular bulbs as well as other smaller, less well-known bulbs. You'll also learn how to grow some types, such as hyacinth, directly in water.

You may find seasonal color from bulbs so pleasing that you decide to grow these plants indoors year-round. This is easily done in a greenhouse, but fortunately, quite a few bulbs thrive as house plants too. Some retain their foliage all year; others die down for a re-energizing respite, then grow back to delight you all over again.

Colorful flowering bulbs bring cheer on dreary winter days.

FORCING BULBS

Because newly purchased bulbs already contain the embryonic bloom for the following season, you can—with a bit of extra effort—manipulate conditions to induce flowering before the normal outdoor bloom season. This process, popularly known as "forcing," takes advantage of the fact that bulbs have certain minimum requirements for each stage prior to bloom. Because outdoor climate slows development, bulbs in the ground usually spend more than the minimally necessary time in these prebloom stages. Under a forcing regime, however, you can control conditions so each stage is completed as quickly as possible.

Not all bulbs respond well to forcing, though many of the most popular spring bloomers do (see list at left). When perusing catalogs, look for species and varieties described as "good for forcing." For the most satisfying results, buy the largest top-quality bulbs you can find: they have the most stored energy and thus are most likely to succeed in a process that draws heavily on their food reserves.

To make sure the bulbs bloom when you want them to do so, you'll need to calculate planting time carefully. Natives of mild-winter areas bloom the soonest after planting, since they don't need a prolonged period of cold. The more tender Tazetta narcissus varieties (often sold as "Paper Whites," though 'Paper White' is more properly the name of one variety) will bloom 5 to 7 weeks after planting. Hardy bulbs (those native to cold-winter regions) typically bloom after 13 to 15 weeks of cold treatment for root and early shoot development, followed by 3 to 4 weeks of warmth and light to induce flowering. Some of the hardy types that bloom earliest in nature—glory-of-the-snow (*Chionodoxa*), winter aconite (*Eranthis hyemalis*), and snowdrop (*Galanthus*)—may get by with only 12 weeks of cold before being brought into the light. Hardy bulbs are usually planted in October or November for bloom in January through April.

Some bulbs needing cold treatment, such as hyacinth (*Hyacinthus*) and lily-of-the-valley (*Convallaria majalis*), can be purchased prechilled; you may see the terms "precooled" or

Various plants can fill a single pot.

Smaller-growing kinds of narcissus
are excellent container subjects.

"pretreated." In fact, the bulbs are only partially chilled, saving you 3 or 4 weeks of cold treatment. The supplier should indicate how much longer the bulbs must be chilled after you receive them.

POTTING THE BULBS

Any kind of pot with drainage holes will do for forcing, though wider-than-tall bulb pots and bulb pans are ideal. Do make sure, though, that the pot is at least twice as tall as the bulb to allow adequate space for roots. Fill the pot loosely with either of the soil mixes described for group B on page 23; if you intend to transplant the bulb into the garden after bloom, add 1 tablespoon of 5-10-5 fertilizer per 6-inch pot.

Space the bulbs close together—for example, about 15 crocuses, 6 narcissus or tulips *(Tulipa)*, or 3 hyacinths *(Hyacinthus)* per 6-inch pot—and barely cover them with mix. Plant tulips with the flat side facing the outside of the pot, so that the first and largest leaf will also face that way and cover the rim of the pot. Water to settle the soil, but don't compact it. Label the pot with the bulb name and planting date.

Bulbs that do not need cold treatment can now be placed in a cool, well-lit spot (55° to 60°F/13° to 16°C), then moved to warmer conditions (65° to 75°F/18° to 24°C) when the buds begin to show color. For bulbs requiring cold treatment, follow the directions below.

PROVIDING COLD TREATMENT

The hardy bulbs need a prolonged period in dark, moist, chilly conditions (35° to 50°F/2° to 10°C) to get off to a good start; without this treatment, they tend to produce foliage and no flowers. Possible cooling sites include an old refrigerator, unheated basement or garage, service porch, cold frame, or trench dug in the ground and lined with wire mesh to keep mice away. Pots kept outdoors should be mulched with leaves, sawdust, straw, or other material to protect against freezing and to exclude light. If indoor pots will be exposed to light, put them in closed cupboards or cover them (by inverting baskets over them, for example). Make sure the bulbs don't dry out.

Start checking for top growth after 12 or 13 weeks. The bulbs are ready for forcing when shoots are about 1 inch high or a little taller. The emerging leaves will be white, since they formed in the dark, but they'll color up when exposed to light. Roots growing through the drainage holes are another sign that bulbs are ready for forcing, even if top growth isn't evident. Move the containers to a cool, well-lit spot (55° to 60°F/13° to 16°C); if you want to stagger bloom, bring them out a few at a time, every 2 weeks. When buds begin to show color, shift to a warmer, sunny location (65° to 75°F/18° to 24°C). Once flowers open, though, cooler conditions will lengthen their life. Keep plants well watered.

With the exception of amaryllis *(Hippeastrum;* see "Forcing Amaryllis," page 28), forced bulbs cannot be forced for a second

Dutch hybrid crocus poke through openings in a ceramic pot.

season. After bloom is over, you can set them out in the garden; in a year or two, they may build themselves up enough to flower at the normal time. Forced tulips, however, rarely bloom again.

WATER CULTURE

Some bulbs can be grown with their roots in water. Dutch hybrid hyacinth *(Hyacinthus)* and narcissus are the most familiar examples, though other choices are possible as well. Because bulbs cultivated in this manner expend all their energy, they should be discarded after bloom.

HYACINTH GLASS

The bulb most often grown this way is the hyacinth; in fact, it has lent its name to the special glass forcing vessel, which resembles an hourglass or egg cup. The bulb rests in the smaller upper section, while the roots grow in the larger, water-filled lower part. Other bulbs suited to this type of culture are Dutch hybrid crocus, dwarf early-flowering tulips *(Tulipa)*, snowdrop *(Galanthus)*, grape hyacinth *(Muscari)*, squill *(Scilla)*, and meadow saffron *(Colchicum)*. More petite containers are sold for smaller bulbs,

Hyacinth in glass

which would fall through the opening of a traditional hyacinth glass.

To "plant" the glass, fill it with water to within ⅛ inch of the bulb base, then add a small piece of activated charcoal to discourage the growth of algae. Place the planted glass in a dark, cool place (around 55°F/13°C) until roots are well developed and top growth has begun; add more water as necessary during this time to keep the level just beneath the bulb's base. If the water looks murky, hold the bulb in place as you change the water; don't take the bulb out, since you won't be able to get the roots back into the glass without damaging them. When growth is underway, transfer the glass to a fairly cool spot (65° to 68°F/18° to 20°C) with plenty of light.

PEBBLES AND WATER

This method is most often used to force the fall- and winter-blooming Tazetta narcissus varieties ('Paper White' and similar types) that don't need a prolonged cool, dark period for root growth before they send up leaves. The interval between starting and blooming is 5 to 7 weeks. If you make your first planting in October and plant at 2-week intervals until December, you can have flowering narcissus indoors over a 2-month period. Hardy narcissus varieties and Dutch hybrid hyacinths are sometimes grown this way too.

Fill a shallow pan with pebbles, stone chips, or coarse sand. Crowd in the bulbs, anchoring them by heaping pebbles all around them, leaving only the top ½ inch or so of each bulb exposed. Then add water until the level reaches just below the base of the bulbs. As for bulbs in a hyacinth glass, start plants in a cool, dark spot, then move to a warmer, sunny spot when growth is underway. Add more water as needed.

Narcissus varieties are ideal candidates for growing in pebbles and water.

FORCING AMARYLLIS

With a minimum of effort, you can bring amaryllis *(Hippeastrum)* into bloom for the winter holidays. Nurseries and mail-order firms offer bulbs already planted in special plastic containers; if you buy one of these, all you have to do is water and wait. Or buy bulbs and pot them up yourself.

Nurseries usually offer one or more types of amaryllis bulbs: African, Dutch, Giant Dutch, or Royal Dutch Hybrids. For winter holiday bloom, choose those labeled African. These are grown to blooming size in South Africa, then stored and shipped under controlled conditions. When removed from cold storage, the bulbs sprout quickly and flower in 4 to 6 weeks. For sure bloom at Christmas, plant bulbs around November 15. Most Dutch varieties are dug and shipped from Holland in September; they will bloom 7 to 8 weeks after planting.

For each bulb, choose a container that allows 2 inches between all sides of the bulb and the container edges. Fill containers with one of the soil mixes recommended for group B (page 23); plant so that the neck and top half of the bulb protrude above the soil surface.

Water thoroughly after planting, then give just enough water to keep soil barely moist until active growth begins. Keep containers in a bright, warm room (70° to 75°F/21° to 24°C during the day, 60° to 65°F/16° to 18°C at night); turn them frequently so the flower stems will grow upright rather than leaning toward the light. As each bloom fades, cut it off to prevent seed formation. After all flowers have withered, cut off the entire stem at its base.

Leaves appear either during or after bloom. For good performance the following year, it's important to keep the plant growing vigorously; water regularly and give bimonthly applications of liquid fertilizer diluted to half strength. If you allow the leaves to wither naturally in fall, the plant will bloom at its normal time the following spring. If you'd like to schedule another holiday bloom, however, proceed as follows. Stop fertilizing 5 to 6 months after flowering ends; then taper off watering over the next 3 to 4 weeks. When foliage yellows, cut it off; then store the dry potted bulbs in a cool closet, basement, or garage where temperatures will remain above freezing (ideally around 40° to 50°F/4° to 10°C). About 4 to 8 weeks before bloom is desired, move the pots back into a bright, warm room and resume watering to start the next cycle of growth and flowering.

GROWING BULBS INDOORS YEAR-ROUND

A number of bulbs thrive indoors much or all of the year. In some cases, the climate dictates this treatment: the bulbs you want to grow may not succeed year-round in the garden. Other times, you may simply want to grow bulbs indoors for decorative purposes. Whatever your reasons, you'll enjoy having your favorites close up, where their flowers and foliage can be easily appreciated.

Cyrtanthus elatus 'Snow White'

BULBS AS HOUSE PLANTS

The bulbous plants most commonly grown indoors are the spring bloomers, such as hyacinth *(Hyacinthus),* tulip *(Tulipa),* and narcissus. Although they're breathtaking in bloom, their tenure as house plants is fleeting—especially if they must be hidden away for months of cold treatment before the floral display. After the flowers fade, most types must be planted in the garden or simply thrown away.

For bulbs with more staying power as house plants, look to those from mild-winter areas (many successful choices are native to South Africa). Such bulbs adapt better to indoor conditions than do those from colder regions. This group includes some evergreen kinds that look attractive all year; examples are clivia, Scarborough lily *(Cyrtanthus elatus), Tulbaghia,* and some species of agapanthus. Others die down and should be stashed away for their dormant period; you can store the pot dry in a cool, dark place, then bring it out again after new growth appears.

Check the growing conditions specified for the various bulbs in the encyclopedia (pages 31–107). Plant at the appropriate time, in the soil mix recommended under "Container culture." Like most other house plants, bulbs grown indoors appreciate regular light feedings. Most need bright indirect sunlight during active growth and bloom; a location in a south-facing window is ideal, especially during the winter months, when light is often at a premium. If your house is very dry, raise the moisture level with a humidifier or place the potted plants atop pebbles in trays partially filled with water.

BULBS IN THE GREENHOUSE

You can grow just about any bulb in a greenhouse, though you probably won't want to do so for types that succeed perfectly well year-round in your garden. The value of a greenhouse is in providing growing conditions that your garden doesn't. In cold-winter areas, a greenhouse will protect tender bulbs from freezing; in moist-summer regions, it will keep rain away from bulbs that rot if they get too much moisture; in arid climates, it will elevate the humidity around tropical plants.

If you live in a mild-winter area and your goal is simply to keep rain at bay or provide humidity in summer, an unheated greenhouse may be sufficient. In all other regions, some heat is necessary for year-round use. A fairly cool greenhouse is useful for growing bulbs that experience cool, moist weather in winter and early spring, such as baboon flower *(Babiana),* cape cowslip *(Lachenalia),* and harlequin flower *(Sparaxis tricolor).* Kept warmer, the greenhouse is an ideal place to grow tender bulbs such as achimenes, caladium, and gloxinia *(Sinningia speciosa).*

HOUSE PLANT CANDIDATES

Agapanthus (some)
Begonia × tuberhybrida
Caladium bicolor
Clivia
Crinum
Cyclamen persicum
Cyrtanthus elatus
Eucharis × grandiflora
Eucomis
Gloriosa rothschildiana
Hippeastrum
Hymenocallis narcissiflora
Lachenalia
Ornithogalum thyrsoides
Oxalis
Scadoxus multiflorus katharinae
Sinningia speciosa
Sparaxis tricolor
Sprekelia formosissima
Tulbaghia
Veltheimia bracteata
Zantedeschia aethiopica
Zephyranthes grandiflora

Cyclamen persicum

Zantedeschia aethiopica

From Achimenes *to* Zephyranthes, *a dazzling world of bulbs awaits your discovery in the following 76 pages. Some of the plants presented here are favorites dear to generations of gardeners; others are well-known regional choices or less-familiar bulbs deserving of wider recognition. The descriptions in this chap-*

AN ENCYCLOPEDIA OF
FAVORITE BULBS

ter will help you decide how well each bulb suits your climate and garden conditions. Every entry begins with a list of at-a-glance information—a quick reference to the bulb's plant family, type, height, sun and water needs, and preferred climate. For a line-by-line explanation, see "Reading the entries" (page 32).

see "Reading the entries" (page 32).

Within each entry, you'll find comments on the plant's native territory and its typical appearance, followed by descriptions of the species and varieties you may encounter at nurseries or in catalogs. Next come ideas for using the plant in your garden. "Garden culture" discusses planting techniques and care for bulbs grown in the ground, while "Container culture" covers the same subjects for those in pots. Some entries lack a discussion of container care; for these bulbs, open-ground planting is the only successful treatment. A very few bulbs (Sinningia, for example) are grown exclusively in containers. For these, no garden culture is given.

Spring-blooming bulbs in full splendor include various tulips, dainty
anemones, and a blue wash of grape hyacinths *(Muscari);* lofty red and yellow
crown imperial *(Fritillaria imperialis)* presides over the scene.

THE YEAR IN FLOWERS

Throughout the year, bulbs of one sort or another are in bloom. The greatest number put on a show in spring and summer, but the other seasons are by no means bulb-free. Use these lists to guide your choices for seasonal color impact.

SPRING
Allium
Alstroemeria
Anemone
Arum
Babiana
Bletilla striata
Brodiaea
Calochortus
Camassia
Chionodoxa
Clivia miniata
Colchicum luteum
Convallaria majalis
Corydalis solida
Crinum
Crocus
Cyclamen
Dietes
Eranthis hyemalis
Eremurus
Erythronium
Freesia
Fritillaria
Galanthus
Gladiolus
Hemerocallis
Hippeastrum
Homeria collina

Hyacinthoides
Hyacinthus
Ipheion uniflorum
Iris
Ixia
Ixiolirion tataricum
Lachenalia
Leucojum
Lilium
Muscari
Narcissus
Ornithogalum
Oxalis
Puschkinia scilloides
Ranunculus asiaticus
Rhodohypoxis baueri
Scadoxus multiflorus
  katharinae
Scilla
Sparaxis tricolor
Tritonia
Tulbaghia
Tulipa
Veltheimia bracteata
Watsonia
Zantedeschia
Zephyranthes

SUMMER
Achimenes
Agapanthus
Allium
Alstroemeria
Amaryllis belladonna
Arisaema
Begonia
Belamcanda chinensis
Brodiaea
Caladium bicolor
Calochortus
Canna
Cardiocrinum giganteum
Colchicum
Crinum
Crocosmia
Cyclamen
Cyrtanthus elatus
Dahlia
Dietes
Eucomis
Galtonia candicans
Gladiolus
Gloriosa rothschildiana
Habranthus
Hemerocallis
Homeria collina
Hymenocallis

Iris
Liatris
Lilium
Lycoris
Oxalis
Pancratium maritimum
Polianthes tuberosa
Rhodohypoxis baueri
Scadoxus multiflorus
  katharinae
Sinningia speciosa
Sprekelia formosissima
Tigridia pavonia
Tulbaghia
Watsonia
Zantedeschia
Zephyranthes

AUTUMN
Begonia
Canna
Colchicum
Crocus
Cyclamen
Cyrtanthus elatus
Dahlia
Dietes
Gladiolus
Hemerocallis

Iris
Leucojum
Lycoris
Nerine
Oxalis
Polianthes tuberosa
Schizostylis coccinea
Sternbergia lutea
Tulbaghia
Zephyranthes

WINTER
Chionodoxa
Clivia miniata
Crocus
Cyclamen
Dietes
Eranthis hyemalis
Eucharis ×
  grandiflora
Galanthus
Iris
Lachenalia
Leucojum
Narcissus
Oxalis
Scilla
Tulbaghia
Veltheimia bracteata

READING THE ENTRIES

Each entry begins with the bulb's botanical name, followed by its common name (if one exists) and the name of its plant family. The next line identifies the bulb type: true bulb, corm, tuber, rhizome, or tuberous root. The following line, introduced by the symbol ▲, gives the plant's height range, covering all species and varieties mentioned in the entry.

Exposure needs are stated next. ☼ means bright, unshaded sun; ● means no direct sun at all. ◑ indicates light shade, part shade, or filtered sun. A location in *light shade* receives no direct sun but plenty of light; such a spot is brighter than one in full shade. A location in *part shade* is sunny during the cooler morning hours, shaded in the afternoon. A spot in *filtered sun* receives shade with shafts of light (as under a shade canopy or lath, for example).

Summer moisture needs are highlighted on the next line. ● means the bulb must have summer water to survive, while ○ means it must have dry conditions. ◐ means the bulb can take summer moisture or leave it.

✷ identifies the climate zones (see pages 108–111) where the bulb is known to succeed outside in the ground year-round. A number of bulbs, however, can be grown outdoors beyond the listed zones for the better part of the year if given special treatment, as noted under "Garden culture" and "Container culture" in individual entries.

If the plant or any of its parts is known to be poisonous, this is noted in the last line, next to the symbol ◊. Plants not so marked may have poisonous parts, but their toxicity is not well known.

Derived from species native to Central America and the Caribbean, these plants put on a lavish floral display throughout summer and early fall, often blooming so profusely that the slender stems and hairy, pointed oval leaves are almost obscured from view. Each flower is a five-lobed, flat-faced trumpet, 1 to 3 inches across; colors include purple, orchid, lavender, blue, white, pink, red, and orange. Nurseries offer plants in single as well as mixed colors; specialty growers sometimes carry named varieties and occasionally the species *A. longiflora*.

USES. This plant looks its best when displayed in containers—individual pots, planters, or hanging baskets.

CONTAINER CULTURE. Plant the small, irregularly shaped rhizomes in late winter or early spring, maintaining a minimum temperature of 60°F/16°C to encourage sprouting. Plant about 1 inch deep in a mixture of half moist peat moss, half sand; when plants are about 3 inches tall, transplant them to containers filled with a potting mix of equal parts peat moss, leaf mold, and perlite. Or plant rhizomes directly in their intended containers (using the potting mix just described), setting them ½ to 1 inch deep and about 2 inches apart (plant 6 to 12 in a 6-inch pot).

During the growing season, pinch back new growth if you want plump, bushy plants; leave growth unchecked for hanging basket specimens.

Water growing plants regularly. Once a month, apply a liquid fertilizer diluted to half strength. When day length shortens, flowering will lessen, then cease. As blooming ends, gradually cut back on water and let plants die down. Store dormant rhizomes over winter in a dry, cool location (but no cooler than 40°F/4°C). Leave rhizomes in their containers, or unpot them and store in dry perlite or vermiculite. Rhizomes stored in their containers should be unpotted and replanted in fresh potting mix at the proper planting time the following year.

ACHIMENES
Gesneriaceae
RHIZOME

- ▲ 1 TO 2 FEET (SOME TRAILING)
- ☼ LIGHT SHADE
- 💧 NEEDS SUMMER MOISTURE
- ✎ SOMETIMES GROWN IN BEDS IN ZONES 25, 26

Achimenes 'Minette'

Thanks to their fountainlike clumps of strap-shaped leaves, both evergreen and deciduous agapanthus are attractive foliage plants when not in flower. During bloom time, their cool blue or white blossoms provide a refreshing contrast to yellow and orange in the summer garden. Height of flowering stems ranges from 1 to 5 feet depending on the species or variety, but all plants are built along the same lines: thick stems, each topped by a rounded cluster of tubular to bell-shaped blooms, rise from the leaf clumps.

All agapanthus are native to South Africa's Cape Province. The two most commonly sold species, both evergreen, are *A. orientalis* and *A. africanus*. Both these species are also offered under the name *A. umbellatus*—and to confuse matters further, *A. orientalis,* now properly called *A. praecox orientalis,* is often sold as *A. africanus*. If you're intent on purchasing a particular species, buy blooming plants and check the appearance of the flower clusters carefully (see descriptions below).

A. orientalis is the tallest species, with the broadest leaves and the most flowers (up to 100) per cluster. Some nurseries sell named selections in white and various shades of light to fairly dark blue; 'Flore Pleno' has double blue blossoms. More often, you'll find plants labeled only as "white" or "blue." If you want a particular blue shade, choose plants while they're in bloom.

Narrower leaves, shorter stems (to about 1½ feet), and fewer flowers (up to 30) per cluster characterize *A. africanus*. Its blooms are deep blue.

The Headbourne Hybrids are a group of named varieties that include light through dark blue shades as well as white. Most are deciduous, with flowering stems rising to about 2 feet high. Some nurseries sell selections labeled simply by color.

Listing continues >

AGAPANTHUS
AGAPANTHUS, LILY-OF-THE-NILE
Amaryllidaceae
RHIZOME WITH FLESHY ROOTS

- ▲ 1 TO 5 FEET
- ☼ ☽ FULL SUN; PART OR LIGHT SHADE WHERE SUMMERS ARE HOT
- 💧 PREFERS SUMMER MOISTURE
- ✎ ZONES 3–9, 12–21, 28–31, WARMER PARTS OF 32 FOR DECIDUOUS KINDS; 7–9, 12–31 FOR EVERGREEN KINDS

Agapanthus 'Peter Pan'

The deciduous species *A. inapertus* is as tall and nearly as many-flowered as *A. orientalis,* but its tubular deep blue blossoms are pendent.

For foreground plantings—even small-scale ground covers—choose from among a number of low varieties. Evergreen 'Peter Pan' has blue flowers carried on 1- to 1½-foot stems emerging from foliage clumps no more than a foot high. 'Tinkerbell' looks much the same, but its leaves are margined in creamy white. 'Peter Pan Albus' is white flowered and a bit larger overall than the preceding varieties; it's similar to or the same as 'Rancho White' (also sold as 'Dwarf White' and 'Rancho'). Deciduous 'Queen Anne' has blue flowers carried on 2-foot stems over foliage clumps to 15 inches high.

USES. Use the larger types as accent clumps or in mass or border plantings. Smaller kinds are fine for foreground or pathway plantings.

GARDEN CULTURE. Where summers are cool or mild, choose a planting area in full sun; in hot regions, plants need light shade all day (or at least some shade during the heat of the afternoon). Plants tolerate heavy soils and will put up with infrequent watering once established, but they perform best with good, well-drained soil and regular moisture during active growth and bloom. Protect from slugs and snails.

Agapanthus is sold only in containers. Set out plants in spring or summer, setting them about 1½ feet apart and at the same depth they were growing in their pots. Divide infrequently, only when clumps show a decline in vigor and flower quality—perhaps every 6 years. Early spring is the best time to divide all types, though evergreen types can also be divided in autumn.

CONTAINER CULTURE. All types are superb container plants, and as such are easily grown in areas beyond their hardiness range if given winter protection. All perform best when crowding the container to capacity. Follow directions "C" on page 23. Where winters are too cold for outdoor survival (evergreen types survive to about 20°F/−7°C, deciduous kinds to about 10°F/−12°C), move containers to a sheltered location where plants will receive some light and temperatures will remain above freezing. Water plants just often enough to keep leaves from wilting. Return containers outdoors in spring when danger of frost is past.

Agapanthus orientalis

ALLIUM
ORNAMENTAL ALLIUM,
FLOWERING ONION
Liliaceae
TRUE BULB

▲ 6 INCHES TO OVER 5 FEET
☼ FULL SUN
◐◊ WITHHOLD WATER AFTER BLOOM
✂ ZONES VARY BY SPECIES (SEE "GARDEN CULTURE")

Most people are acquainted with certain alliums without even realizing it: onions, garlic, shallots, chives, and leeks all belong to this genus. Native mainly to the Northern Hemisphere, the numerous species bear rounded, compact or loose clusters of small flowers—in blue, lavender, violet, red, pink, yellow, or white—at the tops of leafless stems in spring or summer. The tallest types reach 5 feet or more, while the shortest top out at under 1 foot; between these extremes are many of intermediate stature. Here, grouped according to height, are the most readily available species. Specialty bulb growers offer even more kinds.

Summer-blooming giant allium, *A. giganteum,* is the skyscraper of the group. Its softball-size clusters of lavender blossoms are borne on 5- to 6-foot stalks; leaves are a modest 1½ feet long. Nearly as tall are *A. macleanii (A. elatum)* and *A. rosenbachianum;* both are violet-flowered species that bloom in late spring. For green-tinted white flowers, look for *A. rosenbachianum* 'Album'. The hybrid 'Globemaster' produces long-lasting violet blossoms in spherical heads to 10 inches across. Spring-flowering *A. aflatunense* also resembles *A. giganteum,* but its stems are shorter (to 3 to 5 feet) and its heads of lilac blossoms are smaller.

Among the alliums of middling size are three strikingly colored species, all blooming in summer. *A. atropurpureum* and *A. sphaerocephalum* (the latter commonly called "drumsticks") both grow 2 to 2½ feet tall and bear 2-inch flower clusters; the former produces blossoms of dark purple to nearly black, while the latter has very tight clusters of red-purple blossoms. *A. carinatum pulchellum (A. pulchellum)* also has red-purple flowers, but its stems reach only 2 feet at the tallest.

The under-2-foot-tall category offers the greatest variety of floral colors and forms. Summer-blooming *A. narcissiflorum* bears bell-shaped, bright rose to wine red flowers in loose clusters atop foot-tall stems. *A. christophii* (star of Persia), blooming in late spring, has potentially the largest flower clusters of all alliums—from 6 inches to as much as 1 foot across. Individual blossoms are star shaped; color varies from lilac to amethyst purple. Stems are 1 to 1½ feet tall; the 1½-foot-long leaves have silvery white undersides.

Five other worthwhile small species also flower in late spring. The shortest of these is *A. oreophilum (A. ostrowskianum)*; its stems are just 8 to 12 inches tall, topped with 2-inch, rose-colored flower clusters. Its carmine red variety 'Zwanenburg' is only about 6 inches tall. *A. caeruleum,* blue allium, has cornflower blue blossoms in 2-inch rounded clusters on 1- to 1½-foot stems; rose pink *A. roseum* bears its 4-inch flower clusters on 12- to 14-inch stems. Two other species are yellow flowered. Golden garlic, *A. moly*, features loose, 2- to 3-inch clusters of bright yellow blossoms atop 9- to 18-inch stems; its gray-green leaves are nearly as long as the stems. Clusters of pendent straw yellow flowers on 12- to 15-inch stems characterize *A. flavum.*

Midspring flowers are provided by *A. karataviense*, the Turkestan allium. Its 5-inch clusters of pinkish beige to reddish lilac blossoms are carried on 8- to 12-inch stems. Each plant usually produces two purple-tinted leaves, each up to 4 inches wide and nearly prostrate.

Allium giganteum

Another midspring bloomer is pure white *A. neapolitanum,* with loose, 3-inch flower clusters; its stems are about 1 foot tall, rising above 1-inch-wide leaves. 'Grandiflorum' has larger individual flowers and begins blooming a bit earlier than the species.

Allium karataviense

'Cowanii' (often sold as *A.* 'Cowanii') is a superior form, with earlier flowers on longer stems.

USES. The tall and middle-size species provide attractive accents in mixed groupings of annuals and perennials. Shorter species are useful in foreground drifts or clumps and as pathway edgings. *A. caeruleum, A. flavum, A. moly,* and *A. neapolitanum* are the best choices for naturalizing.

GARDEN CULTURE. Grow *A. caeruleum* in Zones 1–24, 28–45; *A. flavum, A. karataviense, A. moly, A. oreophilum, A. sphaerocephalum* in Zones 1–24, 28–43; *A. aflatunense, A. christophii, A.* 'Globemaster', *A. rosenbachianum* in Zones 1–24, 29–43; *A. carinatum pulchellum, A. giganteum, A. macleanii, A. narcissiflorum* in Zones 3–24, 29–41; *A. atropurpureum, A. neapolitanum* in Zones 4–24, 28–34, 39; *A. roseum* in Zones 4–24, 28–32.

All types prefer well-drained soil (preferably on the sandy side), enriched before planting with organic matter. In fall or spring, plant bulbs as deep as their height or width, whichever is greater. Space smaller species 4 to 6 inches apart, larger ones 8 to 12 inches apart. Water regularly during growth and bloom, but when foliage begins to yellow after flowering, water less often or even let soil go dry. Leave plantings undisturbed until vigor and flower quality decline due to overcrowding. At that time, dig clumps after foliage has died down, divide bulbs, and replant in late summer or early autumn. If replanting in the same plot, dig plenty of organic matter into the soil.

Allium moly

Listing continues >

CONTAINER CULTURE. All alliums are suitable container subjects. By growing the plants in pots, you can easily let them dry off after flowering is finished. Container culture also lets you grow species in zones outside their stated hardiness range. The smaller types are good for display on patio or terrace. Pots of larger, taller kinds can be sunk into flower borders, where they can remain until bloom is completed. Follow directions "C" on page 23.

ALSTROEMERIA

ALSTROEMERIA, PERUVIAN LILY
Liliaceae
TUBEROUS ROOT

▲ 1 TO 4 FEET

☼ ◑ FULL SUN; FILTERED SUN OR PART SHADE WHERE SUMMERS ARE HOT

◐ NEEDS SUMMER WATER (EXCEPT AS NOTED)

✇ ZONES 5–9, 14–24, 26, 28, 31; WARMER PARTS OF 32, 34

Alstroemeria

This South American native's airy sprays of azalealike flowers enliven the garden as spring slips into summer. Viewed individually, young plants look rather wispy, so it's best to set them out in groups. As clumps become established, the leafy upright stems multiply, giving the planting a bulkier look.

Most alstroemerias sold in nurseries are hybrid strains with flowers in red, orange, yellow, cream, white, pink, or lavender, often speckled or blotched with a darker color. The older Ligtu and Chilean hybrids (both deciduous groups) are being supplanted by newer, shorter, stockier strains with longer bloom periods; these newer kinds, too, die to the ground after flowering. The Cordu and Meyer hybrids are evergreen; they keep blooming over an especially long season if the spent flowering stems are pulled (grasp each stem and gently twist while pulling upward). The deciduous Constitution Series, bred in Connecticut, makes it possible to grow alstroemerias in colder regions: if mulched heavily in winter, the plants succeed along the Atlantic seaboard.

Some nurseries offer species and named selections. Peruvian lily, *A. aurea* (*A. aurantiaca*), reaches 3 to 4 feet tall, bearing its flowers in loose sprays; varieties include 'Lutea' (yellow), 'Orange King' (yellow-orange petals with brown spots), and 'Splendens' (red). The Brazilian species *A. psittacina* is more or less evergreen, with exotic dark red blossoms marked in green and purple on 1- to 1½-foot stems; it can be invasive. For western dry-summer gardens that receive little or no supplementary water, *A. aurea* and the Ligtu Hybrids are the best choices.

USES. Alstroemeria is showy for weeks in late spring and summer. All kinds, especially the deciduous sorts, are best used in mixed plantings.

GARDEN CULTURE. Plants appreciate well-drained soil enriched with organic matter before planting. The ideal location is a spot where roots are in cool, moist soil during the growing season, while flowering stems receive full sun (in cool to moderate climates) or filtered sunlight or part shade (where summers are hot). To keep soil cool and moist, mulch the planting area or overplant it with nonaggressive ground cover annuals or perennials such as verbena or sweet alyssum.

Choose a site where plants can remain undisturbed for years. Plantings spread over time but usually don't need dividing, and plants reestablish slowly after replanting.

Tuberous roots may be sold bare root from late fall through winter; they're brittle, so handle with extreme care. Space them about a foot apart, setting the growth node about 4 inches beneath the soil surface. Carefully spread out roots as you plant; in time, they will grow to a considerable depth.

During the growing season, some nurseries also sell young plants in 1- or 2-gallon containers, ready for planting.

Water alstroemeria regularly during active growth and bloom, keeping water off flower heads to prevent stems from toppling. As flowers fade and plants enter their dormant period, water less often.

CONTAINER CULTURE. Follow directions "B" (subgroup 2) on page 23, using large, deep wooden boxes or tubs.

Native to the Cape Province of South Africa, this sturdy plant has strap-shaped dark green leaves that form good-looking, fountainlike clumps about 1 foot high and 2 feet wide. Foliage dies down and disappears in late spring or early summer; wine red, 2- to 3-foot flower stalks rise from bare earth about 6 weeks later. Each stalk bears a cluster of 4 to 12 trumpet-shaped, highly fragrant blossoms. Medium rose pink is the most common color, but paler and deeper variations exist; there is also a white-flowered form, 'Hathor'. (For the bulb with the common name "amaryllis," see *Hippeastrum*, page 68).

USES. Because of its tall, bare flower stems, belladonna lily is best planted among lower-growing perennials that will mask its leaflessness.

GARDEN CULTURE. Belladonna lily isn't particular about soil type, but it does require fairly good drainage. Plant bulbs in late summer, immediately after the blooming season ends; set them about 1 foot apart. Where winter temperatures remain above 15°F/−9°C, keep tops of bulb necks at or slightly above the soil line. In colder areas, set tops of bulb necks slightly below ground level and choose a planting location in a southern exposure, even against a south-facing wall. Established plants are quite tolerant of drought, though performance is better if they receive regular moisture until leaves start to die down.

Divide and replant infrequently. Crowded conditions don't hamper bloom, and reset plants may take a year or two to reestablish before they flower.

The words "bright" and "cheerful" are often applied to anemones. And for good reason: their clear, vivid colors—purple, blue, red, pink, and white—seem to capture the essence of springtime. The numerous species are native to many temperate climates of the world. The most widely available types can be separated into two groups, based on size, hardiness, and uses.

Daisylike flowers, stems no taller than 8 inches, and clumps of fernlike or parsley-like foliage characterize rhizomatous *A. apennina* and tuberous *A. blanda.* These are cold-tolerant plants, requiring distinct winter chill for good performance. The bloom period begins in early spring, with *A. blanda* starting several weeks before *A. apennina.* Blossoms of *A. apennina* are usually sky blue, though you may find white and violet variants (some of them with double flowers). Flowers of *A. blanda* also are typically blue, but numerous color variants exist, including 'Pink Star', 'Red Star', and purplish red 'Radar'.

The second group of anemones includes the taller, more frequently planted tuberous types with poppylike and double flowers. The poppy-flowered anemone, *A. coronaria,* has finely divided foliage and leafy stems to 1½ feet tall. Each stem bears a single 1½- to 2½-inch-wide blossom in red, pink, white, or blue, usually with blue stamens. The DeCaen strain of *A. coronaria* is single flowered; the St. Brigid strain has semidouble and double flowers. Specialty growers may offer single-color strains such as Blue Poppy and The Bride.

A. fulgens, the scarlet windflower, grows to 1 foot tall; it bears black-centered, brilliant red blossoms to 2½ inches across. The St. Bavo strain includes blooms in pink, rusty coral, and terra cotta as well as red.

USES. The smaller anemones, *A. apennina* and *A. blanda,* work well as underplanting for tulips, as ground cover drifts beneath deciduous shrubs and trees, and naturalized in short grass. The taller *A. coronaria* and *A. fulgens* make colorful mass plantings and

AMARYLLIS belladonna
BELLADONNA LILY, NAKED LADY
Amaryllidaceae
TRUE BULB

- ▲ 2 TO 3 FEET
- ☼ FULL SUN
- ◐ ACCEPTS SUMMER MOISTURE BUT DOESN'T NEED ANY
- ✎ ZONES 4–24, 28, 29
- ⬧ BULBS ARE POISONOUS IF INGESTED

Amaryllis belladonna

ANEMONE
ANEMONE, WINDFLOWER
Ranunculaceae
TUBER; RHIZOME

- ▲ 2 TO 18 INCHES
- ☼ ◑ FULL SUN, PART SHADE, OR LIGHT SHADE
- ◐◯ SMALLER TYPES ACCEPT SUMMER MOISTURE
- ✎ ZONES VARY BY SPECIES (SEE "GARDEN CULTURE")

Anemone coronaria

accent clumps in borders of spring flowers. These two species and *A. blanda* are good container plants.

GARDEN CULTURE. Grow *A. blanda* in Zones 2–9, 14–23, 30–41; *A. apennina* in Zones 3–9, 14–24, 30–34, 39; *A. coronaria* in Zones 4–24, 30–34; *A. fulgens* in Zones 4–9, 14–24, 32–34.

All anemones need well-drained soil liberally amended with organic matter. Plant tubers or rhizomes top side up, 1 to 2 inches deep and 4 inches apart. To identify the top side (which can be difficult, given the irregular shapes of tubers and rhizomes), look for the depressed scar left by the base of last year's stem; the scarred side is the top.

Plant *A. apennina* and *A. blanda* in fall; where winter temperatures drop below −10°F/−23°C, apply winter protection (see page 21) annually after the first hard frost. Plant *A. coronaria* and *A. fulgens* in fall where they are hardy in the ground; in colder regions, plant in early spring.

Water plants regularly during active growth and bloom. *A. apennina* and *A. blanda* will take summer water, though they can do without it. They can be left undisturbed for many years to form large colonies; dig and divide only when vigor and bloom quality decline. For *A. coronaria* and *A. fulgens*, withhold moisture when foliage yellows; in dry-summer regions where they are hardy in the ground, you can leave them in place from year to year. But where there is summer watering or rainfall (and, for *A. fulgens*, in areas where winter lows dip below 0°F/−18°C), dig tubers when foliage yellows; then dry and store them as for tuberous begonia (page 40).

CONTAINER CULTURE. For *A. coronaria*, *A. blanda*, and *A. fulgens*, follow directions "B" (subgroup 1) on page 23.

Anemone blanda

ARISAEMA
Araceae
TUBER

- ▲ 1½ TO 4 FEET
- ☼● PART OR FULL SHADE
- ◖ NEEDS SUMMER MOISTURE
- ✂ ZONES VARY BY SPECIES (SEE "GARDEN CULTURE")

Arisaema triphyllum

These plants are related to the familiar calla *(Zantedeschia)* and have flowers that are much the same in form: a spikelike spadix sheathed by a petal-like bract called a spathe. But their green, purple, and mottled coloration gives these summer blossoms a curious, almost sinister beauty. As the flowers fade, the spathe withers and the spadix forms orange to red seeds, giving it the look of a small ear of red corn. Plants die to the ground in fall; new shoots emerge in the latter half of spring.

A. triphyllum, known as Jack-in-the-pulpit or Indian turnip, is a denizen of eastern North American woodlands. Each plant bears two 2-foot leafstalks that terminate in three 6-inch leaflets. The cobralike 6-inch spathe is green or purple with white stripes.

Three equally bizarre species hail from eastern Asia. The shortest of these, with two leafstalks to 20 inches tall, is the Japanese *A. sikokianum*, which features a white spadix enveloped by a 6-inch spathe that is purple outside, green inside. The showy cobra lily, *A. speciosum*, produces a single purple-mottled leafstalk to 1½ feet high, above which rises a 2- to 3-foot stem topped by an 8-inch spathe in purple with white stripes; this encloses a white spadix terminating in a thin 2-foot appendage. *A. tortuosum* is the tallest (to 3 to 4 feet) and leafiest species; it bears up to three leaves, each with as many as 15 narrow leaflets. The 6-inch, green or purple spathe curves strongly over the spadix, which bends to emerge from the spathe and rise above it.

USES. Because all species are conversation pieces, place them where their strange charm will be readily apparent. Use them in woodland plantings, but near pathways and with lower-growing plants that won't compete for attention.

GARDEN CULTURE. Grow *A. triphyllum* in Zones 1–6, 26, 28, 31–43; *A. sikokianum* in Zones 3–6, 31–41; *A. tortuosum* in Zones 4–6, 14–17, 31, 32; and *A. speciosum* in Zones 4–6, 14–17, 31.

In nature, these forest plants get a constant renewal of organic matter from fallen leaves and plant remains that decay each year. All prefer acid soil. In the garden, be sure to dig in plenty of organic matter at planting time in fall (set tubers 1 foot apart, about 2 inches deep); keep soil well mulched thereafter. Keep soil moist throughout the growing season, until plants begin to yellow and die down.

CONTAINER CULTURE. These plants make striking (if eerie) potted subjects for the shaded patio or terrace. Follow directions "C" on page 23.

Like their relatives *Arisaema* and calla *(Zantedeschia)*, these plants have the signature flower structure of a cylindrical, vertical spadix loosely enclosed by a petal-like bract called a spathe. But the flowers of the arums are merely unusual or interesting—not unsettling like those of *Arisaema* or elegant like those of calla. Attractively veined leaves are one appealing feature; the bright fruits that follow the flowers are another.

Leaves of Italian arum, *A. italicum,* sprout from summer-dormant tubers in fall or early winter; when mature, the leaves reach about 1 foot long (on a leafstalk of about equal length), with a broad arrow shape and attractive pale veins. Short-

Arum italicum

stemmed, white to greenish white flowers appear in spring. At first, the 1-foot spathe remains erect—like a pale scoop—but later it folds over and conceals the short spadix. After bloom, the leaves die back to the ground, leaving just the flower stems, which hold tight, elongated clusters of bright red fruits. Plants offered as the selection 'Pictum' have foliage conspicuously veined in white.

The fetchingly named black calla, *A. palaestinum,* doesn't disappoint: its 8-inch spathe is green on the outside, but it opens outward and curls back at the tip to reveal a purple interior and a black spadix. Veiny, arrow-shaped leaves reach about 8 inches long, carried on 1-foot leafstalks. Foliage starts growth from dormant tubers in winter; flowers come in spring and early summer. Leaves die to the ground after bloom.

Another species, *A. pictum,* is sometimes also called black calla, but its 8-inch spathe is violet with a white base and encloses a dark purple spadix. Flowers appear in fall—sometimes with the emerging new leaves, sometimes before them. The narrowly arrow-shaped leaves, light green with fine white veins, grow to 10 inches long and are borne on 10-inch leafstalks. Foliage dies to the ground with the onset of hot weather in late spring or early summer.

USES. All three species can be interesting components of a mixed border in shade; Italian arum can be used as a small-scale ground cover or "patch planting" if you don't mind its disappearance in summer.

GARDEN CULTURE. *A. italicum* is adapted to Zones 3–24, 28–34, 39; *A. pictum* to Zones 7–9, 14–24, 28–31; *A. palaestinum* to Zones 14–24. Plant in reasonably good soil amended with organic matter. Set out tubers in late summer or early fall toward the end of their dormant period, planting them 8 to 12 inches apart and about 2 inches deep. Plants can remain undisturbed for years; in favorable situations, Italian arum will spread or naturalize by volunteer seedlings.

CONTAINER CULTURE. Both of the black callas *(A. palaestinum* and *A. pictum)* are easy container subjects. In zones colder than their stated hardiness, container culture is the only way to enjoy their odd beauty. Follow directions "C" on page 23.

ARUM
Araceae
TUBER

▲ 1 TO 2 FEET

☼ ● PARTIAL OR FULL SHADE

◑ ACCEPTS SUMMER MOISTURE BUT DOESN'T NEED ANY

✺ ZONES VARY BY SPECIES (SEE "GARDEN CULTURE")

Arum italicum 'Pictum'

BABIANA

BABOON FLOWER

Iridaceae

CORM

- ▲ 6 TO 12 INCHES
- ☼ ☽ FULL SUN OR PART SHADE
- ◐ ACCEPTS SUMMER MOISTURE BUT DOESN'T NEED ANY
- ✎ ZONES 4–24, 29–31, WARMER PARTS OF 32

Babiana stricta

These natives of sub-Saharan Africa catch the eye with flowers in near-fluorescent shades of blue, lavender, purple, and red; there are also forms with white and blue-and-white blossoms. In mid- to late spring, each flowering stem produces six or more blooms, each up to 2 inches across and shaped like a shallow cup with six equal segments. The hairy, sword-shaped leaves have lengthwise ribbing and are borne in fans, like those of gladiolus. Baboons are said to enjoy eating the corms, hence the plant's common name.

Widely available *B. stricta* and its variously colored named selections bear their arresting blossoms on foot-tall stems. The ruby-throated royal blue blossoms of *B. rubrocyanea* appear on stems just half that height.

USES. Plant baboon flower to be viewed at close range—in rock gardens, along pathways, in foreground drifts.

GARDEN CULTURE. Plant in well-drained soil, in a location that receives sun for at least half the day. For a massed effect, set corms 4 inches deep and 4 to 6 inches apart. In Zones 8–24, 29, plant corms in autumn. In colder zones, plant in early spring, waiting until temperatures will remain above 20°F/−7°C.

Water plants regularly throughout growth and bloom, then taper off as leaves yellow after the bloom period ends. Trim foliage off after it dies back. Where corms can overwinter in the ground, leave them in place for several years—they'll increase and bloom more profusely with each passing year. In colder climates, dig and store corms as for gladiolus (page 64).

CONTAINER CULTURE. Plant corms in a deep pot, setting them about 1 inch deep and 1 inch apart. Follow directions "B" (subgroup 2) on page 23.

BEGONIA

Begoniaceae

TUBER

- ▲ 1 TO 3 FEET
- ☼ FILTERED SUN OR LIGHT SHADE
- ● NEEDS SUMMER MOISTURE
- ✎ ZONES VARY BY SPECIES (SEE "GARDEN CULTURE")

Begonia grandis

The two familiar begonias that grow from tubers could hardly be more different. One is a flamboyant showstopper with masses of large blossoms in a great variety of colors and combinations; the other makes a case for subtle beauty, offering profuse small flowers in just two colors.

Hardy begonia, *B. grandis (B. evansiana, B. grandis evansiana)*, an Asian species, reaches 2 to 3 feet tall, its upright, branching red stems bearing wing-shaped, coppery green leaves backed in red. Pink or white flowers, each slightly more than an inch across, bloom in drooping clusters during summer and early fall. Stems die to the ground with the onset of chilly weather; tubers resume growth the next spring after the danger of frost is past. After bloom—but before stems die down—small bulbils are produced where the leaves join the stems. You can detach these, store them over winter as for the tubers, and plant in spring for growth and bloom the same year.

For general magnificence and great range of hues (pink, red, orange, yellow, cream, white, and multicolors), tuberous begonias—sometimes sold as *B.* × *tuberhybrida*—are second to no other summer-flowering bulb. And for number of blossoms to size of plant, they clearly lead the pack. Starting with the original South American species, hybridizers have refined colors and patterns. Flower form has been tailored, too: a number of modern varieties have blossoms resembling those of other plants, such as rose, camellia, and carnation.

Well-grown plants of tuberous begonia may reach 1 to 1½ feet tall and produce saucer-size flowers. The irregularly shaped, pointed leaves grow to about 8 inches long. A special group of hybrids, sometimes sold as *B.* × *t.* 'Pendula', has drooping stems and downward-facing flowers. These are plants for hanging baskets and are best displayed at eye level, where their blossoms can be appreciated.

USES. Both types of begonias are useful as accents or in mixed plantings in the shady summer garden. For color impact, try mass plantings or groupings of tuberous begonias alone.

GARDEN CULTURE. *B. grandis* is hardy in Zones 3–33 (in colder zones, it can be grown in containers or dug and stored as for tuberous begonia). Tuberous begonias (those sometimes sold as *B. × tuberhybrida*) flourish when given an ideal combination of moist air and "tepid" temperatures: neither too hot nor too cool. They grow best in Zones 4–6, 15–17, 21–24, 38, 39, and 43, areas where bloom-time night temperatures remain above 60°F/16°C—along the Pacific and North Atlantic coasts, in the Great Lakes coastal areas, and in parts of northern Minnesota and Michigan. Heat plus high humidity, typical of summers in the Southeast and along the Gulf Coast, create the most trying conditions. At the end of the bloom season, when stems yellow and die, dig and store the tubers over winter as described below.

Although most gardeners grow both these begonias in containers (see below), the plants can also go directly in the ground for seasonal display. Amend the existing soil with the potting mix described below, using 1 part soil to 2 parts potting mix. With both begonias, sprout tubers in pots or flats as described below, then set them into the ground when plants have a few leaves. The leaves on sprouted tuberous begonias all point in one direction; when flowers come, they too will face that way. As you set these plants into the ground, position them so you'll see the fronts of the flowers.

For tuberous begonias planted in the ground (or hardy begonias to be stored over winter), follow the same regime of withholding water and fertilizer and of digging and storing as for container-grown plants.

CONTAINER CULTURE. Plant tubers of *B. grandis* about ¼ inch deep, 3 to 4 inches apart, directly into pots of potting mix (see directions "A" on page 23). Set the pots in light shade or dappled sun and keep soil moist but not saturated while tubers root and sprout. Apply a liquid fertilizer every 3 to 4 weeks during the growing season—through mid-August in colder zones, into mid- or late September where the season is longer. When growth and flowering cease, treat plants as outlined below for tuberous begonias.

Tuberous begonia plants can be set outdoors whenever night temperatures are sure to remain above 50°F/10°C. Start them 6 to 8 weeks in advance of the time you can put them outside, setting the tubers directly into pots of potting mix (see directions "A" on page 23); be sure the containers are large enough to leave 2 inches between all sides of the tubers and the container edges. Set tubers indented side up, covering them with no more than ¼ inch of mix. If you're planting a number of tubers, it's easiest to start them in a flat or shallow box, spacing them about 4 inches apart. Place pots or flats in a well-lit spot (but not in direct sun) where temperatures will remain above 65°F/18°C; keep soil moist but not saturated during the rooting period.

Tuberous begonia hybrids

When the tubers have produced two leaves, you can move them outside if temperatures are warm enough; this is also the stage when plants sprouted in flats can be potted up.

Tuberous begonias need protection from wind but require freely circulating air: still, moist air will lead to mildewed foliage. Plenty of light (but no direct sun) is another requirement. Choose a spot in filtered sun or light shade—under high-branching trees, on the east or north side of a house, wall, or fence, or under light-modifying overhead structures of lath, shade cloth, or fiberglass.

As plants grow, keep soil moist but not soggy. Too much water will cause tubers to rot; too little will check growth. In dry climates, you'll also need to raise humidity around plants—set up a permanent mist or fog system, or use such attachments on your hose. Except for misting, however, keep water off leaves and flowers: the weight of the water droplets can topple blooming plants or break their stems.

Listing continues >

Tuberous begonia hybrid

Begin applications of liquid fertilizer a week or two after young plants have reached the two-leaf stage. Gardeners who are going for the largest possible blossoms use a half-strength solution every other week, but you can easily grow fine plants with monthly regular-strength applications.

In late summer to midautumn, flower production will slow and then cease. When you notice this slowdown, stop fertilizing and cut back on water, keeping soil just moist enough to prevent foliage from wilting (you want tubers to store as much food as possible before they enter dormancy). When leaves begin to turn yellow, withhold water. If frosts are likely to occur before plants die down completely, move containers into a well-lit, frost-free location.

When leaves fall off and stems separate easily from tubers, the tubers are ready for storage. Place containers in a cool, dark spot where temperatures will remain above freezing (preferably in the range of 40° to 50°F/4° to 10°C). You can also store tubers out of their containers. Knock them from their pots, remove stems and all soil, and let them dry for several days in a shaded, dry location. Then give covered storage (see page 21) over winter.

BELAMCANDA chinensis, PARDANCANDA × norrisii
BLACKBERRY LILY, CANDY LILY
Iridaceae
RHIZOME

- ▲ 2 TO 3 FEET
- ☼ ◑ FULL SUN OR LIGHT SHADE
- ◗ NEEDS SOME SUMMER MOISTURE
- ✄ ZONES 1–24, 26, 28–43

Belamcanda chinensis

Native to China and Japan, blackberry lily (*Belamcanda chinensis*) produces iris-like foliage clumps which give rise to branched flowering stems 2 to 3 feet high. These bear swarms of 2- to 3-inch, red-spotted orange flowers, each with six petals arranged in pinwheel fashion. Though each bloom lasts just one day, each slender stem produces numerous flowers over several weeks in summer. When the seed capsules mature in fall, they split open to reveal clusters of shining black seeds resembling blackberries.

Plants cataloged as candy lily (designated as *Pardancanda × norrisii*) are hybrids between *Belamcanda chinensis* and its near relative *Pardanthopsis dichotoma*, a native of northern Asia. Candy lily resembles blackberry lily in plant habit and size, but its flowers come in blue, purple, pink, and yellow as well as orange.

USES. Blackberry lily and candy lily are good accent plants. Their vertical foliage clumps and masses of airy blossoms mix well with a variety of annuals and perennials.

GARDEN CULTURE. Plant rhizomes in well-drained soil in fall (early spring where winter temperatures fall below 10°F/−12°C); space them 1 foot apart, with their tops just beneath the soil surface. Fall planting is best in Zones 4–24, 26, 28, 29; plant in spring in Zones 1–3, 30–43. Water plants regularly during growth and bloom; after flowering, they'll get by with less frequent watering.

Established clumps give the best display, so divide and reset infrequently.

BLETILLA striata
CHINESE GROUND ORCHID
Orchidaceae
RHIZOME

- ▲ 1½ TO 2 FEET
- ◑ FILTERED SUN OR PART SHADE
- ◗ NEEDS SUMMER MOISTURE
- ✄ ZONES 4–9, 12–24, 26, 28–31, WARMER PARTS OF 32

This easy-to-grow plant from East Asia is unmistakably an orchid—its 2-inch flowers look much like the cattleya orchids of corsage fame. Lavender is the typical color, but a white-flowered variety ('Alba') is sometimes available. *B. s. albostriata* bears light pink flowers above leaves striped in green and white.

Plants break dormancy in early spring, sending up three to six lance-shaped, plaited-looking light green leaves. Bare flower stems to about 2 feet tall follow in late spring; each produces three to seven blossoms, spaced apart from each other toward the stem end.

USES. Plant in clumps, patches, or drifts. The delicate blooms look especially attractive in combination with rhododendrons or azaleas.

GARDEN CULTURE. Plant rhizomes at any time during the dormant period from late fall to early spring, setting them 1 inch deep and 1 foot apart in good, well-drained soil enriched with organic matter. When leaves emerge, put out bait for slugs and snails. Water regularly during growth and bloom, then taper off when leaves begin to yellow in fall. After foliage has died back completely, rhizomes become dormant and don't need much water.

Large, crowded clumps give the best display of blooms, but you may dig and divide as needed during dormancy.

CONTAINER CULTURE. A thriving clump of Chinese ground orchid makes a striking container plant, attractive during bloom and afterwards—until the leaves die back. Follow directions "C" on page 23.

Bletilla striata

BRODIAEA, DICHELOSTEMMA, TRITELEIA
Liliaceae
CORM

- ▲ 10 TO 30 INCHES
- ☼ FULL SUN
- ◊ WITHHOLD SUMMER MOISTURE
- ✀ ZONES VARY BY SPECIES (SEE "GARDEN CULTURE")

In recent years, botanists have transferred a number of species from *Brodiaea* to *Dichelostemma* and *Triteleia*. But because many nurseries still offer all these plants as *Brodiaea*—and many gardeners still refer to them as such—all are treated together here. The correct botanical name is given first; the old name appears in parentheses. For the plant once called *Brodiaea uniflora* (spring star flower), see *Ipheion uniflorum* on page 72.

The brodiaeas (and former brodiaeas) are native to the western United States, where they experience a hot, dry, and usually long summer dormant period. In the wild, these are field and meadow plants, often waving their heads of blue, purple, white, or yellow flowers above or among the dry grasses of fields and hillsides. Each plant produces a few grasslike leaves and a single slender stem topped by a loose cluster of bell-shaped or funnel-shaped blossoms in spring or summer.

Harvest brodiaea, *B. elegans,* bears 1-inch-wide dark blue blossoms on 10- to 20-inch stems in late spring and early summer; *B. coronaria* is very similar, but a bit smaller and shorter.

Dichelostemma capitatum (Brodiaea capitata) blooms in early to midspring, producing tight clusters of deep blue to violet flowers on 2-foot stems.

Two formerly separate *Brodiaea* species, *B. hyacinthina* and *B. lactea,* have been merged as one species with a totally new name: *Triteleia hyacinthina.* Flowering stems to 2½ feet tall arise in early to midsummer, bearing bell-shaped white flowers in open clusters. Golden brodiaea, *T. ixioides* (formerly *B. ixioides*), flaunts inch-long yellow blossoms on foot-tall stems in late spring. Ithuriel's spear, *T. laxa* (formerly *B. laxa*) flowers in mid- to late spring, its 2½-foot stems carrying profuse clusters of bluish purple flowers nearly 2 inches long. 'Queen Fabiola' is usually sold as a selected, superior form of *T. laxa.*

USES. The various brodiaeas are good choices for naturalizing at garden fringes and at the edges of uncultivated property. They can also be used to lend a wildflower-type accent to groupings of other drought-tolerant plants.

GARDEN CULTURE. Grow *B. elegans* and *T. hyacinthina* in Zones 1–9, 14–24, 29–43; *D. capitatum* in Zones 1–3, 5–12, 14–24; *T. laxa* and 'Queen Fabiola' in Zones 3–9, 14–24, 29, 30, 33; *B. coronaria* in Zones 4–9, 14–24, 29, 30; *T. ixioides* in Zones 5–9, 14–24. Under "native" conditions—hot, absolutely dry summer weather—these bulbs will accept heavy soils as well as light and well-drained ones. But if summer moisture is inevitable, good drainage is a necessity—and even then there's no guarantee of success. If you live in a moist-summer region and want to try growing

Brodiaea 'Queen Fabiola'

any of these species in the garden, *T. hyacinthina* is probably your best bet. Container culture (see below) is another option.

Plant corms in fall, 2 to 3 inches deep and 2 to 4 inches apart. All species need regular moisture during their winter and spring growing period. Digging and dividing are necessary only infrequently, when clumps show a decline in vigor and bloom quality.

CONTAINER CULTURE. The various species aren't difficult to grow in containers, though they look rather wispy. Follow directions "B" (subgroup 2) on page 23.

CALADIUM bicolor
FANCY-LEAFED CALADIUM
Araceae
TUBER

- ▲ 2 TO 3 FEET
- ☼ FILTERED SUN OR LIGHT SHADE, EXCEPT AS NOTED
- ● NEEDS SUMMER MOISTURE
- ⚡ ZONES 25–27

Caladium bicolor

No one would look twice at a caladium flower, which resembles a small calla *(Zantedeschia)*. What these tropical South American plants provide is crowd-stopping summer foliage in combinations of red, pink, white, green, silver, and bronze. Each tuber gives rise to numerous slim leafstalks, each of which supports a thin-textured leaf shaped like an elongated heart, up to 1 foot wide and 1½ feet long when well grown. Patterns are almost too varied to describe; veining, dotting, splashing, washing, and edging are some of the ways in which one color is contrasted against another.

Though all types need bright light, most do not tolerate direct sun. Varieties that do take sun include 'Fire Chief', 'Red Flash', 'Rose Bud', and 'White Queen'.

USES. Potted caladiums often decorate terraces and patios; they're greenhouse favorites, too. To simulate garden planting, you can sink the potted plants into the ground.

GARDEN CULTURE. Caladiums need a growing season of at least 4 months, with temperatures above 70°F/21°C during the day and ideally no lower than 60°F/16°C at night. As garden plants, they perform best in Florida and some areas of the Gulf Coast, where they can get rich soil, high humidity, heat, and plenty of water. Plant in early spring, in filtered sun or light shade (sun-tolerant types can take at least a half day of sun). Replace the top 6 inches of garden soil with the potting mix recommended for "A" on page 23. Set out plants (from the nursery or from tubers you started as for tuberous begonia, page 40) 8 to 12 inches apart, keeping tops of tubers even with the soil surface.

Keep soil moist but not soggy, and water more generously as more leaves develop. If humidity is low, mist foliage daily with a fine spray of water. For best performance, apply a liquid fertilizer diluted to half strength every other week. Put out bait for slugs and snails. Remove any blossoms, since these will divert energy from leaf production. When leaves begin to die down in late summer or early fall, cut back on watering. Tubers can stay in the ground where hardy; elsewhere, dig and store as for tuberous begonia (page 40).

CONTAINER CULTURE. Start tubers indoors a month before outside temperatures normally reach the levels noted under "Garden culture" (above), using soil mix described under "A" on page 23 and following directions for tuberous begonia (page 40).

CALOCHORTUS
Liliaceae
TRUE BULB

- ▲ 4 INCHES TO 3 FEET
- ☼ ◐ FULL SUN OR LIGHT SHADE
- ◊ WITHHOLD SUMMER MOISTURE
- ⚡ ZONES VARY BY SPECIES (SEE "GARDEN CULTURE")

Among bulbous plants, these rank near the top for delicacy and floral beauty in spring or early summer. However, the various species are also among the more challenging for the garden, since they demand the long, warm, dry summers of their native habitats in western North America.

Sparse, grasslike foliage is common to all members of the genus, but flower forms can be divided into three distinct groups. Globe tulips or fairy lanterns have nodding flowers, the petals turning inward to form a globe. Star tulips have upward-facing, cup-shaped flowers, with petal tips often rolled outward; those with long straight hairs on the inner flower parts are called "cat's ears" or "pussy ears." Mariposa lilies are generally the tallest types, with striking cup- or bowl-shaped flowers.

Bulb specialists may offer various species, representing some or all of the three basic flower types. Among the globe tulips are *C. albus* (white), *C. amabilis* (yellow), and *C. amoenus* (rosy purple). Star tulips and cat's ears include *C. nudus* (white or lavender), *C. tolmiei* (white or cream, tinged with purple), and *C. uniflorus* (lilac). Most variable of the mariposa lilies is *C. venustus;* its blossoms may be white, pink, light to dark red, purple, or yellow, usually centered with contrasting markings that sometimes extend onto the petals. Other mariposa lilies are *C. clavatus* and *C. luteus* (yellow), *C. splendens* (lilac with purple), *C. nuttallii* (white with purple), and *C. vestae* (white, lilac, or pink, with a contrasting color in the flower center).

USES. Where conditions favor success in the ground, all species can be conversation-piece ornaments in rock gardens or naturalized on sunny, grassy hillsides. As container plants, they are striking in bloom, but the foliage is rather wispy.

GARDEN CULTURE. Grow *C. nuttallii* in Zones 1–3; *C. splendens* and *C. venustus* in Zones 1–3, 7, 9, 14–24; *C. nudus* in Zones 1–3, 7–9, 14; *C. tolmiei* in Zones 1, 4–6, 7, 15–17; *C. amabilis* and *C. uniflorus* in Zones 4–7, 9, 14–24; *C. amoenus* and *C. vestae* in Zones 7, 9, 14–21; *C. albus, C. clavatus,* and *C. luteus* in Zones 7, 9, 14–24.

Plant bulbs in fall, setting them 3 to 4 inches deep and about 6 inches apart. The keys to success are well-drained soil and no water at all from the time leaves start to yellow after bloom until midautumn (when rainfall begins in native habitats). Under ideal conditions, plantings can remain undisturbed for years.

In areas with summer rainfall, try digging bulbs as soon as leaves turn yellow, then holding them in dry sand until fall. Some gardeners have successfully used this method year after year. An alternative is container culture; be sure to keep the soil mix completely dry during the long summer dormant period.

CONTAINER CULTURE. Follow directions "B" (subgroup 2) on page 23.

TOP: *Calochortus albus*
BOTTOM: *Calochortus luteus*

Camassia leichtlinii

CAMASSIA

CAMASS
Liliaceae
TRUE BULB

▲ 1 TO 4 FEET
☼ ◑ FULL SUN OR LIGHT SHADE
◖ NEEDS SOME SUMMER MOISTURE
✚ ZONES 1–9, 14–17, 31, 32, 34, 39

You don't grow this western North American native for flamboyant, show-stopping floral displays. Instead, it offers the charm of a meadow wildflower—which is just what it is. Rosettes of grasslike to strap-shaped leaves send up slender spikes of loosely spaced, starlike blossoms in spring; after flowering, foliage dies down completely for the summer dormant period.

Bulb specialists offer several species and varieties. *C. cusickii* bears blue flowers on stems to 3 feet tall. *C. leichtlinii*, the tallest camass, reaches a height of 4 feet; its blossoms are creamy white. *C. l. suksdorfii* is blue flowered; *C. l.* 'Alba' is nearer to white than the species, while 'Plena' has double greenish white blossoms. For deep blue blooms on 1- to 2-foot stems, choose *C. quamash* or its varieties 'Orion' and 'San Juan Form'.

USES. Though camass is at home in meadowlike situations, the tall flower spikes also look attractive in mixed plantings of spring flowers. Since plants die down after bloom, set camass where the foliage of other plants will hide its yellowing leaves (and fill in the bare spots left after leaves are entirely gone).

GARDEN CULTURE. Camass never requires digging and dividing, so plant bulbs where they can remain undisturbed. In fall, set the large bulbs about 6 inches apart and 3 to 4 inches deep in good, moisture-retentive soil. Plants like ample water during growth and bloom, but can get by with less during the summer dormant period.

CANNA
Cannaceae
RHIZOME

▲ 1½ TO 6 FEET

☼ FULL SUN

● NEEDS SUMMER MOISTURE

✄ ZONES 6–9, 12–31, WARMER PARTS OF 32

Canna

For showiness and productivity, you can't go wrong with cannas. Choose from several heights and a wide range of flower colors, including red, orange, yellow, pink, cream, white, and bicolors. Rhizomes produce clumps of upright stems sheathed in broad, lance-shaped, decidedly tropical-looking leaves that may be green, bronze, or variegated. In summer and fall, each stem bears a spike of large, bright flowers resembling irregularly shaped gladiolus.

Virtually all cannas in the nursery trade are hybrids of mixed ancestry, originating from species found in the American tropics and subtropics. The old-fashioned garden favorites reach 4 to 6 feet, but lower-growing, more compact strains are also available. The Grand Opera strain grows a bit over 2 feet tall, while the Pfitzer Dwarf strain reaches 2½ to 3 feet. Shortest of all is the 1½-foot Seven Dwarfs strain.

USES. Cannas are particularly dramatic as color accents, but their bright blossoms and bold leaves also add a striking tropical touch to the garden. They make stunning container plants.

GARDEN CULTURE. Cannas thrive in good, moist soil and a hot, bright location. Choose a sunny area where plants can receive regular moisture during growth and bloom; incorporate a generous amount of organic matter into the soil before setting out rhizomes.

Where rhizomes are hardy in the ground (they survive to about 0°F/−18°C), plant after the normal last-frost date in spring, spacing rhizomes 1½ to 2 feet apart and covering them with 2 to 4 inches of soil. In colder regions, start rhizomes indoors 4 to 6 weeks before the usual last-frost date, so that plants will bloom sooner after being planted outdoors.

As each stem finishes flowering, cut it to the ground; new stems will continue to grow throughout summer and early fall.

Where the climate is mild enough for cannas to remain in the ground from year to year, cut back faded flower stalks in fall after new flowering stems cease to appear. Clumps usually become overcrowded every 3 or 4 years; when this happens, dig in early spring and cut the rhizomes apart. Let the cuts dry and heal over (this takes about 24 hours), then replant in newly enriched soil.

In regions where winter temperatures fall below 0°F/−18°C, dig cannas after the first hard frost kills foliage. Cut off stems; knock soil from rhizomes and let them dry for several days in a dry, shaded spot. Give covered storage (see page 21) over winter.

CONTAINER CULTURE. Displayed in large pots or wooden planters, the shorter kinds of cannas are effective summer patio and terrace decorations. Follow directions "C" on page 23.

CARDIOCRINUM giganteum
Liliaceae
TRUE BULB

▲ 6 TO 12 FEET

☼ FILTERED SUN OR LIGHT SHADE

● NEEDS SUMMER MOISTURE

✄ ZONES 4–6, 14–17, 32

If ever a plant needed a common name, this Himalayan aristocrat is the one. It looks like a towering lily; and indeed, only small botanical niceties keep it from being classed as a lily species. One distinct difference is the foliage: the glossy dark green leaves are 1½ feet long, broadly oval to heart shaped, with a texture like that of spinach.

Every summer, the foliage rosette gives rise to a leafy, vertical stem. The stem is flowerless for several years, dying back to the ground each fall. In 3 or 4 years, however, a massive flowering stalk rises to bear its majestic beauty high overhead: a tier of up to twenty 6- to 8-inch, fragrant white trumpets with red markings in their throats, reminiscent of alien Easter lilies. The flowers set seed, after which the entire plant dies—but not before producing numerous small offset bulbs that will grow to flowering size within several years.

USES. This plant is the nonpareil of exclamation points in a woodland garden. Plant it among other shade-loving plants where you want a compelling late-summer floral display. It's best to set out bulbs of different sizes; this gives you a better chance of having one or more flowering stems each year while the immature plants build up strength for bloom in the future.

GARDEN CULTURE. Choose a location in light shade or dappled sun, with fertile, organically enriched soil that can be kept moist throughout the growing season. Set out bulbs in fall (in milder-winter regions) or early spring, spacing them about 2 feet apart and placing the tops just beneath the soil surface. Bulbs break dormancy early in spring; if late frosts are likely, mulch the planting location and protect emerging plants with cut conifer branches.

A plant that has flowered usually produces quite a few offset bulbs. If these are left in place, they will be too crowded to turn in a top-notch performance when they mature; for better results, dig, separate, and replant these offspring after the flowering stem dies, giving each enough space to grow to considerable size. You can also obtain new plants by sowing the seeds produced after flowering, but seedlings may take up to 7 years to reach blooming size.

Cardiocrinum giganteum

Chionodoxa sardensis

In their native lands of Crete, Cyprus, and Turkey, these charming little plants begin flowering as the snow melts at winter's end. Each bulb produces a stem to 6 inches tall, with blossoms spaced along its upper part: six-pointed blue, white, or pink stars about an inch across. The straight, narrow leaves are slightly shorter than the stem.

C. luciliae is the most frequently grown species. Each stem carries about 10 bright blue blossoms with white centers. Varieties include 'Alba', pure white and a bit larger flowered; 'Gigantea', with larger leaves and larger blossoms of violet blue; and pink-flowered 'Pink Giant' and 'Rosea'. *C. sardensis* produces blooms of deep gentian blue, each centered with a tiny white eye.

USES. Naturalized under deciduous shrubs, glory-of-the-snow will in time create a carpet of flowers. It's also good in rock gardens and pathway border plantings.

GARDEN CULTURE. Where summers are cool or mild, grow plants in full sun. In hot-summer climates, however, be sure the growing area is in filtered sun or light shade after the bloom period ends.

In fall, plant bulbs 2 to 3 inches deep and about 3 inches apart, in well-drained soil enriched with organic matter. Plants need regular moisture during growth and bloom, less when foliage begins to die back. If bulbs are planted where soil is shaded and relatively cool during summer, they can get by with little or no water during their summer dormancy. Where summers are hot and dry, make sure that any bulbs in full-sun locations receive moderate watering during summer.

Bulbs increase rapidly and may be dug and separated for increase in early fall, whenever plantings have declined in vigor and bloom quality. Plantings often also increase from self-sown seedlings.

CHIONODOXA
GLORY-OF-THE-SNOW
Liliaceae
TRUE BULB

- ▲ 6 INCHES
- ☼ ◑ FULL SUN; FILTERED SUN OR LIGHT SHADE AFTER BLOOM WHERE SUMMERS ARE HOT
- ◖ MAY NEED SOME SUMMER MOISTURE (SEE "GARDEN CULTURE")
- ✀ ZONES 1–7, 14–20, 31–43

Chionodoxa luciliae 'Pink Giant'

CLIVIA miniata

CLIVIA, KAFFIR LILY
Amaryllidaceae
TUBEROUS ROOT

- ▲ 2 FEET
- ☼ ● FILTERED SUN, PART SHADE, OR FULL SHADE
- ● NEEDS SUMMER MOISTURE
- ✂ ZONES 12–17, 19–27

Clivia miniata, Solomone Hybrid

This evergreen South African native is striking in both foliage and flowers. Broad, strap-shaped, lustrous dark green leaves grow to about 1½ feet long, arching outward to form a fountainlike clump. In winter and spring, the clump sends up thick stems to 2 feet tall, each crowned by a cluster of funnel-shaped, 2-inch blossoms, typically in vivid orange with a yellow center. Decorative red berries ripen after the flowers fade.

With a bit of nursery or catalog searching, you can find variations on the basic theme. 'Flame' has blooms of a particularly deep orange red; French and Belgian hybrids have notably wide leaves and thick flower stalks carrying blossoms ranging from yellow to orange red. The Solomone Hybrids offer yellow flowers in pale to deep shades.

USES. Clivia makes a good year-round accent plant for patio or shady garden—in a single clump or a mass planting, in containers or in the ground.

GARDEN CULTURE. Where winters are frost free (or nearly so), plant at any time of year, in filtered sunlight to shade. Dig a liberal amount of organic matter into the soil before planting. Set plants 1½ to 2 feet apart, at the depth they were growing in their pots (they are sold only in containers). Provide regular moisture from winter through summer; taper off when growth slows in autumn, but never let leaves wilt.

Plants will not need dividing for many years. When clumps do become overcrowded, dig and reset in spring, after flowering has ended.

CONTAINER CULTURE. Follow directions "C" on page 23. Apply liquid fertilizer monthly during spring and summer to enhance the next season's flowering.

Where winter temperatures drop below about 25°F/–4°C, container-grown plants can overwinter indoors in a brightly lit, cool room (night temperatures from 50° to 55°F/10° to 13°C). Clivia can also be treated as a house plant.

Clivia blooms best when rootbound, so repot (in spring) only when plants look as if they're about to burst out of the container.

COLCHICUM

MEADOW SAFFRON
Liliaceae
CORM

- ▲ 6 TO 8 INCHES
- ☼ FULL SUN
- ● NEEDS SOME SUMMER MOISTURE
- ✂ ZONES 1–9, 14–24, 29, 30, 33–43
- ◊ ALL PARTS ARE POISONOUS IF INGESTED

Colchicum 'Waterlily'

Meadow saffron's delicate flowers rise from bare earth in late summer to early autumn, holding the stage without accompaniment of foliage. The blooms are chalice shaped or starlike, in lavender, violet, pink, white, or yellow; each has six pointed petals atop a slim tube that acts as a stem. After the flowers wither, the plants essentially vanish until spring, when floppy, straplike leaves up to 1 foot long emerge; these aren't especially decorative, but last for just a few months and die back well before the blooming season. (An oddity among the meadow saffrons is yellow-flowered *C. luteum*, which blooms in spring.)

Many species of meadow saffron are native from the Mediterranean region to central Asia and India. Bulb specialists may offer several kinds, but most nurseries stock only *C. autumnale* (often referred to as "autumn crocus") and several named hybrids. Blossoms of *C. autumnale* are about 2 inches wide and typically pinkish lavender in color, though a white form exists (as do double-flowered kinds in both lavender and white). Available hybrids include 'Autumn Queen' (mottled purple on a paler background), 'The Giant' (lilac with a white center), 'Violet Queen' (rich purple with a white center), and 'Waterlily' (double violet).

USES. Meadow saffron looks best when naturalized along paths or walkways. Locate where flowers won't be obscured by taller plants, but where floppy leaves won't be too obtrusive.

GARDEN CULTURE. Plants aren't fussy about soil type, but they do need good drainage. Plant corms in summer, 6 to 8 inches apart and 3 inches deep. Provide some moisture all year: water regularly in spring while plants are in leaf, then more sparingly during the brief midsummer dormant period—but not so sparsely that soil dries out completely. Resume regular watering when flowers appear. Plantings may become overcrowded every 3 or 4 years. Dig and divide in midsummer as necessary.

CONTAINER CULTURE. These accommodating plants will flower even without benefit of a container: dormant corms placed on a sunny (but not hot) windowsill will bloom at the usual time. For standard container culture, see directions "B" (subgroup 2) on page 23.

The common name "elephant's ear" provides a good description of this tropical plant's enormous (to 2½ by 3 feet), heart-shaped green leaves. Leathery to almost rubbery in texture, they are carried aloft at the ends of succulent stalks from spring through fall; an established clump of multiple tubers produces a display that can only be called junglelike. Inconspicuous flowers resembling greenish callas (*Zantedeschia*) appear only in the most temperate climates.

USES. Elephant's ear is a peerless choice for creating tropical effects in light shade. In native Hawaiian and other Polynesian cultures, the tubers are an important dietary source of carbohydrates.

GARDEN CULTURE. In mild-summer regions, plants can take full sun—but everywhere else, choose a location in filtered sun or light shade. Rich soil and plenty of moisture produce the most impressive leaves, but good drainage isn't a requirement; plants will grow in soggy soil, even in standing water.

Where winters are frost free, plant tubers in late winter or very early spring; elsewhere, wait until after the last-frost date. Enrich soil with organic matter before planting; then set out tubers 1 to 1½ feet apart and about 2 inches deep. Water frequently throughout the growing season; for the most impressive leaves, apply fertilizer periodically. When clumps become overcrowded, dig and divide in early spring.

In regions where soil freezes, plants cannot survive the winter outdoors. After foliage is killed by frost, dig and store tubers as for tuberous begonia (page 40).

CONTAINER CULTURE. In a suitably large container, elephant's ear is a spectacular summertime ornament for patio or terrace. Start tubers indoors 4 to 6 weeks before the expected last-frost date. Follow directions "C" on page 23. Fertilize bimonthly with a high-nitrogen liquid fertilizer such as fish emulsion. In zones too cold for year-round outdoor culture, you can move container-grown plants to a protected spot for the winter, then return them outside in spring after all danger of frost is past.

COLOCASIA esculenta
ELEPHANT'S EAR, TARO
Araceae
TUBER

▲ 6 FEET
☼ ◑ FULL SUN; FILTERED SUN OR LIGHT SHADE WHERE SUMMERS ARE HOT
◖ NEEDS SUMMER MOISTURE
▨ ZONES 12, 16–28

Colocasia esculenta

Lily-of-the-valley is a favorite in regions providing enough winter chill for plants to prosper. Highly fragrant, delicate spring flowers account for part of this European native's popularity; good-looking foliage throughout the growing season is another asset.

Each rhizome (called a "pip") produces one slim flowering stem and two or three broad, lance-shaped leaves to 9 inches long. Along the length of the stem, 12 to 20 small, waxy white bells hang from threadlike stalks. Specialty bulb growers offer variations on the basic theme: sorts with double white blooms or light pink flowers, even a form with cream-striped foliage.

Convallaria majalis

Listing continues >

CONVALLARIA majalis
LILY-OF-THE-VALLEY
Liliaceae
RHIZOME

▲ 6 TO 10 INCHES
◑ FILTERED SUN OR LIGHT SHADE
◖ NEEDS SUMMER MOISTURE
▨ ZONES 1–7, 14–20, 31–45; BEST WITH SUBFREEZING WINTER TEMPERATURES
◈ ALL PARTS ARE POISONOUS IF INGESTED

Convallaria majalis 'Aureo-variegata'

USES. Lily-of-the-valley makes a long-lived ground cover beneath deciduous shrubs and among other plants that need the same conditions.

GARDEN CULTURE. Choose a lightly shaded garden location (or one receiving only filtered sunlight) with good soil. Dig a generous quantity of organic matter into the soil before planting in fall; set out pips in clumps or drifts, 1 to 2 inches deep and 4 to 6 inches apart. Plants need regular moisture throughout the year, even during dormancy. Every year before new growth emerges, topdress the planting with compost, leaf mold, peat moss, or ground bark.

Divide plantings infrequently, only when performance starts to decline. Dig and separate rhizomes when leaves yellow in autumn.

CONTAINER CULTURE. Follow directions "B" (subgroup 2) on page 23. Potted lily-of-the-valley makes a charming patio decoration; it can even be kept indoors, as long as it is given bright indirect light (not direct sun) and fairly cool temperatures. Prechilled pips are available for forcing; see pages 26–27.

CORYDALIS solida
Fumariaceae
TUBER

- ▲ 6 TO 10 INCHES
- ☼ FILTERED SUN OR LIGHT SHADE
- ◆ NEEDS SUMMER MOISTURE
- ✂ ZONES 3–9, 14–24, 32–35, 37, 39–43

Corydalis solida 'George P. Baker'

This northern European native gives you all the beauty of a low-growing fern, with the bonus of charming blossoms. Spreading plants bear dissected foliage with rounded lobes, above which rise upright flowering stems to 10 inches tall in spring. The flowers—tubular with a curved spur, a bit less than an inch long—are borne in loose spikes of up to 20. Blossoms are typically light purplish red, but there are varieties in other colors, among them 'Blue Dream' and coral red 'George P. Baker'.

USES. Low growth and a spreading habit suit this plant to the foreground of woodland and shade garden plantings. It's effective spreading among rocks, draping over low walls, even growing from crevices in unmortared stone walls.

GARDEN CULTURE. Give corydalis good, well-drained, organically enriched soil and filtered sun or light shade. Plant tubers in fall, setting them 2 to 3 inches deep and 4 to 5 inches apart; keep soil moist, but not saturated, throughout the growing season. When clumps become crowded or whenever you want to increase your planting, dig tubers after foliage has died back in autumn; then separate and replant them right away.

CONTAINER CULTURE. Follow directions "C" on page 23. For the best display, reverse the container dimensions recommended: grow in a pot at least 1 foot wide and about 8 inches deep.

CRINUM, × AMARCRINUM
memoriacorsii
Amaryllidaceae
TRUE BULB

- ▲ 2 TO 4 FEET
- ☼ ◑ FULL SUN; PART SHADE WHERE SUMMERS ARE HOT
- ◆ NEEDS SUMMER MOISTURE
- ✂ ZONES 8, 9, 12–31; WARMER PARTS OF 32 AND 33
- ☠ ALL PARTS ARE POISONOUS IF INGESTED

Lush foliage and lilylike flowers of impressive size put crinums high on the list of garden attention-getters. Each bulb tapers to an elongated stemlike neck, from which radiate long, broad, strap-shaped leaves. At some point from late spring through summer—the exact time depends on the species or hybrid—thick stems to 4 feet tall rise from the foliage, each bearing a cluster of long-stalked flowers. The blossoms resemble those of belladonna lily *(Amaryllis belladonna)*, but they're twice as big and open out a bit wider. Most are highly fragrant; colors include white and many shades of pink, from light to dark.

Crinums are native to many warm and tropical parts of the world. Specialty bulb growers, especially those in the South and Southeast, may offer a number of species and hybrids, but only a few are widely available. *C. moorei*, found along streamsides in South Africa, is one of the better-known species; it has wavy-edged bright green leaves and pinkish red blossoms to 4 inches or more across. You may also be able to find forms with white or soft pink flowers. *C. bulbispermum,* also from moist areas of South Africa, has the same general appearance as *C. moorei,* but it is somewhat smaller in all parts and has narrower leaves. The typical flower color is white flushed with red on the outside, but pure white and pink forms also exist.

Among hybrids, the best known is *C. × powellii,* a cross between *C. bulbispermum* and *C. moorei.* It resembles *C. moorei,* but its flowers are deep rose pink, carried on shorter (2-foot-tall) stems. Its variety 'Album' is pure white. Another *C. moorei* hybrid is *C. × herbertii,* bearing flowers that are typically white with a rosy red stripe down the center of each flower segment—a coloration that explains the common name "milk and wine lily." Among hybrids of more complex ancestry, three widely available choices are rose to wine red 'Ellen Bosanquet', rose pink 'J. C. Harvey', and lavender pink 'Peachblow'.

Another hybrid occasionally offered by bulb specialists is the autumn-blooming × *Amarcrinum memoriacorsii* (sometimes sold as *Crinodonna corsii*), a cross between *Amaryllis belladonna* and *C. moorei.* It resembles *Crinum* in growth habit and foliage, but its flowers look more like those of belladonna lily, having a narrower funnel shape than the blooms of most crinums.

USES. These plants make attractive semipermanent accents among shrubs, perennials, and annuals.

GARDEN CULTURE. The bulbs may be planted in any season, but early spring and autumn are the preferred times of year. Where summers are mild, choose a full-sun location; in hot-summer climates, find a spot that receives midday or afternoon shade or a location in filtered sun. Soil need not be especially well drained, but it should be liberally amended with organic matter prior to planting. Set bulbs 2 to 4 feet apart, with tops of bulb necks even with the soil surface. Plants are somewhat drought tolerant, but for best performance, provide regular to copious moisture.

Divide crinums infrequently: the larger the clump becomes, the more impressive its display of foliage and flowers. Protect foliage from slugs and snails.

CONTAINER CULTURE. Follow directions "C" on page 23. Where winter temperatures fall below 20°F/−7°C, overwinter plants indoors in a bright, cool room (night temperatures from 50° to 55°F/10° to 13°C).

Crinum × powellii 'Album'

These South African natives clearly show their relationship to gladiolus, freesia, ixia, and harlequin flower *(Sparaxis tricolor).* The foliage clumps resemble those of gladiolus, with sword-shaped leaves growing in upright fans. In *C. × crocosmiiflora* (formerly *Tritonia × crocosmiiflora*), leaves may reach a height of 3 feet; the upright, branching stems grow in zigzag fashion to 3 to 4 feet. In summer, each branch bears flat sprays of vivid orange-scarlet blossoms similar in form to those of ixia.

Leaves of *C. masoniorum* are shorter (to 2½ feet) and broader than those of *C. × crocosmiiflora;* the 2½- to 3-foot flower stems bend at nearly a right angle, much like those of some freesias. The horizontal part of each stem carries a double row of ½-inch orange to scarlet blossoms.

Hybrid montbretias offer interesting variations. Three 2-foot-tall choices are 'Citronella', with yellow flowers; 'Emily MacKenzie', bearing red-throated deep orange blossoms; and 'Solfatare', with soft saffron yellow flowers above bronze foliage. 'Lucifer' is a robust 4-foot selection with bright red blooms.

Listing continues >

CROCOSMIA
MONTBRETIA
Iridaceae
CORM

- ▲ 2 TO 4 FEET
- ☼ ◑ FULL SUN; PART SHADE WHERE SUMMERS ARE HOT
- ◗ NEEDS SUMMER MOISTURE
- ✇ ZONES 5–24, 28–39; HYBRIDS ALSO GROW IN ZONES 4, 26

Crocosmia 'Lucifer'

CROCUS
Iridaceae
CORM

▲ 3 TO 6 INCHES

☼ ◑ FULL SUN; FILTERED SUN OR
LIGHT SHADE AFTER BLOOM WHERE
SUMMERS ARE HOT

◐ ACCEPTS SUMMER MOISTURE BUT
DOESN'T NEED ANY

✄ ZONES 1–24, 30–45; BEST
WITH SUBFREEZING WINTER
TEMPERATURES

USES. Plants look attractive naturalized on sloping ground or set out to provide drifts of color among other plants. Single clumps also provide effective accents in mixed plantings.

GARDEN CULTURE. In cool- and mild-summer regions, grow in full sun; where summers are hot, give some afternoon shade. In spring, set out clumps of corms in well-drained soil enriched with organic matter, planting them about 2 inches deep and 3 inches apart. Once clumps are established, they'll perform with only casual watering—but for best results, water regularly throughout growth and bloom.

Where winter temperatures remain above 10°F/−12°C, corms are hardy in the ground; where lows range from 10° to −5°F/−12° to −21°C, protect plantings with a mulch of straw or cut conifer boughs. In colder regions, dig corms in early autumn after foliage yellows and store as for tuberous begonia (page 40).

Plantings increase in beauty as clumps grow thicker and larger; *C. × crocosmiflora* can even become invasive. Divide and replant only when vigor and flower quality begin to deteriorate.

If you live in the right climate (one with some subfreezing winter temperatures), you can enjoy blooming crocuses for 7 months out of the year. Autumn-flowering species may come into bloom as early as late August; winter-blooming types continue the show where the climate allows. And as their season draws to a close, the species and hybrids that flower in late winter and early spring take the stage.

Most crocuses are native to the Mediterranean region. All have rather grasslike leaves, often with a silvery midrib. In the autumn-flowering group, flowers appear before foliage; the rest develop leaves before or during flowering. The flower tube flares at the top into a six-segmented, typically chalice-shaped blossom. The flowers appear to be stemless, since the short true stems are hidden underground.

Retail nurseries typically stock various named Dutch hybrids derived from *C. vernus*. These are the most vigorous kinds, bearing flowers in white, cream, and shades of purple, lavender, and yellow—often streaked or penciled with a contrasting color. They bloom in February where winters are mild, in April in the coldest regions.

The various crocus species and their hybrids generally are available from mail-order specialty bulb growers. These kinds usually have smaller blossoms than the familiar Dutch hybrids, but they often produce more flowers from each corm. Here are some of the more widely available species, beginning with the spring-blooming group.

C. ancyrensis. Orange-yellow blossoms; extremely early blooming.

C. angustifolius (formerly *C. susianus*). Called cloth-of-gold crocus for its brilliant orange-gold, starlike flowers; each segment has a dark brown stripe down the center.

C. biflorus. White or pale lilac flowers with purple striping on the exterior of the petals. Crossed with *C. chrysanthus* (below), it produced the hybrids 'Advance' (yellow petals with violet backs) and 'Blue Bird' (white petals with violet backs rimmed in white).

C. chrysanthus. The typical flower is sweet scented, with orange-yellow petals and black-tipped anthers. A number of named selections and hybrids are available, including 'Blue Pearl', palest blue; 'Cream Beauty', pale yellow; 'E. A. Bowles', bronzed yellow with a dark throat; 'Gipsy Girl', yellow with maroon-striped petal backs; 'Ladykiller', cold white with petal exteriors stained and marked in violet; and 'Snow Bunting', yellow-throated white with purple-feathered petal backs.

C. imperati. Saucer-shaped blossoms in bright lilac, with buff petal backs veined in violet.

C. korolkowii. Bright yellow blossoms (sometimes tinged buff or green) open out to a nearly flat star shape.

C. sieberi. Delicate lavender blue flowers with golden throats.

C. tomasinianus. Among the easiest to grow, with slender buds and star-shaped flowers in silvery lavender blue. Petal tips may be marked with a dark blotch. Named selections in solid violet or purple are available. Extremely prolific when well established, covering the ground with bloom.

Autumn-flowering species include:

C. goulimyi. Globe- to chalice-shaped blossoms are lilac to violet shading to a white throat. A native of southern Greece, this grows best where summers are hot and dry.

C. kotschyanus (formerly *C. zonatus*). Its blossoms usually are pale lavender with darker veins running the length of the petals; the flower center is either yellow or white.

C. speciosus. The showiest and largest of the autumn bloomers, this has blue-violet blossoms with brilliant orange stigmas; the petals may be as long as 3 inches. Named selections are available in pale blue, dark blue, lavender, and white.

Crocus tomasinianus

USES. For patches and drifts of color at ground level, crocuses are unsurpassed. Just a few corms can create small, jewel-like spots of color in rock gardens, between paving stones, in rock walls, and in gravel pathways. In addition, you can plant corms of Dutch *C. vernus* hybrids, *C. chrysanthus, C. speciosus,* and *C. tomasinianus* beneath deciduous trees and shrubs, or naturalize them in grassy areas that can remain unmowed until crocus foliage ripens.

GARDEN CULTURE. Crocuses are not particular about soil type, but they do require good drainage. All need sun when in bloom. In hot-summer climates, they will need a bit of light shade or filtered sun in summer; in cooler regions, summer sun is best in order to ripen the corms.

Plant corms as soon as they are available in autumn, setting them 2 to 3 inches deep and 3 to 4 inches apart. Provide regular moisture during growth and bloom; taper off when foliage begins to yellow. Crocuses prefer a dry dormant period, but they'll accept watering during that time if soil is well drained. The corms increase rapidly and will be ready for dividing after 3 to 4 years.

CONTAINER CULTURE. Follow directions "B" (subgroup 1) on page 23. You also can force crocuses for earlier bloom, following the methods outlined on pages 26–27.

TOP: *Crocus chrysanthus* 'Cream Beauty'
BOTTOM: *Crocus* 'Advance'

The large-flowered florists' cyclamen *(C. persicum)* is familiar to gardeners and nongardeners alike as a container-grown gift plant, often sold during the winter holiday season. Less well known, but much more successfully adapted to outdoor culture in many regions, are the various smaller species, most of them native to Europe, the Mediterranean region, and Asia.

All cyclamens have purple, lavender, pink, red, or white flowers resembling those of the perennial shooting star *(Dodecatheon):* elongated, somewhat twisted petals flare back sharply from a central ring that is often darker than the petals (or in a contrasting hue). Leaves are heart shaped to rounded, each carried at the end of a long, fleshy stalk. In many species, the foliage is marbled or patterned in silvery white or light green, and beautiful in its own right. Most cyclamens go through a leafless or near-leafless dormant period at some time during summer.

Listing continues >

CYCLAMEN
Primulaceae
TUBER

- ▲ 3 TO 12 INCHES
- ☼ LIGHT SHADE OR FILTERED SUN
- ◗ NEEDS SUMMER MOISTURE
- ✷ ZONES VARY BY SPECIES
  (SEE "GARDEN CULTURE")

TOP: *Cyclamen hederifolium*
BOTTOM: *Cyclamen coum*

C. persicum, the florists' cyclamen, is the largest (to 1 foot tall) and showiest of the group, available in the greatest color range: lavender, purple, red shades, pink shades, and white. Bloom begins in late autumn and continues until early spring. Leaves may be solid green or patterned in light green or silver. Dwarf or miniature strains, including Dwarf Fragrance and Mirabelle, are one-half to three-fourths the size of the standard plant. Careful gardeners can get these to bloom in 7 to 8 months from seed.

Though *C. persicum* can endure a bit of frost (to about 25°F/−4°C), it's usually grown as a container plant, spending its winter bloom period indoors in a bright, cool room.

The hardier species of cyclamen, smaller than *C. persicum*, will survive to about 0°F/−18°C. Two easy-to-grow types, both flowering on 4- to 6-inch stems, are widely available. *C. hederifolium (C. neapolitanum)* blooms in late summer or early autumn, its rose pink or white flowers appearing before the leaves. The ivylike foliage—light green marbled with silver and white—is especially handsome. *C. coum* and its numerous subspecies begin flowering with the new year and continue to bloom until earliest spring. A typical plant has solid green leaves and rosy crimson flowers, but pink- and white-blossomed forms and subspecies are also sold, some with silver-patterned foliage.

With a little nursery searching, you may also be able to find several other hardy cyclamens. Spring-blooming *C. repandum* has narrow-petaled crimson flowers on 6-inch stems; its ivylike, tooth-edged leaves are marbled with silver. The same description nearly covers midsummer-blooming *C. purpurascens (C. europaeum)*, but its blossoms are fragrant and its red-backed leaves are nearly evergreen. *C. cilicium* blooms from early autumn into midwinter; its pale pink flowers (or white blooms, in the case of 'Album') are carried on 3- to 6-inch stems. Leaves are marked with silver and appear very early in the blooming season.

USES. The hardy cyclamens are fine "woodland wildflower" plants for locations in light shade or filtered sun. Plant them in small groups or large drifts, or even as a ground cover beneath trees or shrubs.

In regions where outdoor culture is possible, florists' cyclamen can be used as a bedding plant along pathway borders and in the foreground of lightly shaded gardens. In pots or planters, it adds winter color to patios and decks.

GARDEN CULTURE. Grow the hardy species as follows: *C. coum* and *C. hederifolium* in Zones 3–9, 14–24, 32–34, 37; *C. cilicium* in Zones 3–9, 14–24, 32–34; *C. purpurascens* and *C. repandum* in Zones 4–9, 14–24, 32.

Hardy cyclamens need well-drained soil liberally amended with organic matter prior to planting in late summer or early fall. Space tubers 6 to 12 inches apart, covering them with ½ inch of soil. Plants need moisture all year, so water regularly during rainless periods. Each year, just after flowers finish, topdress the soil with about ½ inch of leaf mold or compost; this will provide enough nutrition for continued good performance the following year and keep soil in top condition for the plants' shallow roots.

Tubers grow a bit larger each year, producing more and more flowers and leaves as time goes on. They do not produce increases, but can multiply by self-sown seeds. If you need to transplant a cyclamen, do so during the brief summer dormant period.

In mild-winter Zones 15–24, *C. persicum* can be grown outdoors in the same manner as the hardy species. Don't cover tubers with soil, though: plant so that the upper one-third to one-half is above the soil surface.

CONTAINER CULTURE. Florists' cyclamen grows well in containers. Use one of the soil mixes described under "B" on page 23. Plant each tuber in a pot big enough to leave 2 inches of soil between all sides of the tuber and the container edges. As described above for in-ground planting of florists' cyclamen, the top part of the tuber should be exposed.

During the growing and blooming season, water plants regularly, but never let the container sit in a saucer of water. Once a month, apply a liquid fertilizer diluted to half strength. When you take plants indoors to escape freezing weather, give them a well-lit location (in a north- or east-facing window, for example) in a cool room—ideally about 50°F/10°C at night, no warmer than 65°F/18°C during the daytime.

Plants go nearly dormant in summer; at that time, place containers in a cool, shaded spot and water infrequently. Topdress containers annually with a light application of soil mix with complete fertilizer added, being careful not to cover the top of the tuber with the mix.

S carborough lily looks much like a more delicate version of its close relative the Dutch hybrid amaryllis *(Hippeastrum)*. In summer and early fall, each thick flower stalk is topped with a cluster of up to 10 broad, funnel-shaped blossoms; the typical color is orange red, but you'll sometimes find white- or pink-flowered forms. The glossy evergreen leaves, strap shaped and 1 to 2 feet long, are attractive throughout the year.

Where winters are very mild, this South African native can be planted in the ground. But most gardeners, even those living within the plant's hardiness range, prefer to grow Scarborough lily in containers.

USES. Garden plants make attractive accent clumps or ground covers for small areas. Use container-grown plants for accents indoors or on patio, deck, or terrace.

GARDEN CULTURE. Select a spot receiving plenty of bright, indirect light—in light shade under deciduous trees, for example (bulbs will almost always survive competition from tree roots). Except where summers are cool and overcast, don't plant in direct sun. In spring, plant bulbs in well-drained soil enriched with organic matter prior to planting, setting them 1 to 1½ feet apart and positioning the tips just beneath the soil surface. Water regularly during growth and bloom; give less water during the dormant period, but never let soil go completely dry.

Divide clumps infrequently, only when overcrowding causes a decline in vigor and bloom quality. Small bulbs will eventually form around the larger bulbs; to increase your planting, remove these in summer, before the bloom season begins, and plant them separately.

CONTAINER CULTURE. Plant bulbs in early summer, in a container large enough to leave 2 inches between all sides of the bulb and the container edges. Plant the bulb so its neck and top half are above the soil surface, using the potting mix recommended for "C" on page 23. Firm the mix thoroughly, then water well. Throughout growth and bloom, water regularly and apply liquid fertilizer monthly. During winter and spring, when bulbs are dormant, keep the soil mix just barely moist and do not fertilize at all. When the plant fills its container, repot just as growth begins, moving it into a larger pot with fresh soil mix.

D ahlias are among the most varied and variable of the summer-flowering bulbous plants. Heights range from 1 foot to over 7 feet, flower diameters from about 2 to 12 inches. Colors include all but blue and true green, and many varieties are patterned or shaded with a second color. And though dahlias are native to Mexico, they are amazingly adaptable: they grow from coast to coast and in a great latitudinal range, encompassing both short- and long-summer climates.

Listing continues >

CYRTANTHUS elatus
(C. purpureus, Vallota speciosa)
SCARBOROUGH LILY
Amaryllidaceae
TRUE BULB

▲ 2 FEET

☼ LIGHT SHADE, EXCEPT AS NOTED

◆ NEEDS SUMMER MOISTURE

✄ ZONES 16, 17, 23–27

Cyrtanthus elatus

DAHLIA
Asteraceae
TUBEROUS ROOT

▲ 1 TO 7 FEET

☼ ☼ FULL SUN; PART SHADE WHERE SUMMERS ARE HOT

◆ NEEDS SUMMER MOISTURE

✄ ALL ZONES (SEE "GARDEN CULTURE")

The American Dahlia Society has divided flower types into 12 groups (formal decorative, anemone, and cactus, for example), each including plants of varying heights. Specialists use these classifications in describing available varieties—but the general nursery trade may not do so, nor do we use them in the discussion here.

USES. Plant dahlias in separate beds or in combination with other plants. Use smaller types as low borders, short accents, or container plants; taller ones make striking accents or temporary screens and hedges.

GARDEN CULTURE. Dahlias can be grown in all zones. Though the roots can be left in the ground where winter temperatures remain above 20°F/−7°C, gardeners in most areas prefer to dig them annually.

Plant dahlias in spring, after air and soil have warmed. The easiest gauge is this: when the time is right to plant tomatoes, corn, and potatoes, it's right for dahlias. Except where summers are hot, choose a location in full sun; in hot-summer regions, plants need light shade during the hottest part of the day. Also keep in mind that flowers face the source of light.

Dahlias grow best in well-drained soil liberally enriched with organic matter. Space roots of larger dahlias (over 4 feet tall) 4 to 5 feet apart, those of smaller types 1 to 2 feet apart. For each root, dig a 1-foot-deep planting hole—about 1½ feet across for larger dahlias, 9 to 12 inches across for smaller ones. (This deep-planting method gives the plant more stability as it grows taller.) Incorporate about ¼ cup of granular low-nitrogen fertilizer into the soil at the bottom of the hole. Then add a layer of pulverized native soil—about 4 inches if the soil is on the sandy side, about 6 inches if it's more claylike.

If you're planting a tall variety, drive a 5- to 6-foot stake into the hole just off center; place the root horizontally in bottom of hole, 2 inches from the stake and with the growth bud pointing toward it. Cover the root with 3 inches of soil and water well. Unless weather is dry and soil loses its moisture, don't water again until growth begins.

As the shoots grow, gradually fill in the hole with soil. For tall-growing varieties, thin out shoots when they're about 6 inches tall, leaving only the strongest one or two. When these shoots have three pairs of leaves, pinch out the growing tip just above the upper set of leaves to encourage bushy growth. Varieties with small flowers need just one pinching, but if you're growing large-flowered dahlias, pinch again after subsequent growth has produced three pairs of leaves.

TOP: *Dahlia* 'Apache'
BOTTOM: *Dahlia* 'Prince Valiant'

Dahlias grow rapidly, so they need a steady supply of water after shoots emerge; be sure to moisten the soil to a depth of at least 1 foot each time you water. Mulch soil to conserve moisture. Properly prepared soil should contain enough nutrients to last plants through the season. But if your soil is light or if roots remained in the ground the previous year, apply a granular low-nitrogen fertilizer when the first flower buds show. During growth and bloom, watch for mildew on foliage.

In fall, after plants turn yellow or have been frosted (whichever comes first), cut stalks down to 6 inches. Where dahlias can overwinter in the ground, you can leave the roots undisturbed through a second and sometimes even a third bloom season before you dig and separate. To lift dahlias, carefully dig a 2-foot-wide circle around each plant and gently pry up the clump with a spading fork. Shake off loose soil, being careful not to break roots apart; then let the clump dry in the sun for several hours.

At this point, you have two choices. You can divide roots immediately; or you can store clumps intact, then divide them several weeks before planting in spring. Fall division is simpler, since growth buds are easier to recognize and separated roots are easier to store. However, fall-separated roots are more likely to shrivel in storage and are also more susceptible to rot. To divide clumps, cut them apart with a sharp knife, making sure that each separate root is attached to a portion of stalk with a visible growth bud (see page 21). Dust each cut with sulfur to prevent rot during storage.

To store divided roots (or intact clumps) over winter, place them in a single layer and cover with dry sand, sawdust, peat moss, vermiculite, or perlite. Keep in a dark, dry, cool place (40° to 45°F/4° to 7°C) until spring. Check occasionally for signs of shriveling; lightly moisten the storage material if necessary.

About 2 to 4 weeks before planting time, separate intact clumps, cutting them apart as directed above. Then place all roots—whether fall-divided or spring-divided—in moist sand to plump them up and encourage sprouting.

CONTAINER CULTURE. Smaller types are best for containers, since they don't require pinching or staking. Use one of the soil mixes described under "B" on page 23. Plant one tuberous root or cluster to a 10-inch pot, three to a 15-inch pot. When plants die down, knock them from pots; cut off tops and store clumps as directed above, then divide and repot in fresh soil mix at planting time. Or store plants in their pots over winter; then knock from pots, divide, and repot in fresh soil mix at planting time.

Dahlia flower forms, clockwise from top left: ball, anemone, formal decorative

DICHELOSTEMMA.
See BRODIAEA

These South African natives are irislike in both foliage and blossom. The narrow, flat, evergreen leaves are arranged in fans; the branching stems carry flattish, six-segmented blossoms that could pass for beardless irises. Though each flower lasts for only one day, each blossom stalk carries a seemingly inexhaustible supply of buds. Flowering comes in bursts through spring, summer, and fall—and even in winter, in very mild climates. To prolong bloom and prevent self-sowing, break off any seedpods that develop.

For many years, these plants were grouped with *Moraea,* and some nurseries still offer them under their old names. *D. vegeta* (formerly known as *D. iridioides*) is the most widely grown species; it's also one of the tallest (2 to 3 feet) and largest flowered. Each 3-inch, waxy white blossom has an orange-and-brown blotch and some blue shading on the three outer segments. Variety 'Johnsonii' is larger and more robust. Flower stems are productive for several years. To groom plants, just break off developing seedpods; cut out stems only when they die.

The plant sold as *D. catenulata* is now considered merely a small-growing form of *D. vegeta.* Foliage and flowering stems reach 1½ to 2 feet; the stems frequently produce offsets that weigh them to the ground, where the offsets take root. This form is more sensitive to cold than the standard *D. vegeta,* its foliage suffering damage at 30°F/–1°C.

The blooms of *D. bicolor* are light yellow with dark brown blotches; they're slightly smaller and more rounded than those of *D. vegeta.* The 2- to 3-foot flower stems each last just 1 year.

Two white-flowered hybrids of *D. vegeta* and *D. bicolor* are occasionally sold. 'Orange Drops' has an orange spot on three of the six flower segments; 'Lemon Drops' has yellow spots. Both hybrids resemble *D. vegeta* in stem and foliage size, but have smaller, rounder blossoms more like those of *D. bicolor.*

USES. The thick clumps of narrow leaves, good looking all year, make effective accents; they're especially attractive in Japanese gardens and near water or rocks.

GARDEN CULTURE. Though all species and hybrids look their best with good soil and regular water, one of their virtues is toughness: once established, they'll turn in a satisfactory performance even in poor soil and with infrequent or erratic watering. Plant

DIETES
AFRICAN IRIS, FORTNIGHT LILY
Iridaceae
RHIZOME

▲ 1½ TO 3 FEET
☼ ☽ FULL SUN OR LIGHT SHADE
◗ NEEDS SOME SUMMER MOISTURE
✎ ZONES 8, 9, 12–28

Dietes vegeta

from containers (bare rhizomes are not sold) at any time of year. Choose a sunny or lightly shaded spot; set plants about 2 feet apart, at the depth they were growing in their pots.

Clumps can remain undisturbed for many years. If you need to divide or move them, do so in fall or winter.

CONTAINER CULTURE. The smaller plant sold as *D. catenulata* can be a conversation-piece hanging basket plant; plantlets will droop from its arching stems in the fashion of spider plant *(Chlorophytum)*. Follow directions "C" on page 23.

ENDYMION.
See HYACINTHOIDES

ERANTHIS HYEMALIS
WINTER ACONITE
Ranunculaceae
TUBER

- ▲ 2 TO 8 INCHES
- ☼ ◐ FULL SUN DURING BLOOM, PART SHADE DURING REST OF YEAR
- ● NEEDS SOME SUMMER MOISTURE
- ✻ ZONES 1–9, 14–17, 32–43

Eranthis hyemalis with *Crocus*

This little European and Asian native is one of the harbingers of spring: blossoming stems often come up through snow, appearing before the leaves. Each stem bears its 1½-inch, buttercuplike yellow flower on a leafy collar. Rounded basal leaves, each divided into narrow lobes, emerge later.

USES. Rock gardens, pathway borders, and woodland plantings are all good settings for winter aconite. For an attractive mixed planting, combine it with other bulbs that bloom at around the same time.

GARDEN CULTURE. The best planting site is one receiving full sun during bloom time, part shade for the rest of the year. Set out tubers in late summer, as soon as they are available in nurseries; if they look dry or shriveled, plump them up in wet sand before planting. Set them about 3 inches deep and 4 inches apart, in good, well-drained soil enriched with organic matter. Throughout growth and bloom, keep soil moist but not saturated. Tubers will get by with less moisture during summer dormancy, but the soil should not dry out completely.

Divide clumps infrequently, since it takes plants a year or more to reestablish. Separate into smaller clumps rather than individual tubers.

Eranthis hyemalis

EREMURUS
FOXTAIL LILY
Liliaceae
TUBEROUS ROOT

- ▲ 3 TO 9 FEET
- ☼ FULL SUN
- ● NEEDS SOME SUMMER MOISTURE
- ✻ ZONES 1–9, 14, 32–43; BEST WITH SUBFREEZING WINTER TEMPERATURES

Native to western and central Asia, foxtail lily is an impressive plant. Its flowering stems reach 3 to 9 feet tall, rising from fountainlike rosettes of narrow, strap-shaped leaves in late spring or early summer. The upper one-third to one-half of each stem is packed with starlike blossoms ½ to 1 inch wide; buds open in sequence from the bottom of the stem, giving half-open spikes the look of a fox's tail. After bloom is over, the foliage yellows and dies back to the ground; new leaves don't emerge until early the following spring.

Specialty bulb growers offer various species as well as hybrid strains and selected named varieties. Among the species, pink-flowered *E. robustus* easily attains 8 to 9 feet when in bloom; white-flowered *E. himalaicus* is only 1 to 2 feet shorter. The runt of this group, at a mere 3 to 5 feet, is yellow-blossomed *E. stenophyllus* (formerly known as *E. bungei*).

Several hybrid strains—both long-established groups and newer ones—are now grouped under *E. × isabellinus*. The well-known Shelford Hybrids reach 4 to 5 feet, bearing flowers in pink, yellow, buff, orange, or white; the Highdown Hybrids, based on the Shelford work, include plants of shorter stature. The Ruiter Hybrids, developed in the Netherlands, feature bright, clear flower colors; some named selections are available, such as orange-and-red 'Cleopatra', chartreuse 'Obelisk', and salmon red 'Romance'.

USES. These imposing plants add vertical accents to the late-spring garden. Plant them where other perennials and annuals will fill in the blank spots left after the foliage dies down in summer.

GARDEN CULTURE. Plant in fall, in a sunny location with good, well-drained soil enriched with organic matter. Space the roots 2 to 4 feet apart. To plant each, dig a hole large enough to accommodate it easily; form a cone of soil and spread the roots over it and downwards, positioning the growing point about 1 inch below ground. Then cover with soil. Handle roots carefully: they are brittle and may rot if damaged.

Water regularly from the onset of growth until foliage has died back, then less often throughout late summer and fall. Roots will rot if soil is overly moist in winter, making well-drained soil especially critical in regions where winter rainfall is plentiful.

New growth can be harmed by freezing nights. To prevent damage, give winter protection (see page 21); remove after the danger of hard frosts is past.

Eremurus stenophyllus

Most *Erythronium* species are woodland plants with lilylike spring flowers and broad, tongue-shaped, brown-mottled leaves. Because many are fairly exacting in their cultural requirements, they are generally sold only by bulb specialists—particularly those in western North America, where a number of species are native.

The various species have acquired a variety of common names, many of which describe the leaves. *E. americanum,* one of several species from eastern North America, is called trout lily or adder's tongue—the first name referring to leaves' mottled appearance, the second to their shape. Each 6-inch leaf is splotched with purplish brown and near-white; one nodding, yellow, 2-inch flower tops each 9- to 12-inch stem.

Dog-tooth violets take their name from the plants' fang-shaped corms. *E. denscanis,* a European native, has 4- to 6-inch leaves mottled brown and white. Each 6- to 12-inch flower stem bears a single 1-inch blossom; the typical color is deep pink to purple, but specialists offer other choices, such as pure white 'Snowflake'. North American native *E. albidum,* another dog-tooth violet, has 6-inch leaves lightly mottled in silvery green; its foot-tall flower stems bear solitary yellow-centered white blossoms.

Western North America is home to a number of species, many of which are known as fawn lilies from the brown mottling on their leaves. All of these prefer little or no moisture from the time leaves yellow until autumn.

E. californicum sends up 6- to 10-inch stems from clumps of mottled, 6-inch leaves; each stem carries up to three white flowers, yellow at the base. *E. revolutum* is similar, but its foliage and flowers are larger and its stems can reach 16 inches. Its blossoms are usually lavender, but 'Rose Beauty' and 'White Beauty' are variants.

The brown-mottled, dark green leaves of *E. hendersonii* may grow to 8 inches long; each of its foot-tall stems bears one to four nodding lavender blossoms. *E. tuolumnense* has yellowish green, foot-long leaves and 12- to 15-inch stems, each carrying several starlike yellow blossoms.

Several named selections are available, variously listed as forms of *E. revolutum* or *E. tuolumnense,* or as hybrids of the two. 'Citronella' has lemon yellow blossoms; 'Kondo' and 'Pagoda' feature yellow flowers with brown centers. All are vigorous growers, better adapted to ordinary garden culture than the species.

Listing continues >

ERYTHRONIUM
Liliaceae
CORM

- ▲ 6 TO 16 INCHES
- ☼ FILTERED SUN OR LIGHT TO MODERATE SHADE, EXCEPT AS NOTED
- ◐○ ALL BUT WESTERN NATIVES NEED SUMMER MOISTURE
- ✂ ZONES VARY BY SPECIES (SEE "GARDEN CULTURE")

Erythronium 'Kondo'

Erythronium hendersonii

USES. Plant clumps or drifts in woodland gardens, rock gardens, along pathways, or under deciduous trees and shrubs.

GARDEN CULTURE. Grow *E. albidum* in Zones 1–6, 32–43; *E. dens-canis* in Zones 1–7, 15–17, 31–43; *E. americanum* in Zones 1–7, 15–17, 28, 31–43; *E. californicum, E. hendersonii, E. revolutum* in Zones 2–7, 14–17, 33–41; *E. tuolumnense* and above-listed hybrids in Zones 2–7, 14–17, 32 (colder parts), 33–41.

With the exception of *E. dens-canis,* which needs only partial shade (preferably during the hot afternoon hours), all species do best in filtered sunlight or light to moderate shade. In fall, plant corms in well-drained soil liberally amended with organic matter; arrange them in clumps or drifts, setting them 2 to 3 inches deep and 4 to 5 inches apart. Withhold summer moisture from the western North American species and their hybrids (noted on previous page); all other species need moisture the year around. Divide plantings of all types infrequently—only when vigor and bloom quality decline.

EUCHARIS × grandiflora
AMAZON LILY
Amaryllidaceae
TRUE BULB

- ▲ 1½ TO 2 FEET
- ☼ LIGHT SHADE
- ● REGULATE WATER TO INDUCE FLOWERING (SEE "CONTAINER CULTURE")
- ✄ ZONE 25

Eucharis × grandiflora

Except in absolutely frost-free areas, this native of the South American tropics is strictly a container plant to be brought inside during cold weather (or kept indoors all year long). Its thin-textured, glossy, tongue-shaped leaves grow to 1 foot long, supported by equally long leafstalks. The 1½- to 2-foot flowering stems support clusters of up to six fragrant white blossoms, each resembling a 3-inch daffodil. It blooms primarily in winter, though it can flower periodically throughout the year under ideal conditions.

USES. Good-looking foliage and flowers make Amazon lily an excellent choice for a house plant. It's also attractive on patio, deck, or terrace in warm weather.

GARDEN CULTURE. To try Amazon lily in the garden, choose a spot where plants will receive as much light as possible without direct sun. Because dormancy is induced by withholding water (see "Container culture"), bulbs may be planted at any time of year. Set them 4 inches apart, tips even with the soil surface, in well-drained soil liberally amended with organic matter. Crowded clumps give the best performance.

CONTAINER CULTURE. Follow directions "C" on page 23. Water bulbs thoroughly just after potting, then sparingly until growth begins. Increase water as leaves grow, keeping soil moist; every other week, apply liquid fertilizer diluted to half strength.

After bloom finishes, stop fertilizing and cut back on water, giving just enough to keep leaves from wilting. When new growth begins, resume regular watering and fertilizing. This technique may induce plants to bloom several times in a year.

Repot or divide only when a plant crowds its container to capacity.

EUCOMIS
PINEAPPLE FLOWER
Liliaceae
TRUE BULB

- ▲ 1½ TO 3 FEET
- ☼ ☽ FULL SUN; FILTERED SUN OR LIGHT SHADE WHERE SUMMERS ARE HOT
- ● NEEDS SUMMER MOISTURE
- ✄ ZONES 4–29

As its common name suggests, this native of tropical southern Africa presents a convincing imitation of a pineapple fruit: the upper portion of each summer-flowering spike is topped with a tuft of leafy bracts and surrounded by a tight, cylindrical cluster of fragrant, starlike blossoms. Decorative purplish seed capsules follow the flowers.

E. bicolor has green blossoms with purple petal edges; flower spikes reach about 2 feet, rising from rosettes of broad, wavy-edged leaves. *E. comosa* (sometimes sold as *E. punctata*) grows to 3 feet tall, with leaves to 2 feet long; its greenish white blossoms are tinged with pink or purple. The shortest species, at 1½ feet, is *E. autumnalis;* it bears pale green flowers that fade to white.

USES. Pineapple flower is an attractive foliage plant at all times, and a conversation piece when in bloom. Grow it in containers or at the foreground of garden plantings.

GARDEN CULTURE. Choose a location in full sun (filtered sun or light shade where summers are hot) and enrich the soil with organic matter. Set out bulbs in fall, 4 to 6 inches deep and 1 foot apart. When growth begins in spring, apply a granular fertilizer. Water regularly during growth and bloom, but give little or no water during winter dormancy—plants can usually survive on rainfall. Divide plants infrequently, perhaps every 5 or 6 years.

CONTAINER CULTURE. Plant bulbs in spring, following directions "C" on page 23; set bulbs with tips just beneath the surface. For best results, repot yearly in fresh soil mix.

Eucomis autumnalis

To people who know them, freesias and fragrance are synonymous. In spring, the wiry, 1- to 1½-foot-tall stems bear trumpet-shaped flowers that reach 2 inches long and flare to 2 inches across. Each stem bends at nearly a right angle just beneath the lowest bud, so a double rank of blossoms faces upward (or nearly so). Narrow, swordlike leaves to 1 foot tall grow in irislike fans.

The most widely available freesia in times past was creamy white, powerfully sweet-scented *F. alba*, from South Africa's Cape Province. In favorable climates, it naturalizes easily, both from offsets and self-sown seedlings. Today, though, the most popular freesias are hybrids offering larger blossoms (both single and double) in a color range that includes yellow, orange, red, pink, lavender, purple, and blue as well as the traditional white. Not all of these, however, are as fragrant as the old-fashioned favorite. Dutch and Tecolote hybrids represent the majority of the new kinds sold in the retail trade; you can buy mixed-color assortments as well as named varieties in specific colors.

USES. Try naturalizing freesias in clumps or drifts, or use them in borders of drought-tolerant plants.

GARDEN CULTURE. Freesias need well-drained soil and little or no water during their summer dormant period. Plant corms in fall, setting them 2 inches deep and about 2 inches apart. Close spacing—and planting in clumps or drifts—lets the somewhat floppy flowering stems prop each other up. Plants need moisture during growth and bloom, but you should cut back on watering when leaves start to yellow in late spring. In regions with dry summers and mild winters, you can leave corms in the ground if the soil can be kept fairly dry until autumn. In rainy-summer areas, it's best to dig corms when foliage yellows; store them over summer as for gladiolus (page 64), then replant in early fall.

Freesia corms increase rapidly. Dig and divide them for increase after several years, if you wish; or leave plantings in place until vigor and bloom quality decline. Unless you remove faded flowers, freesias tend to set seed and provide you with volunteer seedlings; many of these, however, will have white or creamy white flowers.

CONTAINER CULTURE. Plant corms 2 inches deep and 1 inch apart, following directions "B" (subgroup 2) on page 23. In cold-winter climates, you can grow freesias indoors in a cool room—60° to 65°F/16° to 18°C during the day, around 55°F/13°C at night. Bulb growers produce cold-treated corms that can be potted in spring to bloom in summer the first year. In subsequent years, these will bloom at the normal time in early spring.

FREESIA
Iridaceae
CORM

- ▲ 1 TO 1½ FEET
- ☼ ◑ FULL SUN OR PART SHADE
- ◌ WITHHOLD SUMMER MOISTURE
- ✇ ZONES 8, 9, 12–24, 28

Freesia hybrids

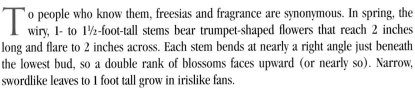

FRITILLARIA

FRITILLARY

Liliaceae

TRUE BULB

- ▲ 6 INCHES TO 4 FEET
- ☼ FILTERED SUN OR LIGHT SHADE, EXCEPT AS NOTED
- ◑◐○ SUMMER MOISTURE NEEDS VARY BY SPECIES (SEE "GARDEN CULTURE")
- ✎ ZONES VARY BY SPECIES (SEE "GARDEN CULTURE"); BEST WITH SUBFREEZING WINTER TEMPERATURES

Fritillaria imperialis

Native to temperate regions of the Northern Hemisphere, these spring bloomers are a contradictory group. Most have a wildflower charm, though the blossoms—in red, orange, yellow, maroon, purple shades, cream, and white—are often rather strangely and intricately marked.

The best-known species—*F. imperialis,* the crown imperial—is the exceptional individual and would hardly fit anyone's idea of a woodland wildflower. Its thick stems grow 3 to 4 feet tall, clothed for about half their height in whorls of lance-shaped 6-inch leaves. At the top of each stem is a circular cluster of drooping, bell-shaped flowers topped by a thick tuft of leaflike bracts. Blossoms are 2 to 3 inches long; the usual color is a clear and brilliant red, but orange and yellow forms are also available. Both bulb and plant have a musky odor that some people find objectionable.

The 2- to 3-foot stems of *F. persica* also are clothed in whorls of leaves over their lower half, but there the similarity to crown imperial ends. The upper portion of the stem is a spike of up to 30 pendent, 1-inch bells in a somber but alluring dark plum purple. *F. camschatcensis,* appropriately called black lily or chocolate lily, also has a leafy flowering stem; it reaches 1½ feet tall, with one to eight brownish maroon to black bells dangling from the top.

Most other fritillaries are more diminutive (though no less unusual or striking), bearing small, pendent bells atop slender, fairly short stems. Well-known European native *F. meleagris,* the checkered lily or snakeshead, produces stems to 15 inches high that rise above three or more narrow, 3- to 6-inch leaves. The nodding, bell-shaped 2-inch blooms, carried one to three per stem, are typically marked in an unusual checkerboard pattern. The most common color combination is light with dark maroon, but there are variations (pale gray with brownish purple, white with light violet) as well as solid colors of dark purple, lilac, and white. In *F. acmopetala,* one to three flowers nod from a 1½-foot stem; each green bell is brushed or striped purple on the outside. About the same size is *F. pallidiflora,* with one to six greenish yellow flowers per stem. *F. michailovskyi* is the shortest fritillary—just 6 inches high, with one to six flowers nodding from each stem. The blossoms are purple over the lower two-thirds, then yellow to the petal tips.

The western United States is home to several appealing fritillaries. Checker lily, *F. affinis,* has bell-like blossoms with a checkerboard pattern like that of *F. meleagris.* In *F. affinis,* however, the colors are brownish purple and yellow, while the stems, clothed in whorls of leaves on their lower part, reach 2½ feet. Scarlet fritillary, *F. recurva,* has the same general appearance as checker lily and grows about as tall, but its bell-shaped blossoms are bright red with yellow centers. Mission bells, *F. biflora,* produces 16-inch stems with leafy whorls, each bearing one to six purple-tinged brown blossoms; its selection 'Martha Roderick' has rusty orange bells centered in white.

Bulb specialists may offer other, less well-known species—some strikingly beautiful, some intriguing looking, and all worth growing.

USES. Naturalize fritillaries in grassland or meadow areas; the smaller species are also attractive in rock gardens and at the margins of woodland plantings. Crown imperial makes a striking and stately color accent in mixed perennial, bulb, and annual groupings.

GARDEN CULTURE. Grow *F. imperialis* in Zones 1–7, 14–17, 32–43; *F. camschatcensis* and *F. meleagris* in Zones 1–7, 15–17, 32–43; *F. pallidiflora* in Zones 1–7, 33–43; *F. michailovskyi* and *F. persica* in Zones 2–7, 14–17, 32 (colder parts), 33–41; *F. affinis, F. biflora,* and *F. recurva* in Zones 3–7, 14–17; *F. acmopetala* in Zones 7–9, 14–21. All fritillaries appreciate some winter chilling and tend to perform poorly where summers are hot and dry.

F. imperialis and *F. persica* can take full sun where summers are cool and overcast; elsewhere, locate them where they will get light shade in summer. The other species prefer filtered sunlight or light shade everywhere.

Fritillaries need good, well-drained soil enriched with organic matter. In fall, set the large bulbs of *F. imperialis* 4 to 5 inches deep, 8 to 12 inches apart; set those of the smaller species 3 to 4 inches deep, 6 inches apart. Give plants regular moisture during growth and bloom; cut back as foliage dies back in summer. After foliage is gone, withhold water entirely from the western natives *(F. affinis, F. biflora, F. recurva)* until fall. The other species prefer reduced summer moisture—except for *F. meleagris,* which requires regular to moderate watering during summer.

Established bulbs seldom need dividing; dig and separate only when you want to increase plantings.

Fritillaria meleagris

GALANTHUS
SNOWDROP
Amaryllidaceae
TRUE BULB

▲ 6 TO 12 INCHES

☼ ◗ FULL SUN DURING BLOOM, LIGHT SHADE DURING REST OF YEAR

◖ NEEDS SUMMER MOISTURE

✂ ZONES 1–9, 14–17, 31–45; BEST WITH SUBFREEZING WINTER TEMPERATURES

I n the cold-weather climates they prefer, snowdrops are among the first bulbs to bloom as winter draws to a close. Even if a snowfall catches plants in flower, the blossoming stems will pop back up again—as long as the snow melts quickly.

The various snowdrops are native to deciduous woodlands of Europe and Asia Minor. In all types, each bulb produces two or three slender leaves and one flower stem. Each stem bears one pendent, six-petaled white flower; the three inner petals are always shorter than the three outer ones, and are usually marked or infused with green.

Though all snowdrops need a climate in which at least some winter night temperatures drop below 32°F/0°C, the giant snowdrop, *G. elwesii*, is adapted to regions without too much winter chill. Its rather egg-shaped flowers are up to 1½ inches long, their inner petals heavily infused with green. Stems reach 1 foot tall, rising above two or three narrow 8-inch leaves.

Common snowdrop, *G. nivalis*, grows 6 to 9 inches tall; it has inch-long bell-shaped flowers, the inner petals marked at the tips with a precise green crescent. 'Flore Pleno' has double blooms; 'Viridapicis' is a vigorous form with green marks on all floral parts.

USES. Snowdrops find their niche in woodland landscapes and rock gardens. An ideal location is near deciduous trees or shrubs, where the planting area will be sunny during the bulbs' bloom period but lightly shaded later in the year.

GARDEN CULTURE. Plant in fall. Enrich the soil with organic matter; then set bulbs 3 to 4 inches deep and 3 inches apart. Snowdrops prefer moisture all year, so water periodically when rainfall doesn't do the job for you.

Snowdrop bulbs may stay in place for many years, naturalizing into large drifts. If you need to divide or move plants, do so in spring, just after flowers fade. Try to keep plenty of soil around bulbs; replant immediately and water regularly.

Galanthus nivalis

GALTONIA candicans
SUMMER HYACINTH
Liliaceae
TRUE BULB

▲ 2 TO 4 FEET

☼ ◗ FULL SUN; LIGHT SHADE WHERE SUMMERS ARE HOT

◖ NEEDS SUMMER MOISTURE

✂ ZONES 4–32

D espite its common name, this summer bloomer from southern Africa doesn't look much like the familiar spring-blooming hyacinth *(Hyacinthus)*. Each bulb produces a stout, erect stem that carries a spire of 20 or more sweet-scented, pendent white bells about 1½ inches long. The floppy, strap-shaped leaves reach a length of 2 to 3 feet.

USES. The white flower spikes add height and a welcome dash of coolness to the summer garden.

Listing continues >

Galtonia candicans

GLADIOLUS

Iridaceae

CORM

- ▲ 1½ TO 6 FEET
- ☼ FULL SUN
- ● NEEDS MOISTURE UNTIL LEAVES YELLOW
- ✄ ZONES VARY BY TYPE (SEE "GARDEN CULTURE")

Gladiolus tristis

GARDEN CULTURE. Summer hyacinth revels in rich soil and lots of water. Dig plenty of organic matter into the soil in advance of planting; choose a sunny spot if your summers are cool to moderate, a lightly shaded location in hot-summer regions. Plant bulbs 6 inches deep, 1 foot apart—in fall where winter lows won't fall below 10°F/−12°C, in spring in colder regions. Water plants regularly during growth and bloom; provide protection from slugs and snails.

Summer hyacinth gives the best display if allowed to remain undisturbed from one year to the next. Where winter lows range from 10° to −20°F/−12° to −29°C, protect the planting area with a mulch after foliage dies down. In colder regions, dig bulbs annually and store them over winter as for gladiolus (below).

If you need to divide or move plantings, do so at the best planting time for your climate.

The word "gladiolus" automatically brings to mind the large, tall, variously colored hybrids so familiar in summer gardens and as cut flowers. Derived from a number of species over a century of hybridization, these magnificent flowers are collectively known as grandiflora hybrids. Less well known, but no less lovely or desirable, are smaller hybrids and several species gladiolus. Whatever the size or flamboyance, all these plants conform to a general pattern. Funnel-shaped flowers are arranged alternately on either side of a slender blossom spike, all facing the same direction; the blooms open in sequence from the bottom to the top of the spike. The leaves are shaped like a sword blade (hence the name *gladiolus,* Latin for "little sword") and arranged in narrow, upright fans.

Grandiflora hybrids. Blooming in late spring and summer, these plants produce spikes that reach 3 to 6 feet tall, depending on the variety and growing conditions. The flowers (up to 30 per spike) are widely flaring and up to 8 inches across; colors include white, cream, yellow, orange, apricot, salmon, red, rose, lavender, purple, smoky shades, buff, and even green. Smaller selections from grandiflora breeding are grouped as small and miniature gladiolus; these grow 3 to 4 feet high and bear up to 18 flowers on each spike.

Primulinus and butterfly hybrids. These summer bloomers derive in part from *G. dalenii* (formerly *G. primulinus*), an African species with primrose yellow flowers that are hooded rather than funnel shaped. Named varieties grow 3 to 4 feet high, each spike bearing up to 18 blossoms spaced apart from one another; flowers are at least somewhat hooded, in a wide color range. The group known as butterfly gladiolus has 2- to 3-foot flowering stems, the blossoms more closely spaced; distinct throat markings or blotches of contrasting color give them the "butterfly" appearance.

Baby gladiolus. This group of hybrids derives in part from *G. × colvillei,* an early 19th-century hybrid that bore dark red blossoms on a spike a bit under 2 feet high; its pure white selection 'The Bride' is still available. Modern baby gladiolus are late spring bloomers with stems to 1½ feet tall and flaring flowers (like those of the large grandiflora types) to about 3 inches across; the color range is extensive, with some varieties showing throat blotches in a contrasting color. Plants listed under Nanus Hybrids are part of this group.

Species gladiolus. Several appealing gladiolus species are available from specialists. The tropical African native *G. callianthus* blooms in late summer and fall; it was classed as *Acidanthera bicolor* until recently, and some growers may still offer it under that name. Borne on 2- to 3-foot stems, its fragrant, creamy white blossoms are blotched with chocolate brown at the base; the elongated, pointed petals produce flowers of a more starlike shape than the blooms of other species. The selected variant 'Murielae' is taller, with crimson-blotched petals. Summer-blooming South African

G. tristis has 1½-foot stems bearing scented blossoms, typically in light yellow with purple veins. Byzantine gladiolus, *G. communis byzantinus,* is a southern European species; it blooms in summer, bearing flared maroon flowers on 2- to 3-foot stems that rise from clumps of distinctly narrow leaves.

USES. Many gardeners grow gladiolus for cut flowers, planting them in space-efficient rows. But clumps of gladiolus are much more pleasing to the eye: the plants' stiffness becomes an asset, providing a vertical accent in plantings of annuals and perennials.

GARDEN CULTURE. Grow grandiflora hybrids in Zones 4–9, 12–24, 29–33; primulinus and butterfly hybrids, *G. callianthus, G. communis byzantinus,* and *G. tristis* in Zones 4–9, 12–24, 29–31; baby gladiolus in Zones 4–9, 12–24 (baby glads sold as "winter-hardy" can also be grown in Zones 2, 3, 33–41).

Plant baby gladiolus in fall or early spring for flowers in late spring. Plant corms of all others from midwinter (in the mildest regions) into spring, after soil has warmed. The showy grandiflora hybrids will flower about 100 days after planting; the smaller hybrids and species will bloom in about 80 days. If you plant corms at 1- to 2-week intervals over a period of 4 to 6 weeks, you can enjoy an extended flowering season.

During warm to hot summer weather, thrips can seriously disfigure gladiolus blossoms. Many growers prefer to plant corms as early as possible, so that bloom will be over before thrips can become a problem (systemic insecticides, however, can virtually eliminate a thrips problem). If you want gladiolus to flower before the onset of hottest weather, plant at these times: *mild West Coast:* January through March; *Pacific Northwest:* April through June; *Southwest low desert:* November through January; *Southeast:* April through June; *Midwest, Mid-Atlantic, and Northeast:* May and June.

For the best-looking plants and flowers, purchase corms that are high crowned for their width; broad, flat corms are older and less vigorous. Choose a bright, sunny planting area, preferably with sandy loam soil; then dig a generous amount of organic matter into the soil before you set out corms.

Planting depth varies according to soil type and corm size. Set corms deeper in light soils than in heavy ones; set thicker corms deeper than thinner ones. As a general rule, plant each corm about four times as deep as it is thick, making some adjustment for soil type. For example, you might set a 1-inch-thick corm 4 inches deep in its preferred sandy loam, only 2 to 3 inches deep in a heavy soil. Spacing depends on corm diameter; position broader corms about 6 inches apart, smaller ones about 4 inches apart.

Water regularly from the time leaves emerge until bloom is over (this will entail providing moisture for some part of the summer, depending on when you planted). If you cut flowering stems for display indoors, leave at least four leaves on each plant; these will build up the corm for the next year's performance. Stems left to bloom out in the garden should be trimmed off beneath the lowest flower after blossoms fade. Uncut stems will set seeds, diverting energy from food storage in the corm.

Some time after flowering, leaves will begin to turn yellow. When this begins, withhold water and let foliage yellow completely. At this point, you face the question of digging or not digging. In zones beyond the stated hardiness, you must dig corms and store them over winter in a frost-free location. Within the stated hardiness zones, corms can remain in the ground over winter without risk. Nevertheless, many growers in these regions still prefer to dig corms each year, figuring that performance is better when corms are separated and replanted the next year in reworked or fresh soil. When you dig corms, shake off soil, then cut off stems and leaves just above each corm. Destroy cut-off tops to get rid of any thrips. (In rainy-summer areas, some growers dig plants before foliage yellows to prevent botrytis infection, which could ruin corms in storage.)

Gladiolus × colvillei 'The Bride'

Gladiolus, grandiflora hybrid

Listing continues >

Gladiolus callianthus

Place corms on a flat surface in a dark, dry area and let them dry for 2 to 3 weeks. Then examine corms carefully; discard those showing lesions, irregular blotches, or discoloration, all of which could indicate disease. Remove the old, spent base from each healthy corm. If you'd like to increase a particular variety, save the small offsets (cormels) for replanting; they should reach blooming size in 2 to 3 years.

Dust all corms and cormels with a powdered insecticide and keep them in a dry, cool place (40° to 50°F/4° to 10°C) until planting time. To store corms, place them in onion sacks or in discarded nylon stockings or pantyhose, then hang them up; or arrange them in a single layer on shallow trays. Stack the trays if necessary, placing spacers between them to allow for air circulation.

CONTAINER CULTURE. The smaller gladiolus make interesting container subjects. Use one of the soil mixes described under "B" on page 23. When plants die down, knock them from pots; cut off tops and store corms as directed above, then repot in fresh soil mix at planting time. Or store corms in their pots over winter; then knock from pots, separate, and repot in fresh soil mix at planting time.

GLORIOSA rothschildiana
GLORY LILY, CLIMBING LILY
Liliaceae
TUBER

- ▲ 6 FEET (CLIMBING)
- ☼ ◑ FULL SUN; FILTERED SUN OR LIGHT SHADE WHERE SUMMERS ARE HOT
- ● NEEDS SUMMER MOISTURE
- ✀ ZONES 24–27
- ◊ ALL PARTS ARE POISONOUS IF INGESTED

Gloriosa rothschildiana

A number of true lilies *(Lilium)* may reach 6 feet or more; this lily relative, native to tropical Africa and Asia, reaches that height in a distinctive manner. The tip of each lance-shaped, 5- to 7-inch leaf tapers to a tendril, which wraps around any handy support to stabilize the plant as it climbs. In summer, the top portion of the plant bears flashy 4-inch-wide blossoms, each with six recurved, wavy-edged segments in brightest red banded with yellow. This plant is now properly called *G. superba* 'Rothschildiana', but most catalogs still list it by its older, more familiar name, *G. rothschildiana*.

In completely frost-free regions, glory lily can survive outdoors all year—but even in these climates, it's best grown in containers. If you want the appearance of a permanent planting, just sink the containers into a garden flower bed, raised bed, or planter.

USES. Glory lily is a certain conversation piece for patio, terrace, or deck.

CONTAINER CULTURE. Plant tubers in a horizontal position, one to a container; set them 4 inches deep in the soil mix described in directions "A" on page 23. For the longest bloom season, start tubers indoors in late winter. After danger of frost is past, move containers to an outdoor spot in full sun (filtered sunlight or light shade in hot-summer regions). Be sure to provide the climbing stems with a support: a trellis, wires, strings, or even loose-growing shrubs or other vines.

During growth and bloom, water regularly and apply a liquid fertilizer every 3 weeks. Withhold water and fertilizer when foliage begins to yellow and die back in fall. After leaves are dry, sever dead stems and move containers to a dry, cool place (55° to 60°F/13° to 16°C) for the winter. In late winter, knock tubers out of containers; repot in fresh soil mix. Or dig tubers in fall and store as for dahlia (page 55) until planting time.

HABRANTHUS
Amaryllidaceae
TRUE BULB

- ▲ 6 TO 12 INCHES
- ☼ ◑ FULL SUN OR PART SHADE
- ● NEEDS SUMMER MOISTURE
- ✀ ZONES 8, 9, 14–28

In their native habitats from Texas to Argentina, these plants sprout and flower almost immediately after the ground has been moistened by summer rainfall—hence one of their common names, "rain lily." The grassy foliage and trumpet-shaped to funnel-shaped blossoms are very similar to those of fairy lily *(Zephyranthes)*, a close relative; but while fairy lily has upward-facing flowers, those of rain lily are angled outward. Each stem usually bears just one blossom.

The best-known species, *H. tubispathus (H. andersonii)*, has 1½-inch-long yellow blossoms veined in red on the exterior of the petals; stems and leaves grow to about 6 inches high. The plant sold as *H. texanus* and known as "copper lily" in Texas is probably a naturally occurring variant of *H. tubispathus,* differing from it in having all-yellow flowers on slightly taller stems. Taller still (to about 9 inches) is *H. robustus.* Like the related belladonna lily *(Amaryllis belladonna),* this species blooms before its leaves emerge, bearing 3-inch flowers—sometimes two to a stem—in light pink with green throats and deeper pink veining. Stems of *H. brachyandrus* can reach a foot tall, each carrying a purple-throated pink flower that faces nearly upward.

USES. Tuck clumps in the foreground of mixed summer annuals and perennials, or plant in rock gardens.

GARDEN CULTURE. In spring, plant bulbs in well-drained soil, setting them with tops at soil level; space at least 3 inches apart. Water regularly throughout growth and bloom. If you live in a frost-free climate and can withhold moisture for about a month after flowers have finished, you may be able to initiate another bloom cycle in fall.

Plantings may be left undisturbed for many years; dig and divide only to increase plantings or when vigor and flower quality decline. Replant divided bulbs immediately.

CONTAINER CULTURE. Follow directions "C" on page 23.

Habranthus robustus

HAEMANTHUS KATHARINAE. See SCADOXUS MULTIFLORUS KATHARINAE

HEMEROCALLIS
DAYLILY
Liliaceae
TUBEROUS ROOT

▲ 1 TO 6 FEET
☼ ◑ FULL SUN; FILTERED SUN OR PART SHADE WHERE SUMMERS ARE HOT
◆ NEEDS SUMMER MOISTURE
✀ ALL ZONES, EXCEPT AS NOTED

Hemerocallis 'Oodnadatta'

I n recent years, the old orange and yellow daylilies from Europe and Asia—indestructible components of grandmother's garden—have undergone a dramatic transformation at the hands of hybridizers. Standard, miniature, and small-flowered types have all been improved, the most obvious change being a greatly expanded color range: the orange and yellow shades now include soft apricot and pale yellow as well as the familiar bright hues, and you'll also find purple, lavender, red, maroon, bronze, all shades of pink, deep to pale shades of cream (some almost white), and various multicolored combinations. Increased petal width and thickness are two other notable improvements. The only part that hasn't changed is the foliage, which gave the plant its old-fashioned name "corn lily": before bloom, daylilies still look like young corn plants. Some kinds are deciduous; others are evergreen or semievergreen.

Hemerocallis 'Metaphor'

Stems of standard-size daylilies generally grow 2½ to 4 feet tall, though some exceptional varieties reach heights of up to 6 feet. Miniature and small-flowered types grow just 1 to 2 feet tall. Since the flowering stems are branched along their upper portion, each one produces an abundance of blooms. The blossoms may be lily shaped or chalice shaped, from 3 to 8 inches across (1½ to 3 inches wide in the smaller varieties); some are fragrant. A typical flower is single, consisting of six petal-like segments—but double-flowered varieties with an indeterminate number of segments are also available, as are "spider" types with narrow, twisted segments. Each flower lasts just one day (hence the common name), but buds open on successive days to prolong the display. Some extended-bloom varieties feature blossoms that remain open into the evening and may even last until the following morning.

Bloom usually begins in midspring, but early and late bloomers are also sold; by planting all three types, you can extend the spring flowering period for a month or more. Scattered bloom may occur during summer, and reblooming types put on a second display in late summer to midautumn.

Listing continues >

TOP: *Hemerocallis* 'Stella de Oro'
BOTTOM: *Hemerocallis* 'Raging Tiger'

Most daylilies offered in retail and mail-order nurseries are named hybrids of complex ancestry, but you can find several species daylilies if you do some searching. All those described below are deciduous.

H. altissima. As the name suggests, this species is tall, with leaves to 5 feet long and stems to 6 feet high. Scented, 4-inch yellow flowers appear in late summer to early fall. 'Statuesque' is a 5-footer that flowers about a month earlier.

H. fulva, tawny daylily, long ago escaped from cultivation to become a familiar roadside "wildflower" in parts of eastern North America. It blooms in summer, its 3- to 5-foot stems topped with 5-inch blossoms in dull, tawny orange. 'Kwanso' ('Kwanso Flore Pleno') is double flowered; it also comes in a form with variegated leaves. 'Rosea', with rosy red blossoms, is the source of pink in modern hybrids. *H. fulva* and its forms all spread to make sizable clumps or colonies.

H. lilio-asphodelus (H. flava). Even among the glut of modern hybrids, this species—commonly called "lemon lily" or "lemon daylily"—deservedly remains a favorite. Rising above foliage clumps about 2 feet high, the 3-foot stems bear delightfully fragrant, 4-inch, pure yellow blossoms in mid- to late spring.

USES. By selecting varieties of different sizes, you can use daylilies as accents in the foreground, middle, or background of any border planting. They're good for drifts as well; for this use, space them about 2 feet apart. They can also function as a tall ground cover, even in some shade (they usually endure competition from tree roots).

GARDEN CULTURE. Grow *H. altissima* in Zones 3–10, 14–24, 26–34, 39. Other daylilies will grow in all zones, according to these guidelines. Where winters are very mild, deciduous types may not get enough chill to turn in a top performance; on the other hand, they are the hardiest without protection (to about −35°F/−38°C). Evergreen kinds are entirely at home in mild-winter regions, but they need protection (see page 21) to survive where lows dip below −20°F/−29°C. Semievergreen types are intermediate between the two in hardiness; some perform better than others in mild-winter areas.

Though daylilies have a reputation for toughness and adaptability, they more than repay the gardener who gives them extra attention. Where summers are dry and hot, plant in filtered sun or part shade; in cooler regions, give full sun. Set out bare-root plants in fall (in colder zones) or early spring; plant ½ to 1 inch deep, 2 to 2½ feet apart. Plant from containers at any time from early spring through midautumn (even in winter, in mild-winter regions). For best results, use well-drained soil amended with organic matter. Plants need regular moisture from spring through fall. Divide when clumps become crowded, usually after 3 to 6 years; do this in fall or early spring in hot-summer regions, in summer in cool-summer areas or where the growing season is short.

CONTAINER CULTURE. The smaller daylilies are suited to container life on sunny patios, terraces, and decks. Follow directions "C" on page 23.

HIPPEASTRUM
AMARYLLIS
Amaryllidaceae
TRUE BULB

▲ 2 FEET
☀ ◖ FULL SUN OR PART SHADE
◖ NEEDS SUMMER MOISTURE
⟋ ZONES VARY BY SPECIES
   (SEE "GARDEN CULTURE")

The modern amaryllis sold as "Dutch hybrids" are the products of many European, American, and South African hybridizers, who developed them from various species native to Central and South America. In spring, each plant produces one or two thick stems, each bearing a cluster of three to six trumpet-shaped blossoms to 9 inches across. The broad, strap-shaped leaves usually appear after bloom; they may be nearly as long as the stems, but they're arching rather than upright. Flower colors range from pure white through blush and light pink to assertive, dramatic shades of crimson and orange scarlet; the lighter-colored blooms often have green throats. Many varieties are boldly veined—white veins on background colors of dark pink to red, reddish veins on white backgrounds. More recent developments include double-flowered varieties in white, creamy yellow, and pink, as well as miniature types with stems 12 to 15 inches high and flowers 3 to 5 inches across.

One Brazilian species, *H. papilio,* is also available; its 5-inch, greenish white trumpets are streaked with lavender to dark red. In parts of Texas and the lower South, *H.* × *johnsonii* is a reliable garden plant. A progenitor of the modern Dutch hybrids, it has stems to nearly 2 feet high and flowers with narrower petals than those of its hybrid descendants; the blossoms are bright red with white stripes.

USES. Pots of blooming amaryllis provide a focal point indoors or out. Where plants are hardy in the ground, you can set them out in large clumps or dramatic drifts.

GARDEN CULTURE. Grow *H.* × *johnsonii* in Zones 4–9, 14–29; *H. papilio* in Zones 8, 9, 14–28; Dutch hybrids in Zones 15–17, 21–28, and (with some shelter) in Zones 8, 9, 14, 18, 20.

In fall, set out bulbs 1 foot apart in well-drained soil enriched with organic matter; keep tops of bulb necks even with the soil surface. Water thoroughly, then keep soil just barely moist until leaves emerge. Increase watering after plants have sprouted, making sure that soil is moist at all times. Protect from slugs and snails.

After flowers have faded, cut off stalks. The leaves will grow through summer and disappear in fall if plants are dried off; otherwise, some foliage will remain. Divide infrequently—only when vigor and bloom quality decline or when you want to move or increase plantings. The best time to divide is early fall, just before growth begins.

CONTAINER CULTURE. Plant bulbs from midautumn through winter; the earlier you plant, the sooner flowers will appear (see also information on forcing, page 28). Select a container large enough to leave 2 inches between all sides of the bulb and the container edges. Use a soil mix described in "B" on page 23; plant bulb so its neck and top half are above the soil surface. Firm soil thoroughly and water well.

Move pots to a room receiving plenty of light (morning sun is fine, but not hot afternoon rays), with temperatures around 60° to 65°F/16° to 18°C at night, 70° to 75°F/21° to 24°C during the day. Keep soil mix just slightly moist until growth begins; then water regularly during growth and bloom. After blossoms fade, cut off flower stalks to prevent seed formation. Continue to water regularly and apply half-strength liquid fertilizer bimonthly until late summer. At that point, cut back on watering; when leaves are completely yellow, withhold water to give bulbs a dry dormant period. About 4 to 6 weeks before regular planting time, knock the plants out of their pots, scrape off part of the old soil mix, and replant in the same containers, using fresh mix (or, if bulbs have outgrown their original pots, replant in larger containers). Then resume watering as directed for newly planted bulbs.

TOP: *Hippeastrum,* Dutch hybrid
BOTTOM: *Hippeastrum papilio*

Homeria is a wispy, ephemeral plant, well adapted to the dry-summer, scant-rainfall region of South Africa from which it comes. Each corm produces a single lax, grasslike leaf, from which rises one slender, 1- to 1½-foot flowering stem in early to midspring. Each stem is topped with three or four flowers like those of ixia in warm pastel colors: soft orange, salmon to peach pink, or soft yellow. Soon after bloom, the foliage yellows and dies down, signalling the start of a long dormant period that lasts until late winter or early spring of the following year.

Listing continues >

HOMERIA collina
Iridaceae
CORM

▲ 1 TO 1½ FEET

☼ FULL SUN; PART SHADE WHERE SUMMERS ARE HOT

◊ ACCEPTS SUMMER MOISTURE BUT DOESN'T NEED ANY

✄ ZONES 4–29

Homeria collina

HYACINTHOIDES
(Endymion)
BLUEBELL
Liliaceae
TRUE BULB

- ▲ 12 TO 20 INCHES
- ◑ FILTERED SUN OR LIGHT SHADE
- ● NEEDS SOME SUMMER MOISTURE
- ⚡ ZONES VARY BY SPECIES
  (SEE "GARDEN CULTURE")

Hyacinthoides hispanica

HYACINTHUS
HYACINTH
Liliaceae
TRUE BULB

- ▲ 6 TO 12 INCHES
- ☀ FULL SUN
- ◐ ACCEPTS SUMMER MOISTURE BUT
  DOESN'T NEED ANY
- ⚡ ZONES VARY BY SPECIES (SEE "GAR-
  DEN CULTURE"); MOST NEED SUB-
  FREEZING WINTER TEMPERATURES

USES. In regions where soil does not freeze and corms can remain in the ground all year, homeria is a charming component of wildflower-type plantings. Plant corms in patches or drifts to gain color impact and compensate for the scant foliage.

GARDEN CULTURE. Where homeria is adapted, plant corms in a sunny location at any time from fall through winter, setting them 2 inches deep, 3 inches apart. Corms can remain in place for many years. In areas beyond the hardiness limits, set out corms in early spring for early summer bloom; dig them after leaves have died down and store over winter as for gladiolus (page 64). If corms are to accept moisture during their long dormancy, soil must be very well drained; if drainage is less than excellent and you can't keep the planting area dry, dig and store corms over summer or grow them in pots.

CONTAINER CULTURE. Follow directions "B" (subgroup 2) on page 23.

Both Spanish bluebell (*H. hispanica*) and English bluebell (*H. non-scripta*) are trouble-free spring-blooming bulbs. Botanists, however, have made them a bit troublesome by changing their names three times; before being given their current identity as *Hyacinthoides,* they were classed as *Scilla,* then moved to *Endymion.* Under any name, Spanish bluebell is the taller of the two, with straplike leaves and erect flower stems to 20 inches tall. Twelve or more ¾-inch, bell-shaped flowers hang from the upper part of each stem. English bluebell's flower stalks reach only about 1 foot and are gently arching rather than upright; the fragrant blossoms are slightly smaller and narrower than those of Spanish bluebell. Both species are available in blue, white, and pink forms. Wherever the two species grow near one another, hybrids are likely to appear, bearing appealing flowers intermediate in character between those of the two parents.

USES. Plant these bulbs in drifts or naturalize them at edges of woodland areas.

GARDEN CULTURE. Grow *H. hispanica* in Zones 1–11, 14–24, 28–43; plant *H. non-scripta* in Zones 3–6, 31–35, 37, 39–41. English bluebell is more climate specific, preferring cool to mild summer temperatures and definite winter chill. The more amenable Spanish bluebell is definitely the choice for hot-summer regions.

Choose a location in filtered sunlight or light shade. In fall, set bulbs 3 inches deep and 6 inches apart in clumps or drifts. Plants need regular moisture from planting time until foliage dies, and at least some moisture in summer. Divide infrequently, since the display grows in beauty as the plantings increase.

CONTAINER CULTURE. Follow directions "B" (subgroup 2) on page 23.

To most gardeners, a hyacinth is just one plant: the highly fragrant, fat-spiked Dutch hybrids of *H. orientalis,* a native of the eastern Mediterranean region. These grow to 1 foot tall, with straplike leaves that may be either erect or arching. The spikes of spring blossoms look like flowering drumsticks—they're tightly packed with small, outward-facing blooms shaped like flaring bells. Colors include pure white, cream, buff, yellow, pink, salmon, red, blue, and purple.

The largest bulbs (called exhibition size) produce the largest spikes; they're the best choice for container-grown and forced flowers. The next largest size is satisfactory for outdoor planting. The smallest bulbs produce smaller, looser flower clusters—the same results you'll get from larger bulbs left in the ground from year to year.

Native to the south of France, the Roman or French Roman hyacinth, *H. orientalis albulus,* is smaller than the *H. orientalis* hybrids and blooms earlier in the season. It thrives (and naturalizes easily) where winters offer little or no chill. Each bulb may produce several slender, foot-tall stems, each carrying loose spikes of white, pale blue, or pink flowers.

A third hyacinth is now classed as *Brimeura amethystina*, though most catalogs still list it as *H. amethystinus*. In bulb and leaf, it resembles the preceding species, but the 10-inch spikes of pendent bells that bloom in spring to early summer look just like those of bluebell *(Hyacinthoides)*. Bright blue is the standard color, but a pure white form is also available.

USES. All but the Dutch hybrids are good for naturalizing or for informal drifts beneath deciduous trees and shrubs. The hybrids provide an impressive display when massed in beds or borders, but because of their rather stiff appearance, they look rigidly formal when planted in rows. All hyacinths can be grown in containers; the Dutch hybrids are the showiest.

Hyacinthus orientalis 'Gypsy Queen'

GARDEN CULTURE. Grow *H. amethystinus (Brimeura amethystina)* in Zones 1–24, 29–43; grow *H. orientalis albulus* in Zones 4–24, 29–33. The Dutch hybrids can be grown in all zones, but bulbs left in the ground will persist only in regions where there is distinct winter cold. Where winters are mild, in-ground Dutch hybrid bulbs do not last long: if summers are dry, they soon dwindle and vanish for lack of winter chill; if summers are warm and moist, they are likely to rot during the first summer after flowering. In these regions, treat Dutch hybrid hyacinths as annuals.

TOP: *Hyacinthus orientalis* in container
BOTTOM: *Hyacinthus orientalis albulus*

The Dutch hybrids and *H. orientalis albulus* must be planted early enough to establish vigorous roots before the ground freezes. Where winter temperatures drop below 20°F/−7°C, set bulbs out in earliest fall; in warmer regions, delay planting until mid- to late fall, when summerlike warmth is sure to be gone. Keep bulbs cool in the meantime; if you're planting only a few, store them in the vegetable crisper of your refrigerator.

Choose a sunny planting area with well-drained soil (preferably on the sandy side); dig plenty of organic matter into the soil prior to planting. Set the largest Dutch hybrid bulbs 4 to 5 inches deep, about 5 inches apart; the smaller hybrid bulbs and those of *H. orientalis albulus* should go about 3 inches deep and 4 to 5 inches apart.

Keep soil moist after planting so roots will become established; continue to water regularly from the time leaves emerge until the flowers fade. If bulbs are to remain in the ground for more than one flowering, apply a granular fertilizer just as blossoms fade; remove the spent flower spikes and continue to water regularly until foliage yellows. After foliage has died down, keep soil fairly dry during summer and into fall, until cool weather returns.

H. amethystinus (Brimeura amethystina) is more widely adapted than the other hyacinths. Plant bulbs in mid- to late fall (before ground freezes), 2 inches deep and 3 inches apart. In Zones 1, 2, and 41–43, mulch soil after the first hard frost. Give the same watering regime as for other hyacinths.

CONTAINER CULTURE. Follow directions "B" (subgroup 1) on page 23. For information on growing bulbs indoors in a hyacinth glass, see page 27.

HYMENOCALLIS
Amaryllidaceae
TRUE BULB

- ▲ 2 FEET
- ☼ ☽ FULL SUN; FILTERED SUN OR PART SHADE WHERE SUMMERS ARE HOT
- ◖ NEEDS SUMMER MOISTURE
- ✇ ZONES 5, 6, 8, 9, 14–31
- ◓ BULBS ARE POISONOUS IF INGESTED

Hymenocallis 'Sulfur Queen'

Imagine a fanciful hybrid between a belladonna lily *(Amaryllis belladonna)* and a daffodil, and you'll come close to visualizing this summer-blooming bulb. Like belladonna lily, it has strap-shaped leaves (usually about 2 feet long) and thick flower stems, each topped with several fragrant blossoms—though leaves and flowers appear simultaneously in hymenocallis. Like daffodils, the flowers have two sets of segments: the inner ones form a funnel, while the outer ones are longer, spidery, and recurved.

The most common species is *H. narcissiflora* (formerly known as *H. calathina* and *Ismene calathina*), the Peruvian daffodil. Its white flowers, striped green in the throat, are carried in clusters of two to five per stem. Its selected form 'Advance' has pure white flowers only faintly lined green in the throat. The hybrid 'Sulfur Queen' has a more circular cup surrounded by broader, less spidery segments; the color is soft primrose yellow, with green stripes in the throat. *H. × festalis* is at the more spidery end of the spectrum: its outer segments are like curled white ribbon, surrounding a broadly chalice-shaped inner cup with fringed lobes. Each stem bears about four flowers, held horizontally, over foliage like that of *H. narcissiflora*.

USES. Hymenocallis is attractive in border plantings of summer-flowering annuals and perennials. It's also a good choice for containers.

GARDEN CULTURE. Where bulbs are hardy in the ground, plant in fall or early winter. In colder regions, plant in spring, after all danger of frost is past; when foliage yellows and dies down after flowering, dig the bulbs and store them as for dahlia (page 55) until planting time the following spring.

Select a sunny location (filtered sun or part shade where summers are hot) with well-drained soil; dig a generous amount of organic matter into the soil before planting. Set tops of bulbs just beneath the soil surface, spacing bulbs about 1 foot apart. Plants need regular moisture during growth and bloom; leaves will remain green throughout summer if watering continues. At some point, leaves will start to turn yellow; at this point, withhold moisture and let them die down.

CONTAINER CULTURE. Follow directions "C" on page 23.

IPHEION uniflorum
SPRING STAR FLOWER
Liliaceae
TRUE BULB

- ▲ 6 TO 8 INCHES
- ☼ ☽ FULL SUN, PART SHADE, OR LIGHT SHADE
- ◖ ACCEPTS SUMMER MOISTURE BUT DOESN'T NEED ANY
- ✇ ZONES 3–24, 27–34

Ipheion uniflorum

This rugged little spring bloomer from Argentina has an understated, wildflowerlike charm. Each bulb produces several slender stems, each bearing a ½-inch blossom with six overlapping petals arranged in star fashion. The usual color is white tinged with blue, but bulb specialists may offer selected variants such as white 'Album', bright blue 'Rolf Fiedler', and dark blue 'Wisley Blue'. All types have narrow, nearly flat bluish green leaves that give off an oniony odor when bruised.

USES. Plant spring star flower in borders or under deciduous shrubs. Or naturalize it in woodland areas or among low grasses.

GARDEN CULTURE. Though spring star flower prefers well-drained soil, it is not particular about the type; anything from light, sandy soil to clay is satisfactory. It is similarly unfussy about planting location, performing equally well in sun, part shade, and light shade.

Plant bulbs in early to midautumn, 2 inches deep and 2 inches apart. Water regularly during growth and bloom. The bulbs prefer dry conditions during their summer dormancy, but will accept moisture if drainage is good. Dig and divide infrequently, since plantings become more attractive over the years as bulbs multiply.

CONTAINER CULTURE. Follow directions "B" (subgroup 2) on page 23.

M ention iris, and most people will think of the showy tall bearded irises that are mainstays of the midspring flower display. But though these may be the most widely planted, they constitute only one part of a highly diverse group of plants.

Despite their considerable differences, all irises have the same basic flower structure. All blossoms have three true petals (the standards) and three petal-like sepals (the falls). Standards may be upright, arching, or flaring, while falls range from flaring to drooping. Flower types fit into two broad groups: *bearded*, with a caterpillarlike tuft of hairs on each fall; and *beardless*, without such hairs. In growth habit, irises are either *rhizomatous* or *bulbous*.

RHIZOMATOUS IRISES

Irises that grow from rhizomes may be bearded or beardless. Leaves are swordlike, overlapping each other to form a flat fan of foliage.

BEARDED IRISES

Bearded irises are available in a dazzling array of colors and color combinations. Irises of this type are divided into the four main classes outlined below: *tall, median, dwarf,* and *arils and arilbreds*. Except for the arils and arilbreds, which have special needs, all bearded irises require the same basic care (see "Bearded iris culture," page 74).

TALL BEARDED IRISES. Plants bloom in midspring, bearing large, broad-petaled blossoms on branching stems that grow 2½ to 4 feet tall. Reblooming (remontant) types will flower again in summer, fall, or winter (depending on the variety) if grown in a favorable climate and given cultural encouragement.

MEDIAN AND DWARF IRISES. Blossoms resemble those of tall beardeds, but on a smaller scale; stems and foliage are smaller as well. Median is a collective term for the first four types listed below.

Border bearded irises. These are segregates from tall bearded breeding with 15- to 28-inch stems and proportionately sized flowers and foliage. The bloom period is the same as for tall bearded irises.

Miniature tall bearded irises. Height range is the same as for border beardeds (15 to 28 inches), but miniature tall beardeds have pencil-slim stems, rather narrow and short leaves, and relatively tiny flowers—only 2 to 3 inches wide. The bloom time is the same as for tall beardeds; the color range is more limited. Members of this group usually have more stems per clump than the average tall bearded.

Intermediate bearded irises. Modern intermediates are hybrids of tall beardeds and standard dwarfs. Flowers are 3 to 5 inches wide, carried on 15- to 28-inch stems. Plants come into bloom 1 to 3 weeks before tall beardeds; some varieties bloom a second time in fall. In addition to modern types, this group includes the old, familiar "common purple" and "graveyard white" irises that flower in early spring.

Standard dwarf bearded irises. Most modern members of this group were developed from crosses of tall bearded varieties with a miniature dwarf species from central Europe. Standard dwarfs bloom even earlier than intermediates, producing a great profusion of 2- to 3-inch-wide flowers on stems 8 to 15 inches tall. There's a wide range of available colors and patterns.

Miniature dwarf bearded irises. These are the shortest and earliest blooming of the bearded irises, reaching just 2 to 8 inches high. They bear a wealth of flowers in a great variety of colors; blooms are often a bit large in proportion to the rest of the plant. Established, well-grown plants can form cushions of bloom—attractive in rock gardens, borders, and foreground plantings.

Listing continues >

IRIS
Iridaceae
RHIZOME; TRUE BULB

- ▲ 2 INCHES TO 7 FEET
- ☀ ◑ FULL SUN, FILTERED SUN, LIGHT SHADE, OR PART SHADE, DEPENDING ON TYPE AND CLIMATE
- ◐ ◑ ○ SUMMER MOISTURE NEEDS VARY (SEE DESCRIPTIONS)
- ✿ ZONES VARY BY TYPE (SEE DESCRIPTIONS)

TOP: Standard dwarf bearded iris 'Sarah Taylor'
BOTTOM: Tall bearded iris 'Cinderella's Coach'

ARIL AND ARILBRED IRISES. The word "exotic" might have been coined especially for the aril species, which take their name from the collarlike white cap (the aril) on their seeds. These irises comprise two groups, Oncocyclus and Regelia; both are native to arid regions of the Near East and central Asia. Hybrids between the two groups are called Oncogelias. For all, bloom comes during midspring.

Oncocyclus species typically feature 4- to 7-inch-wide, domed or globe-shaped blooms with a base color of gray, silver, lavender, gold, or maroon. In many types, the petals are intricately veined and dotted with darker hues. Flower stems are fairly short, usually reaching only about 1 foot; leaves are narrow, lightly ribbed, and typically sickle shaped.

Regelias have smaller and more vertical blossoms than the Oncocyclus types; both base colors and contrasting veining are in brighter shades (though *I. hoogiana* is pure blue), often with a lustrous sheen. Flower stems reach 1½ to 2½ feet, depending on care. The narrow, ribbed leaves are usually straight rather than curving.

All the aril species have strict cultural needs: perfect drainage (no standing water), alkaline soil, and a hot, dry summer dormant period. Oncocyclus species are the fussiest; Regelias and Oncogelias are more adaptable. All three are hardy in the ground to about −20°F/−29°C.

Arilbred irises are hybrids of aril types and tall or median bearded irises; a number of named

Arilbred iris 'Jeweled Veil'

varieties are sold, with varying percentages of aril "blood." In general, those with more aril in their ancestry have a more exotic look. Many arilbreds are nearly as easy to grow as tall beardeds, or require only the addition of lime to the soil and a little extra attention to drainage.

BEARDED IRIS CULTURE. These irises are grown in Zones 1–24, 30–45; where winter temperatures are likely to drop below −20°F/−29°C, many gardeners give plantings winter protection (see page 21) just after the ground freezes. Bearded irises demand good drainage; as long as rhizomes don't sit in saturated soil, they'll do well in anything from light sand to clay. If you're growing irises in heavy soil, plant them in a raised bed or raised planting area to promote drainage.

In cool-summer climates, plants must have full sun from spring through fall. Where summers are hot, however, they may appreciate afternoon filtered sunlight or high shade—but too much shade will greatly decrease bloom production and interfere with the necessary summer ripening of rhizomes.

Plant rhizomes between July 1 and October 21 (limit planting to July or August in cold-winter climates, September or October where summer temperatures are high). Space rhizomes 1 to 2 feet apart; set them with tops just beneath the soil surface, spreading roots well. Growth proceeds from the leafy end of the rhizome, so point that end in the direction in which you want growth to occur initially. If the weather turns hot, shade newly planted rhizomes to prevent sunscald and subsequent rot.

After planting rhizomes, water the planting area to settle the soil and start root growth; thereafter, water judiciously until new growth appears, signalling that plants have taken hold. Water regularly unless rain does it for you or freezing weather arrives. From the time growth starts in late winter or early spring, water regularly until about 6 weeks after flowers fade (increases and buds for the following year are formed during the post-bloom period). During summer, plants can get by with less frequent watering—every other week in warm climates, once a month where summers are cool.

Apply a granular fertilizer as plants begin growth in late winter or early spring, then again right after the blooming season ends.

Clumps become overcrowded after 3 or 4 years, producing fewer flower stalks and blooms of poorer quality. When this occurs, dig clumps at the best planting time for your climate and separate old, woody rhizomes from healthy ones with good fans of leaves. Then trim leaves and roots to 6 to 8 inches and replant. If you're replanting in the same plot, dig plenty of organic matter into the soil before you plant.

BEARDLESS IRISES

Only two main characteristics are common to all irises in this category: the lack of a beard on the falls, and roots that are generally fibrous rather than fleshy. The most widely sold beardless irises are the four hybrid groups (the first four listings) described below.

JAPANESE IRISES. Zones 1–10, 14–24, 32–45. Derived from *I. ensata* (formerly *I. kaempferi*), these irises are graceful, moisture-loving plants which, when grown under ideal conditions, bear the largest flowers of all irises. The narrow, upright leaves, each with a distinct midrib, are reminiscent of rushes. Above the foliage clumps, 4- to 12-inch flowers float on stems up to 4 feet tall. Blossoms are fairly flat, either single (standards small and distinct in appearance from falls) or double (standards and falls of about equal size, shape, and markings). Colors include white and all shades of purple, violet, blue, and pink; light-colored blooms are often intricately marked, veined, or striped. Flowering begins in late spring.

Japanese irises must have rich soil and copious nonalkaline moisture from the time growth begins until the blooming season ends. Grow them at pond edges, or plant them in boxes, pots, or buckets of soil sunk halfway to the rim in the water of a pond or pool. If you water them very faithfully, they can also succeed in heavy garden soil. Where summers are cool, plant in full sun; in warm-summer regions, choose a spot receiving high shade or dappled afternoon sun.

Set out rhizomes in fall or spring, 2 inches deep and 1½ feet apart, pointing the leafy ends in the direction you want growth to take. (Or plant up to three rhizomes per 12-inch-wide container.) Divide crowded clumps in late summer or early fall, then replant as quickly as possible.

LOUISIANA IRISES. Zones 3–24, 26–43. The progenitors of this group are three or more species native to swamps and moist lowlands, primarily along the Gulf Coast. Leaves are long, linear, and unribbed; graceful, flattish blossoms are carried on 2- to 5-foot stems in spring. The range of flower colors and patterns is nearly as extensive as that of the tall beardeds.

Though the species come from milder climates, some varieties have succeeded as far north as South Dakota. Plants thrive in rich, well-watered garden soil as well as at pond margins; both soil and water should be neutral to acid. Full sun is best in cool- and mild-summer areas, but where heat is intense, choose a spot receiving light afternoon shade. Plant in late summer; set rhizomes 1 inch deep, 1½ to 2 feet apart. Where ground freezes in winter, give plants winter protection (page 21).

Tall bearded iris 'Mother Earth'

Japanese iris

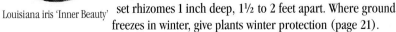

Louisiana iris 'Inner Beauty'

Listing continues >

Siberian iris

Spuria iris 'Barbara's Kiss'

SIBERIAN IRISES. Zones 1–10, 14–23, 32–45. The most widely sold members of this group are named hybrids derived from *I. sibirica* and *I. sanguinea*. All have narrow, almost grasslike deciduous foliage and slender flower stems. Depending on the variety, leaf length ranges from 1 to 3 feet, stem height from about 14 inches to nearly 4 feet. In midspring, each stem bears two to five blossoms with upright standards and flaring to drooping falls. Colors include white and every shade of violet, purple, lavender, wine, pink, and blue; several recent hybrids are light yellow.

Plant Siberian irises in early spring or late summer in cold-winter regions, in fall where summers are hot and winters mild to moderate. Plant in sun (light shade where summers are hot) in good, neutral to acid soil; set rhizomes 1 to 2 inches deep, 1 to 2 feet apart. Water generously from the time growth begins until the bloom period is over. Divide infrequently; plants look most attractive in well-established clumps. Dig and divide (in late summer or early fall) only when old clumps begin to show hollow centers.

SPURIA IRISES. Zones 2–24, 28–43. In general flower form, Spurias are almost identical to florists' Dutch irises. The older members of this group have yellow or white-and-yellow flowers, but modern hybrids show a greatly expanded range of colors: blue, lavender, gray, orchid, tan, bronze, brown, purple, earthy red, and near black, often with a prominent yellow spot on the falls. Plants come into bloom a little later than tall bearded irises, their blossoms held closely against 3- to 6-foot flower stems. The narrow dark green leaves grow upright to 3 to 4 feet.

Plant these irises in late summer or early fall, in a full-sun location with good soil. Set rhizomes 1 inch deep, 1½ to 2 feet apart; water regularly from the time growth begins until flowering is over. Most Spurias need very little water during summer. Give plants winter protection (see page 21) where temperatures drop below −20°F/−29°C.

Divide plantings infrequently—only when they become overcrowded. Dig and replant rhizomes in late summer or early fall.

ADDITIONAL BEARDLESS SPECIES. Several beardless iris species that do not fit into the previous categories are good garden plants offered by specialty growers. The following three will grow in shallow water as well as in moist to boggy, acid garden soil. Plant all in late summer, setting them 1 inch deep and 2 feet apart.

I. laevigata grows in Zones 1–10, 14–24, 32–45. Handsome clumps of evergreen, glossy leaves grow to 2½ feet high; flower stems reach about the same height. Typical blossoms are blue violet, with upright standards and drooping falls with a yellow blaze. Named variants offer flowers in white, magenta, and combinations of purple and white, and those in which standards have the shape and carriage of falls, giving the effect of a double flower. The bloom period comes after that of tall bearded irises.

I. pseudacorus, yellow flag, succeeds in Zones 1–24, 28–45. Impressive foliage, deciduous in winter, may reach 5 feet tall under ideal conditions, with flower stems attaining 4 to 7 feet. The bloom period coincides with the latter part of the tall bearded season. Blossoms are bright yellow, though there are selected forms with flowers in ivory and light yellow; other forms include those with double petals, shorter or taller leaves, and creamy yellow young foliage.

I. versicolor, blue flag, grows in Zones 1–9, 14–17, 28–45. This familiar North American native grows wild in bogs and swamps in the Great Lakes region, the Ohio River Valley, and the Northeast. Narrow deciduous leaves grow 1½ to 4 feet high; leaves of shorter types are upright, while those of taller kinds recurve gracefully. Light violet blue is the typical color, but darker and lighter forms are available; 'Kermesina' is wine red, while 'Rosea' and 'Vernal' have pink flowers. Flowers of all appear during the latter part of the tall bearded season.

Bulbous irises

Like bearded irises, all bulbous irises have foliage that grows in flattened fans, but the leaves tend to be more grasslike and rounder in cross section. In summer, the foliage dies back and the bulbs enter dormancy. At this time, they can be dug and stored until planting time in fall.

GARDEN CULTURE. For details on growing bulbous irises in the ground, see the individual listings below and on page 78.

CONTAINER CULTURE. All bulbous irises are appealing, easy-to-grow container subjects. See directions "B" (subgroup 1) on page 23.

DUTCH AND SPANISH IRISES

Bulb growers in Holland developed the Dutch hybrids from several Mediterranean species. All have stiff, 1½- to 2-foot stems bearing sturdy, rather stiff, 3- to 4-inch-wide blossoms with erect standards and down-curving falls. Colors include white and various bright, clear shades of blue, purple, mauve, bronze, yellow, and orange; some types have bicolored blooms. In warm-winter climates, flowering comes in March and April; where winters are colder, blossoms appear in May and June.

Dutch irises grow in Zones 3–24, 30–34. Choose a sunny planting area with well-drained soil, preferably in a part of the garden that can remain unwatered over the summer. Plant bulbs in October or November, 4 inches deep and 3 to 4 inches apart. Give plenty of water from the time leaves emerge until about a month after flowers finish; then withhold water and let foliage die.

Where summers are dry (and the planting area won't be watered in summer), you can leave bulbs in the ground for several years. Dig and divide when plants show a decline in vigor and bloom quality. But where there is summer watering or rainfall, dig bulbs after leaves die back and hold until planting time in fall.

Though it is usually sold as a Dutch iris and needs the same care, the variety 'Wedgwood' is larger, taller, and earlier blooming by about 2 weeks (at 'King Alfred' daffodil time). It succeeds only where winter temperatures remain above 10°F/−12°C.

Spanish irises are derived from species native to Spain. They grow in the same zones Dutch irises do (Zones 3–24, 30–34) and have the same cultural needs and general appearance, but the plants tend to be smaller flowered, shorter, and slimmer. Spanish irises come into bloom about 2 weeks later than the Dutch types.

ENGLISH IRISES

All the available named varieties and color variations of English irises are derived solely from *I. xiphioides* (sometimes sold as *I. latifolia*). This species gained the name "English iris" because it was first grown as an ornamental plant in England; its true home, though, is in the moist meadows of northeastern Spain and the Pyrenees Mountains.

Flower stems may reach 1½ feet tall. In early summer, each bears two velvety-textured blooms of white, mauve, maroon, bluish purple, or blue (bulb specialists may list varieties in specific colors). Flower form is similar to that of Dutch irises, but blossoms are a bit larger, with much broader falls.

Grow English irises in Zones 3–6, 15–17, 21–24, 32, 34, 39. They perform best in a climate with cool to moderate summers. Plant bulbs as soon as they arrive in nurseries (usually October or November); choose a location in full sun (or in part shade, where summers are warm to hot), with cool, moist, acid soil. General cultural requirements are the same as for Dutch irises, but English irises don't need complete dryness after flowering.

Iris versicolor

Dutch iris hybrids

Listing continues >

Reticulata iris

RETICULATA IRISES

The several species and varieties belonging to the Reticulata section are characterized by a netted outer covering on the bulb. They are small, slim plants (most no taller than 8 inches), classic choices for rock gardens and pathway border plantings.

Depending on the severity of the winter, flowering time varies from midwinter to early spring. Blossoms are 2 to 3 inches across. Slender, sometimes spikelike leaves may emerge simultaneously with the flowers or appear just after bloom ceases.

The group's best known member is *I. reticulata*, with flowers of pale to violet blue, red violet, or white. Blossoms of *I. histrioides* and its variety *I. h. major* are light to medium blue, with darker blue spots on the falls. Bright yellow *I. danfordiae* differs from the others in both flower color and form—the standards are almost nonexistent. Bulb specialists may offer other species and varieties.

Grow reticulata irises in Zones 3–24, 30–34; bulbs are hardy in the ground to about −10°F/−23°C, but do need some subfreezing winter temperatures to thrive. Reticulata irises appreciate a full-sun location with well-drained soil. Set out bulbs in fall, 3 to 4 inches deep and as far apart. Plants need regular water from fall through spring, but soil should be kept dry during the bulbs' summer dormant period. Dig and divide only when vigor and flower quality deteriorate.

Reticulata iris

IXIA
IXIA, AFRICAN CORN LILY
Iridaceae
CORM

▲ 16 TO 24 INCHES
☼ FULL SUN
◊ WITHHOLD SUMMER MOISTURE
✂ ZONES 7–9, 12–24

Ixia

Ixia's clumps of narrow, almost grasslike leaves give rise to wiry stems topped by short spikes of bright, cheery, 2-inch flowers in late spring. Each six-petaled blossom opens out nearly flat in full sun, but remains cup shaped or closed on overcast days.

Most of the ixias available at nurseries are hybrids involving the South African *I. maculata*; the color range is extensive, including cream, yellow, red, orange, and pink, typically with dark centers. A lovely curiosity is *I. viridiflora*, with purple-centered bluish green flowers.

USES. Ixia offers a bright wildflower charm in the foreground of mixed plantings or naturalized in sunny drifts where summers are dry.

GARDEN CULTURE. Plant *I. maculata* and *I. viridiflora* in a sunny spot with light, well-drained soil (*I. viridiflora* in particular demands good drainage). In regions where winter lows usually remain above 20°F/−7°C, plant corms in early fall, setting them about 2 inches deep and 3 inches apart. Where temperatures may dip to 10°F/−12°C, plant after November 1; set corms 4 inches deep, then cover the planting area with a mulch (see page 16). The later planting time, greater planting depth, and mulch keep corms from sending up leaves that would be damaged by cold. Where temperatures fall below 10°F/−12°C, plant corms in spring for flowers in early summer.

Water plants regularly during growth and bloom, then let soil go dry when foliage yellows. If corms are planted among drought-tolerant plants or by themselves, you can leave them undisturbed in dry-summer areas where they are hardy in the ground. After several years, or when the planting becomes crowded and flower quality decreases, dig corms in summer and store as for gladiolus (page 64) until planting time in fall.

Where there is summer watering or summer rainfall, and in regions where corms are not hardy in the ground, dig them after foliage dies back and store as for gladiolus (page 64) until the best planting time for your climate.

CONTAINER CULTURE. Plant corms close together and about 1 inch deep in a deep container. Follow directions "B" (subgroup 2) on page 23.

Native to the steppes of central Asia, these floral star sapphires bejewel the garden in late spring. Wiry, 12- to 16-inch stems rise above narrow gray-green leaves, bearing loose clusters of 1½-inch, blue-violet blossoms, each with six narrow petals highlighted by a darker central line. Foliage dies down at some point during summer, not to reappear until the following spring.

USES. In clumps and drifts, these plants provide an effective blue front-of-border accent among other spring-flowering bulbs and perennials.

GARDEN CULTURE. Where ixiolirion is native, its bulbs receive a good baking over a long, dry summer, then get moderate moisture from fall through spring. In the garden, they need good, well-drained soil—especially where winter rain is plentiful or where they'll receive supplemental water after the foliage disappears. In Zones 3, 32 (colder parts), and 33, choose a planting spot where emerging foliage will be sheltered from late spring frosts. Plant in fall, setting bulbs 3 inches deep and about 3 inches apart; plantings can remain in place for many years before they need division. To grow ixiolirion in zones beyond its adaptability, set out bulbs in early spring; dig in fall and give covered storage (see page 21) until planting time the following spring.

CONTAINER CULTURE. Follow directions "B" (subgroup 2) on page 23.

Mild-winter gardeners searching for a hyacinthlike plant that persists from year to year find just what they want in this South African native. Each bulb usually produces just two broad, succulent, strap-shaped leaves (spotted with brown, in some kinds). Spikes of pendent, tubular blossoms appear at the tips of thick flowering stems in late winter or early spring.

The most common cape cowslip is *L. aloides* (formerly *L. tricolor*), with inch-wide leaves and 10- to 12-inch stems displaying yellow flowers tipped in red and green. Several named selections offer color variations. 'Aurea' has bright orange-yellow blossoms; flowers of 'Nelsonii' are bright yellow tinged green; 'Pearsonii' has yellow-orange blooms with red-orange bases on slightly taller stems.

Larger overall—with stems to 15 inches high, flowers 1½ inches long, and leaves 2 inches wide—is *L. bulbiferum* (formerly *L. pendula*). Its coral red and yellow blossoms are tipped in purple; blooms of 'Superba' are orange red. *L. contaminata* is reminiscent of grape hyacinth *(Muscari):* its flowers (in white tipped red to brown) are nearly spherical, bell shaped, and carried in tight spikes. Both the stems and the narrow, upright leaves reach about 9 inches high. Growers specializing in tender bulbs may offer a number of other species.

USES. Plants are at home in rock gardens and border plantings, as well as in containers.

GARDEN CULTURE. Plant in late summer or early fall. Where summers are cool or mild, choose a sunny spot; in hot-summer climates, pick an area in part or light shade. Set bulbs in well-drained soil, 3 inches apart and 1 to 1½ inches deep. Water sparingly until growth starts, then give regular moisture until foliage yellows after bloom. Then gradually let soil dry out and keep as dry as possible until the next fall. Protect plants from slugs and snails.

CONTAINER CULTURE. Plant bulbs 2 to 3 inches apart, with tips just beneath the soil surface, in the soil mix described under "A" on page 23. Potted plants can grow outdoors all year in the dry-summer zones listed above right. They can also be grown outdoors in Zones 25–27, but must be protected from summer rain. Elsewhere, grow

IXIOLIRION tataricum

Amaryllidaceae

TRUE BULB

▲ 12 TO 16 INCHES

☼ FULL SUN

◐ ACCEPTS SUMMER MOISTURE BUT DOESN'T NEED ANY

✄ ZONES 3–11, 14–21, 29–33

Ixiolirion tataricum

LACHENALIA

CAPE COWSLIP

Liliaceae

TRUE BULB

▲ 9 TO 15 INCHES

☼ ◑ FULL SUN; PART OR LIGHT SHADE WHERE SUMMERS ARE HOT

◑ WITHHOLD SUMMER MOISTURE

✄ ZONES 16, 17, 23, 24

Lachenalia aloides

as a house or greenhouse plant. Outdoors, follow the watering regime described in "Garden culture." After planting for indoor bloom, water thoroughly and keep cool and dark until leaves appear, then bring into a light room with cool night temperatures (50°F/10°C). Apply a dilute liquid fertilizer every 2 weeks throughout the period of active growth. Store bulbs dry in pots over summer.

LEUCOJUM
SNOWFLAKE
Amaryllidaceae
TRUE BULB

- ▲ 6 TO 18 INCHES
- ☼ ◑ FULL SUN; FILTERED SUN OR LIGHT SHADE AFTER BLOOM WHERE SUMMERS ARE HOT
- ◑ NEEDS SOME SUMMER MOISTURE, EXCEPT AS NOTED
- ⟋ ZONES VARY BY SPECIES (SEE "GARDEN CULTURE")

Leucojum aestivum
'Gravetye Giant'

Dainty appearance and delicate fragrance belie a tough constitution: where adapted, these natives of Europe and the western Mediterranean region are among the most tolerant of bulbs.

Of the two commonly grown species, the more widely adapted is *L. aestivum*. It's commonly called "summer snowflake," but the name is misleading: in warmer parts of the West and Southwest, flowering begins in late November and continues into winter. In cold-winter regions, blossoms appear in midspring. Narrow, strap-shaped leaves grow 1 to 1½ feet long; flower stems are equally long (or longer), each carrying three to five pendent, six-segmented white bells. The pointed tip of each blossom segment is marked with green. 'Gravetye Giant' is a bit taller and larger flowered than the species.

Spring snowflake, *L. vernum*, blooms in midwinter to earliest spring, depending on climate. Unlike *L. aestivum*, this species thrives only where it receives definite winter cold: 20°F/−7°C or lower. The blooms are similar to those of summer snowflake, but each foot-tall stem bears just one blossom.

Less widely grown than the preceding two species is *L. autumnale*. In late summer or fall, its 6-inch stems rise from bare earth, each carrying one to four pink-tinted white blossoms; grasslike leaves emerge after the flowers fade.

USES. Naturalize snowflakes under deciduous trees or shrubs; use clumps along lightly shaded pathways.

GARDEN CULTURE. Grow *L. aestivum* in Zones 1–24, 29–43; *L. vernum* in Zones 1–6, 30–43; *L. autumnale* in Zones 4–9, 14–34, 30–32.

In fall, set bulbs in well-drained soil, 3 to 4 inches deep and about 4 inches apart. Water regularly from planting time until foliage yellows and dies down in late spring of the next year. Less water is needed during the summer dormant period; *L. aestivum* can even get by without summer moisture as long as the soil is shaded.

Leave clumps undisturbed until diminished growth and flower quality indicate overcrowding. Dig and separate in summer; replant immediately.

CONTAINER CULTURE. These bulbs are best suited to garden culture, but they can be forced for early bloom (see pages 26–27). Use one of the soil mixes described under "B" on page 23.

LIATRIS
GAYFEATHER
Asteraceae
TUBEROUS ROOT

- ▲ 2 TO 5 FEET
- ☼ FULL SUN
- ◑ NEEDS SUMMER MOISTURE
- ⟋ ZONES 1–10, 14–24, 26, 28–45

Although these summer-blooming eastern and central U.S. natives belong to the daisy family, their appearance is decidedly undaisylike. Clumps of narrow, almost grassy leaves send up leafy stems topped by foxtail-like spikes of small flowers with prominent stamens. Bloom proceeds from the top of the spike down, with the upper flowers opening before the lower ones—an unusual feature, since most blossoms borne in spikes open from the bottom of the spike up. All species and selections are similar in general build; the chief differences are in color and height.

The most widely available species, light purple–flowered *L. spicata* (sometimes sold as *L. callilepis*), grows to about 4 feet high; rosy lilac 'Kobold' (the best-known selection) and white-flowered 'Alba' top out at about 2 feet. 'Silvertips' has shimmering silvery lilac flowers on 3-foot stems.

Two species can send spikes up to 5 feet. *L. ligulistylis* typically has dark red buds and reddish purple flowers. Kansas gayfeather, *L. pycnostachya*, is purplish pink in the standard form, but its selection 'Alba' has white flowers.

The reddish purple flowers of 2½-foot *L. scariosa* differ from those of other gayfeathers in two ways: they're set more loosely on the spike, and they open nearly simultaneously all over the spike. 'September Glory' is a taller-growing selection; 'White Spire' is similar, but with white blossoms.

USES. All gayfeathers are trouble-free assets to the summer perennial border, where they look especially good alongside flowers of white, cream, light yellow, or blue.

GARDEN CULTURE. Gayfeathers need moderately fertile, well-drained soil; they are especially sensitive to soggy soil during their winter dormant period. Set out tuberous roots in early spring, placing them about 2 inches deep and 6 inches apart in clumps or drifts. Although plants tolerate drought, they look better if the soil is kept regularly moist (but not saturated) throughout growth and bloom. After a number of years, when performance declines, divide and reset overcrowded clumps in early spring.

Liatris spicata 'Kobold'

The word "aristocratic" has been aptly used to describe lilies. From foot-tall species in the wild to 9-foot modern hybrids in the summer flower border, all possess a highborn polish and elegance.

Wild lily species have been garden favorites for centuries in many parts of the world. But the lilies most widely grown today were developed only in this century, when growers and hybridizers embarked on intensive breeding programs. By selectively combining species, hybridizers produced varieties and strains with greater health and vigor than their species parents, new flower forms, and new colors: the lily palette now includes yellow, orange, red, maroon, pink, cream, white, lilac, purple, pale green, and multicolors. As the plants themselves were improved, so were the techniques used to grow them. The net result was a great gain for home gardeners: the new, more robust lilies were much easier to grow.

TYPES OF LILIES. Specialists' catalogs list a potentially bewildering assortment of hybrids (and sometimes species) that bloom in spring, summer, and fall. However, the International Lily Register's classification of hybrids and species into nine divisions establishes a logical order. The first eight divisions are reasonably cohesive hybrid categories; the ninth consists of lily species.

The nine divisions are listed below, along with the approximate hardiness of the plants in each group. For fuller descriptions of each division, consult a lily or bulb specialist catalog.

Division 1. Asiatic Hybrids. Hardy to about −30°F/−34°C.
Division 2. Martagon Hybrids. Hardy to about −30°F/−34°C.
Division 3. Candidum Hybrids. Hardy to about −20°F/−29°C.
Division 4. Hybrids of North American species. Hardiness varies, according to parent species, from −10° to −30°F/−23° to −34°C.
Division 5. Longiflorum Hybrids. Hardiness varies; most survive to about −20°F/−29°C.
Division 6. Aurelian Hybrids. Hardy to about −30°F/−34°C.
Division 7. Oriental Hybrids. Hardy to about −20°F/−29°C.

LILIUM
LILY
Liliaceae
TRUE BULB

- ▲ 1 TO 9 FEET
- ☼ ◑ EXPOSURE NEEDS DEPEND ON CLIMATE (SEE "GARDEN CULTURE")
- ◖ NEEDS SUMMER MOISTURE, EXCEPT AS NOTED
- ✍ ZONES VARY BY TYPE AND SPECIES (SEE DESCRIPTIONS)

Lilium 'Golden Splendor' (Aurelian Hybrid)

Listing continues >

Division 8. Miscellaneous hybrids. Hardiness varies.

Division 9. Species lilies. Hardiness varies.

The majority of lilies available nowadays are hybrids that fit into Divisions 1–8, but a limited number of species lilies are sold by bulb specialists. These include:

L. candidum. Madonna lily. Zones 4–9, 14–24, 30–33. In late spring to early summer, fragrant pure white trumpets appear atop 3- to 4-foot stems. The foliage dies down soon after bloom, not to reappear until fall. Plant dormant bulbs in August; since plants do not make stem roots, set tops of bulbs just 1 to 2 inches below the soil surface. Growth begins soon after planting, with each bulb producing a rosette of leaves that persists over winter and gives rise to a flower stem in spring. The seed-raised Cascade strain is free of viral diseases that may affect performance of imported bulbs.

L. henryi. Zones 2–10, 14–21, 32–41. In midsummer, each slender 8- to 9-foot stem carries 10 to 20 bright orange blossoms with sharply recurved segments. This species performs best in light shade in all regions.

L. lancifolium (L. tigrinum). Tiger lily. Zones 1–10, 14–22, 31–43. This easy-to-grow old favorite blooms late in summer, its 4-foot stems bearing pendulous orange flowers spotted in black. Newer kinds are available in white, cream, yellow, pink, and red, all with black spots.

L. longiflorum. Easter lily. Zones 6–9, 14–24, 26–29. Every year at Easter, these lilies are widely sold as potted plants forced into bloom for the occasion. Long, notably fragrant white trumpets are borne on short stems. Named selections include 'Ace', 'Croft', and 'Tetraploid', all in the 1- to 1½-foot range, and 3-foot 'Estate'. Easter lily hybrids also offer flowers in pink, red, and yellow. Enjoy potted plants indoors until flowers fade, then plant them in the garden. The stems will ripen, then die down; growth may resume to produce more blooms in fall. In subsequent years, the plant should acclimate to the outdoors and flower in its normal (unforced) midsummer season.

L. martagon. Turk's cap lily. Zones 2–10, 14–17, 32–41. Easy to grow but slow to establish, this lily will form ever-enlarging clumps that become more beautiful each year. In early summer, 3- to 5-foot stems bear up to 50 pendent flowers with sharply recurved segments. Blossoms are typically purplish pink with darker spots, but darker and pure white variants exist. Flowers are fragrant, but the scent is unpleasant.

L. regale. Regal lily. Zones 3–9, 14–24, 30–34, 39. Modern hybrid trumpet lilies may surpass this species in beauty, but it is a sentimental favorite that is easy to grow. Stems reach 6 feet high; in midsummer, each bears up to 25 funnel-shaped white blossoms that are carried horizontally.

USES. Lilies are splendid components in mixed plantings of annuals, perennials, and even shrubs. And thanks to their great height range, they can be used in the foreground, center, or background. When planted in clumps, many have the mass of a shrub.

Many of the smaller species lilies are excellent candidates for naturalizing; try setting them out in drifts under high shade of deciduous trees, along with smaller types of ferns and other low plants that will keep their roots cool.

GARDEN CULTURE. Lilies have three basic cultural needs: deep, loose, well-drained, fertile soil; ample moisture all year (except for *L. candidum* and the Candidum Hybrids of Division 3); and coolness and shade at their roots, but sun or filtered sun for blooming tops. Begin by choosing a planting area with the right kind of light. Don't plant in full sun except where summers are cool and overcast; filtered sun, light shade, or afternoon shade is preferred in most climates. Don't expose bases of plants to bright, direct sun for any length of time. In all climates, avoid planting in windy locations.

Before planting, prepare the soil well: dig it to a depth of about 1 foot and add plenty of organic matter. The simplest method is this: dig the soil, spread a 3- to 4-inch

TOP: *Lilium* 'Black Dragon' (Aurelian Hybrid)
BOTTOM: *Lilium martagon*

layer of organic matter on the surface, and scatter on a granular fertilizer (using the amount the package directs); then thoroughly dig the organic matter and fertilizer into the loosened soil.

Plant bulbs as soon as you can after you get them. If you must delay, store them in a cool place. Before planting, check bulbs carefully; if they look shriveled, place them in moist sand or peat moss until the scales plump up and roots start to form. Also cut off any injured portions and dust the cuts with sulfur.

All lily bulbs should be planted about 1 foot apart, but planting depth varies according to bulb size and rooting habit. Some lilies send out roots only from their bulbs, but many others produce roots from stems as well (the hybrids in Divisions 1, 2, 4, 5, 6, and 7, for example). Stem-rooting types need deeper planting than those that root from bulbs alone. A general rule for stem-rooting types is to cover smaller bulbs with 2 to 3 inches of soil, medium-size bulbs with 3 to 4 inches, and larger bulbs with 4 to 6 inches. *L. candidum* and its hybrids (Division 3 lilies) root from bulbs only; plant these just 1 to 2 inches deep. If you're uncertain about correct planting depth, set bulbs shallower rather than deeper—lilies have contractile roots that will gradually pull the bulbs down to the proper depth.

Gophers are fond of lily bulbs. If these pests are a problem in your area, see "Foiling the Spoilers" (page 14) for planting methods that will thwart them.

Water well after planting, then mulch the soil with 2 to 3 inches of organic matter to conserve moisture and keep soil cool. Since most lilies never really enter a dormant period, they need constant moisture all year; try to keep soil moist to a depth of at least 6 inches. You can taper off on watering a bit after tops turn yellow in fall, but never let roots go completely dry. The exceptions to the constant-watering rule are the Candidum Hybrids (Division 3 lilies), *L. candidum* itself, and certain other species native to dry-summer parts of southern Europe, western Asia, and western North America. Let these types go dry during mid- to late summer.

Avoid overhead watering if possible, since it can spread diseases and also topple tall types when they're in flower.

Remove faded flowers to prevent seed formation, but don't cut back stems until leaves have yellowed in fall.

During active growth and bloom, watch for and control aphids, which spread an incurable viral disease that evidences itself as mottling on the leaves and, in many cases, as stunted growth. If you discover any apparently infected plants, dig and destroy them to eliminate sources of potential future infection. Where summers are humid, be watchful for signs of botrytis. For more on these pests and diseases, see page 19.

When clumps become crowded and bloom quality declines, dig and divide them—either in early spring just before growth begins, or in fall after foliage has yellowed. (*L. candidum* and its hybrids in Division 3 are again an exception; dig and divide these during their leafless period in summer.) If you simply need to transplant a lily clump without dividing it, you can do so at any time, even when plants are in full bloom. Just be sure to dig very carefully and replant immediately.

CONTAINER CULTURE. Lily roots need plenty of room, so always use deep containers. Plant one bulb in a 5- to 7-inch pot, up to five in a 14- to 16-inch pot. Follow directions "B" (subgroup 2) on page 23; fill container one-third full of either of the soil mixes described, then set in bulbs, with roots spread out and pointing downward. Add enough additional soil mix to cover tops of bulbs by 1 inch; then water thoroughly and place in a cool, shady spot. Keep soil only moderately moist during the rooting period. When top growth appears, water more frequently; as stems elongate, gradually add more soil until containers are filled to 1 inch beneath the rim. Then move containers to

TOP: *Lilium* 'Casablanca' (Oriental Hybrid)
BOTTOM: *Lilium,* Asiatic Hybrids

a partly shaded location for the bloom period. Apply liquid fertilizer monthly during growth and bloom.

After flowers fade, cut back on water, but never let soil dry out (except for *L. candidum* and Division 3 lilies). Repot when bulbs crowd their containers.

LYCORIS
SPIDER LILY
Amaryllidaceae
TRUE BULB

▲ 1½ TO 2 FEET
☀ FULL SUN
◊ WITHHOLD SUMMER MOISTURE
✄ ZONES VARY BY SPECIES
   (SEE "GARDEN CULTURE")

Lycoris squamigera

S pider lily has much in common with its better-known relative belladonna lily *(Amaryllis belladonna)*. Narrow, strap-shaped leaves appear in fall (in mild-winter regions) or spring; they remain green until some point in summer, then die down completely. The smooth flower stalks emerge shortly afterward, each bearing a cluster of lilylike blossoms in late summer or early fall. The blossoms are funnel shaped or wide open, with narrow, pointed petal-like segments; most have long, projecting, spidery-looking stamens.

The best-known species is 1½-foot *L. radiata*, a showpiece in coral red with a golden sheen, with long, curved stamens protruding from its 1½- to 2-inch trumpets; 'Alba' is a white-flowered selection. *L. sanguinea* reaches 2 feet tall; its 2½-inch, bright red to orange-red blooms lack the prominent stamens of *L. radiata*.

Appearing on 2-foot stems, the 3-inch lilac pink trumpets of *L. squamigera* resemble those of belladonna lily *(Amaryllis belladonna)*—and in fact, the plant was once known as *Amaryllis hallii*. *L. sprengeri* is a similar species with slightly smaller blossoms in a more purple-tinted pink. Both bloom in late summer. Golden spider lily, *L. aurea (L. africana)*, shows off its 3-inch, bright yellow blossoms in early fall.

USES. Spider lily provides a colorful accent among other plants that tolerate dry soil in summer.

GARDEN CULTURE. Grow *L. squamigera* in Zones 3–24, 29–33; *L. sprengeri* in Zones 4–24, 29–33; *L. sanguinea* in Zones 4–24, 29–31; *L. radiata* in Zones 4–9, 12–24, 29–33; *L. aurea* in Zones 16, 17, 19–24, 26, 28.

Choose a sunny planting area that can remain dry during the summer dormant period. In late summer, set bulbs in well-drained soil about 1 foot apart. Keep tops of bulb necks at or just above the soil surface—except in the colder part of the range, where tops of necks should be set just under the surface. Water regularly while plants are growing and again when flower stalks emerge, but withhold water and let soil go dry when foliage begins to wither.

Dig and divide just after bloom, only when you want to move or increase plantings.

CONTAINER CULTURE. In regions beyond their hardiness limits, all species can be grown in containers and overwintered indoors in a brightly lit room or greenhouse where temperatures fall between 40° to 65°F/4° to 18°C. Follow directions "C" on page 23.

While leaves are growing in winter and spring, water regularly and apply

Lycoris radiata

liquid fertilizer monthly. Move containers outdoors when danger of frost is past. Follow watering directions described in "Garden culture." Repot every 3 to 5 years, when bulbs crowd their containers.

Though more modest in flower than its relative the true hyacinth *(Hyacinthus)*, grape hyacinth makes up for the difference in its profusion of early spring blooms and ease of culture. Native to the Mediterranean and southwest Asia, it typically bears fragrant, urn-shaped blossoms carried in short, tight spikes atop short stems; in blue-flowered forms, the blossom clusters resemble bunches of grapes. The fleshy, grasslike leaves usually emerge in fall, but foliage is rarely damaged by low temperatures.

M. armeniacum and its varieties are the most widely available grape hyacinths. The species has floppy foliage and 8-inch stems bearing bright blue flowers; 'Early Giant' is deep blue, while 'Blue Spike' has light blue double blossoms. 'Cantab', another light blue variety, has shorter stems and neater foliage than the species.

Italian grape hyacinth, *M. botryoides*, bears medium blue flowers (white in 'Album') on stems to 1 foot tall. Eight-inch-tall *M. tubergenianum* takes its common name—"Oxford and Cambridge hyacinth"—from its two-tone flower spikes: blossoms are light blue (Cambridge) at the top of the spike, dark blue (Oxford) in the lower portion.

The largest and showiest of the grape hyacinths is *M. latifolium*. Each bulb produces just one leaf and a flowering stem to 1 foot tall; the lower flowers in the spike are deepest violet, the upper ones vivid indigo blue.

M. azureum offers something of a floral difference, as its previous classifications under *Hyacinthus* and *Hyacinthella* suggest: its sky blue blooms, borne on 8-inch stems, are bell shaped, like those of true hyacinth. In its leaves and the form of its blossom spikes, though, it resembles a standard grape hyacinth. Distinctive *M. comosum*, the fringe or tassel hyacinth, is a complete departure from the other species. Its flowers, carried in loose clusters on 1- to 1½-foot-tall stems, have an odd shredded appearance. In the species, blossoms are greenish brown on the lower part of the spike, bluish purple in the upper portion; 'Monstrosum' has petals resembling lilac-colored shredded coconut.

USES. Naturalizing is a natural for grape hyacinths. They'll readily produce a carpet of bloom under deciduous trees and shrubs, along paths, and in transitional areas between garden and meadow. They're also prime container candidates.

GARDEN CULTURE. Grow *M. botryoides* and *M. tubergenianum* in Zones 1–24, 30–45; *M. latifolium* in Zones 2–24, 32–43; *M. azureum* and *M. comosum* in Zones 2–24, 30–43; and *M. armeniacum* in Zones 2–24, 29–43. In early fall, set bulbs about 2 inches deep and 3 inches apart in well-drained soil. Water regularly during fall, winter, and spring; in summer, when leaves have died down and bulbs are dormant, give less water or even no water at all.

Bulbs increase fairly rapidly, and many species also spread by self-sown seeds. When clumps become so crowded that vigor and flower quality decline, dig and divide in early fall.

CONTAINER CULTURE. Follow directions "B" (subgroup 1) on page 23.

MUSCARI
GRAPE HYACINTH
Liliaceae
TRUE BULB

- ▲ 8 TO 18 INCHES
- ☼ ◑ FULL SUN OR LIGHT SHADE
- ◑ ACCEPTS SUMMER MOISTURE BUT DOESN'T NEED ANY
- ✇ ZONES VARY BY SPECIES (SEE "GARDEN CULTURE")

Muscari armeniacum
'Blue Spike'

NARCISSUS

DAFFODIL, NARCISSUS

Amaryllidaceae

TRUE BULB

- ▲ 3 TO 18 INCHES
- ☼ ◑ FULL SUN; PART OR LIGHT SHADE AFTER BLOOM WHERE SUMMERS ARE HOT
- ◖ ACCEPTS SUMMER MOISTURE BUT DOESN'T NEED ANY
- ✇ ZONES 1–24, 28–45, EXCEPT AS NOTED

ABOVE: *Narcissus* 'Ice Follies'

Of all the bulbs that bloom in late winter and early spring, daffodils and other members of *Narcissus* have been judged the most trouble-free by generations of gardeners. Given minimum care at planting time, these natives of Europe and North Africa grow, bloom, increase—in other words, thrive—with virtually no further attention. They do not require summer watering (but will take it), need only infrequent division (and will even survive without it), and are totally unappetizing to the rodents that find tulips, for example, such a treat. They have just two principal enemies: encroaching shade, which can adversely affect performance; and the narcissus bulb fly, which, if unchecked, can seriously erode the bulb population.

All plants variously called "daffodil," "narcissus," and "jonquil" are properly *Narcissus*. In gardener's terms, however, "daffodil" refers only to the large-flowered kinds, while "narcissus" denotes the small-flowered (and usually early-blooming) types that bear their blossoms in clusters of four or more per stem. "Jonquil" correctly refers only to *N. jonquilla* and its hybrids.

All have the same basic flower structure. Each bloom has six outer petal-like segments (the perianth) and a central petal-like structure (the corona), which is usually elongated and tubular or more shallow and cuplike. Color range is also fairly consistent: the perianth may be orange, yellow, cream, or white, while the corona is white, cream, yellow, orange, red, pink, or a light color bordered by yellow, pink, orange, or red.

TYPES OF DAFFODILS. Despite their general similarities, blossoms do vary from one species or hybrid type to another. Based on this variation and on botanical relationships, the Royal Horticultural Society of England has established 12 divisions.

Division 1. Trumpet daffodils. Corona as long or longer than the perianth segments; one flower to each stem. The best-known trumpet daffodil is yellow 'King Alfred', but the newer varieties 'Unsurpassable' and 'William the Silent' bear better flowers. White varieties include 'Mount Hood', 'Cantatrice', 'Empress of Ireland'. White perianth/yellow trumpet combinations are 'Las Vegas' and 'Peace Pipe'; reverse bicolors (yellow perianth/white trumpet) include 'Honeybird', 'Lunar Sea', and 'Spellbinder'.

Division 2. Large-cupped daffodils. Corona shorter than the perianth segments, but always more than one-third their length; one flower to each stem. 'Stainless' is white; 'Carleton' and 'Saint Keverne' are yellow. Varieties with a white perianth and a colored cup include 'Ice Follies' (yellow cup); 'Accent', 'Romance', and 'Salome' (pink cup); 'Johann Strauss', 'Professor Einstein' (orange cup). 'Ambergate', 'Ceylon', 'Fortissimo', and 'Paricutin' all have a yellow perianth and a cup of pink, orange, or red. Reverse bicolors (yellow perianth/white cup) include 'Daydream' and 'Impresario'.

Division 3. Small-cupped daffodils. Corona no more than one-third the length of the perianth segments; one flower to each stem. 'Audubon' (white perianth/pink cup) and 'Barrett Browning' (white/orange-red) are good.

Division 4. Double daffodils. Corona segments greatly multiplied, and separate rather than joined together. Blossom has a fluffy appearance and looks more like a peony than a typical daffodil. One flower to each stem. Examples are 'Christmas Valley' (white with pink), 'Tahiti' (yellow with red), and 'White Lion' (white with yellow). 'Cheerfulness' (white) and 'Yellow Cheerfulness' are like double-flowered tazettas (see Division 8).

Division 5. Triandrus Hybrids. Derivatives of *N. triandrus*. Corona at least two-thirds the length of the perianth segments; several flowers to each stem. White 'Thalia' is an old favorite. Others include 'Hawera' (lemon yellow) and 'Silver Chimes' (white/yellow).

Division 6. Cyclamineus Hybrids. Derivatives of *N. cyclamineus;* early-flowering forms carrying one flower on each stem. Perianth segments are strongly recurved (as though facing a stiff headwind); 'February Gold' is the best-known example. Yellow 'Peeping Tom' has an especially long trumpet; 'Jack Snipe' has a white perianth and a yellow trumpet.

Division 7. Jonquilla Hybrids. Derivatives of *N. jonquilla.* Each stem bears two to four small, fragrant flowers; foliage is often rushlike. A growing number of varieties offer most of the color combinations found in larger daffodils. Choices include 'Bell Song' (white perianth/pink corona); 'Pipit' (yellow/white); 'Suzy' (yellow/orange); 'Trevithian' (all yellow).

Division 8. Tazetta & Tazetta Hybrids. Derivatives of *N. tazetta.* Hardy to about 10°F/−12°C. This division includes all the early-blooming, cluster-flowering types popularly known as "narcissus." Each stem bears four to eight or more highly fragrant flowers with short coronas. Many types have a white perianth and a yellow corona, but there are other color combinations. *N. tazetta* 'Orientalis', the Chinese sacred lily, has a light yellow perianth and a darker yellow corona; 'Paper White' is pure white; 'Early Splendor' is white/orange; 'Grand Soleil d'Or' is yellow/orange. Newer varieties include 'Cragford' and 'Geranium' (white/orange) and 'Hoopoe' and 'Scarlet Gem' (yellow/orange).

Division 9. Poeticus narcissus. Derivatives of *N. poeticus.* Perianth segments are white; very short, broad corona is in a contrasting color, usually with red edges. 'Actaea' and 'Pheasant's Eye' are old favorites.

Division 10. Species, their naturally occurring forms, and wild hybrids. Included here are numerous miniature types popular with collectors and rock garden enthusiasts. Prominent among these are the following:

N. asturiensis (often sold as *N.* 'Miniature'). Pale yellow flowers, only 1 inch long, are miniature trumpet daffodils (see Division 1, facing page). Plants are just 3 inches tall.

N. bulbocodium. Hoop petticoat daffodil. Hardy to about −10°F/−23°C. Six-inch-tall stems bear small yellow flowers with flaring coronas and almost threadlike perianth segments. Foliage is grassy.

N. cyclamineus. Hardy to about −10°F/−23°C. Small flowers, one to each 6- to 12-inch stem, have strongly recurved perianth segments and tubular coronas.

N. jonquilla. Jonquil. Stems to 1 foot tall bear small, fragrant blossoms in clusters of two to six. The cuplike corona is short in relation to the perianth segments; foliage is rushlike.

N. triandrus. Angel's-tears. Plants have rushlike foliage and one to six small, white to pale yellow flowers per stem. Corona is at least half as long as the perianth segments. The tallest forms of this species reach 10 inches.

Division 11. Split-corona hybrids. The corona is split for at least one-third of its length into two or more segments. 'Casata' (white perianth/yellow corona) and 'Palmares' (white/pink) are two of the more readily available varieties in this small but growing class.

Division 12. Miscellaneous. This category contains all types that don't fit the other 11 divisions. 'Tête-à-tête' and 'Jumblie' (both yellow) have Division 6 flowers but are rock-garden dwarfs to about 6 inches tall.

USES. These are among the most versatile of bulbs. Plant them in mixed borders of annuals and perennials, under deciduous trees and shrubs, or even beneath ground covers that grow loosely enough to let plants come through. You can also naturalize bulbs in high shade beneath deciduous trees or in open, grassy meadowland. The small species make good long-term container plants.

Listing continues >

TOP: *Narcissus* 'Early Splendor'
CENTER: *Narcissus bulbocodium*
BOTTOM: *Narcissus* 'Tête-à-tête'

GARDEN CULTURE. When buying daffodil bulbs, look for solid, heavy bulbs with no injury to the basal plate. So-called double-nose bulbs will give you the most and largest flowers the first season after planting. In most regions, it's best to plant in late summer or early fall, as soon as bulbs become available. But in areas with a long, warm autumn and fairly mild winter, put off planting until soil has cooled in midautumn.

Select a planting area that will be in full sun while bulbs are blooming, keeping in mind that blossoms will face the source of light. One traditional and attractive location is under high-branching deciduous trees. After bloom has ended, part or light shade can actually be beneficial to plants, especially in hot-summer regions.

For all members of the genus, good drainage is the primary soil requirement. To improve drainage in heavy soils, dig plenty of organic matter into the soil prior to planting (this will also aid moisture retention in light soils).

Plant bulbs approximately twice as deep as they are tall; this measures out to 5 to 6 inches deep for large bulbs, 3 to 5 inches deep for smaller sizes. Space bulbs 6 to 8 inches apart, so they can increase for a number of years without crowding each other.

Water newly planted bulbs thoroughly to initiate root growth. In many regions, fall and winter will be wet (or snowy) enough to take care of bulbs' water requirements until flowering time or later. But if rainfall is inadequate, keep plantings well watered between rains: plants need plenty of moisture during growth and bloom, especially after foliage has broken through the ground. After flowers have faded, continue to water plants regularly until foliage begins to turn yellow. Then stop watering, let foliage die down, and keep soil dry (or fairly dry) until fall.

The most serious pest is the narcissus bulb fly. An adult fly resembles a small bumblebee. The female lays eggs on leaves and necks of bulbs; when the eggs hatch, the young grubs eat their way into the bulbs, opening the way for rot organisms. See page 19 for controls.

Established clumps need dividing only when flower production and bloom quality decline. It's easiest to dig and divide clumps (or transplant them to another location) just after foliage dies down, when you can still see where plants are. After digging bulbs for division, give them ventilated storage (see page 20) until the best planting time for your climate, as specified above.

CONTAINER CULTURE. Follow directions "B" on page 23. The small species can be permanent container residents. All other types belong to the first subgroup under "B" (page 23): they make attractive pot plants for just one season, after which their performance declines and they should be moved to the garden. To force bulbs for earlier bloom, see pages 26–27.

TOP: *Narcissus* 'Christmas Valley'
BOTTOM: *Narcissus* (Tazetta Hybrid)
in wall container

NERINE
Amaryllidaceae
TRUE BULB

▲ 1½ TO 2 FEET

☼ ◑ FULL SUN; PART SHADE WHERE SUMMERS ARE HOT

◊ WITHHOLD SUMMER MOISTURE

⚡ ZONES 5, 8, 9, 13–28

These South African natives are relatives of spider lily *(Lycoris)*, which they closely resemble. All have strap-shaped leaves to about 1 foot long that complete their growth and die back well before the late-summer or early-fall bloom period, then reappear later in the year (typically around bloom time or shortly afterwards). The broad, funnel-shaped flowers appear in clusters atop smooth stems; each has six spreading segments, recurved at the tips.

Soft pink, 3-inch-long trumpets of *N. bowdenii* typically have a darker pink stripe down each segment; 8 to 12 of these blossoms are clustered atop 2-foot stems. Bulb specialists may offer named selections, such as larger, later-blooming 'Pink Triumph' or pink-blushed white 'Alba'. The inch-wide leaves reappear shortly before or during the bloom period. This is the best species to try in marginally cold regions, where temperatures may occasionally dip below 10°F/–12°C.

Guernsey lily, *N. sarniensis,* is similar to *N. bowdenii* in size and height. The species has flowers of iridescent crimson, but its forms and hybrids bear blossoms in a wider range of colors: pink, coral, orange, scarlet, and white, usually with a silvery or golden sheen. Leaves reappear after the bloom period ends.

Prominently extended stamens, as in spider lily, distinguish the gold-dusted scarlet blossoms of *N. curvifolia* 'Fothergillii Major'. The bloom clusters are carried on 1½-foot stems; leaves re-emerge after flowering finishes.

Blossoms with narrow, curved, crinkled segments are the signature of rose pink *N. undulata* (sometimes sold as *N. crispa* or *N. sarniensis* 'Crispa'). Its 1½-foot stems bear clusters of 8 to 12 flowers; leaves reappear at flowering time.

USES. Like spider lily, nerine provides a bright accent among perennials or shrubs that tolerate (or require) dry soil in summer. It's also an excellent container plant.

GARDEN CULTURE. Nerine needs well-drained, preferably sandy soil. Plant in full sun; where summers are hot and dry, choose a planting area in partial shade.

In late summer or early fall, set bulbs 1 foot apart. Keep tops of bulb necks at or just above soil surface except in the colder part of range, where tops of necks should be just below the surface. Water thoroughly after planting, but wait until growth begins before starting regular watering.

When foliage starts to yellow and die down in late spring, cut back on water; after foliage has died back completely, withhold all water and keep soil dry until flower stalks emerge. Then resume a regular watering routine. Leave established clumps undisturbed unless you need to increase or move plantings.

CONTAINER CULTURE. All types of nerine can be grown in climates beyond their hardiness limits if planted in containers and overwintered indoors. Follow directions "C" on page 23. Handle as for spider lily *(Lycoris)*.

Nerine sarniensis

Ornithogalum dubium

Six species are generally available from bulb growers. All bear starlike blossoms in white or nearly white (with one exception), and two take their common name, "star of Bethlehem," from the flower shape. True to the name, these last two (along with *O. nutans*) are native to the southern and eastern Mediterranean region; the remaining species come from South Africa. All flower in spring; *O. dubium* may start in late winter, while bloom of *O. saundersiae* may extend into early summer.

The most widely grown species is *O. umbellatum,* one of the two commonly known as star of Bethlehem. It increases rapidly, which can be an asset or a liability: plants quickly spread to fill bare areas, but may naturalize to the point of becoming weedy. Foot-tall stems bear loose clusters of inch-wide white flowers; the back of each narrow petal is striped green. Grasslike leaves are about as long as the flower stems.

Fragrant *O. arabicum,* Arabian star of Bethlehem, has the most striking blooms: broad-petaled, 2-inch blossoms of solid white, each centered with a shiny, beadlike black eye. Blossom clusters are carried on 2-foot stems; bluish green, strap-shaped leaves may reach the same length as the stems, but they're usually floppy rather than upright. Plants perform best where summers are warm and dry. Giant chincherinchee, *O. saundersiae,* is essentially a larger version of *O. arabicum,* with flower stalks to 3 feet tall rising above upright leaves that grow to about 2 feet.

Listing continues >

ORNITHOGALUM
Liliaceae
TRUE BULB

- ▲ 8 INCHES TO 3 FEET
- ☀ ◑ FULL SUN OR PART SHADE
- ◐◐○ SUMMER MOISTURE NEEDS VARY BY SPECIES (SEE "GARDEN CULTURE")
- ✂ ZONES VARY BY SPECIES (SEE "GARDEN CULTURE")
- ◊ ALL PARTS ARE POISONOUS IF INGESTED

O. thyrsoides, commonly called chincherinchee, produces elongated clusters of 2-inch flowers with brownish green centers. Stems grow 1½ to 2 feet tall; upright, bright green, 2-inch-wide leaves are shorter than the stems (to just 1 foot) and usually start to die back while the plants are in bloom.

Charming *O. nutans,* sometimes called silver bells, bears nodding, starlike to nearly bell-shaped blossoms with a pronounced central cluster of stamens; up to 15 blooms are spaced along the upper portion of each 1½- to 2-foot flower stalk. In color, the flowers combine light green and white. The narrow leaves are rather floppy. Like *O. umbellatum,* this species spreads rapidly and may become weedy.

Flower color makes *O. dubium* easy to recognize: though the blooms resemble those of *O. arabicum* and appear in similar rounded clusters, the petals surrounding the beady black eye come in shades of yellow or orange. Stems grow just 8 to 12 inches high; leaves are lance-shaped, to about 4 inches long.

USES. *O. nutans* and *O. umbellatum* are ideal choices for naturalizing. The other four species make attractive accent clumps in foreground locations, though three of them— *O. arabicum, O. dubium,* and *O. thyrsoides*—die down over summer and need a relatively dry dormant period.

GARDEN CULTURE. Grow *O. umbellatum* and *O. nutans* in Zones 4–33; *O. saundersiae* in Zones 4–32; *O. thyrsoides* in Zones 4–24; *O. arabicum* in Zones 5–24; and *O. dubium* in Zones 8, 9, 14–24. Choose a planting area with well-drained soil; dig in plenty of organic matter prior to planting in early fall. Set bulbs 3 inches deep, 3 to 4 inches apart. *O. nutans, O. saundersiae,* and *O. umbellatum* can take moisture all year round. *O. arabicum, O. dubium,* and *O. thyrsoides* need moisture throughout growth and bloom, but once flowering has finished and leaves have died down, withhold moisture until new foliage begins to emerge.

Dig and divide plantings only when a decline in vigor and bloom quality tells you that clumps have become overcrowded.

CONTAINER CULTURE. In areas with summer rainfall, growing *O. arabicum, O. dubium,* and *O. thyrsoides* in pots is the best way to cater to the plants' needs for a dry dormant period. Follow directions "C" on page 23.

Ornithogalum umbellatum

OXALIS
Oxalidaceae
TRUE BULB

- ▲ 4 TO 20 INCHES
- ☼ ◑ FULL SUN; FILTERED SUN OR LIGHT SHADE WHERE SUMMERS ARE HOT
- ● SUMMER MOISTURE NEEDS VARY BY SPECIES (SEE "GARDEN CULTURE")
- ✣ ZONES VARY BY SPECIES (SEE "GARDEN CULTURE")

Gardeners familiar only with the weedy, invasive *Oxalis* species will find the following attractive, well-mannered bulbous kinds a pleasant surprise. (Other species may grow from rhizomes or tubers.) All those described below are native to South Africa or South America, and all have cloverlike leaves and five-petaled flowers with a broad funnel shape.

O. adenophylla forms a dense tuft of foliage just 4 inches tall. Each gray-green leaf is divided into 12 to 22 crinkly leaflets. In late spring, 4- to 6-inch-high stems appear, each bearing up to three 1-inch-wide, lavender pink blossoms centered and veined with deeper lavender.

Summer-blooming *O. bowiei* has downy, 2-inch green leaves and foot-tall stems topped with clusters of 3 to 12 pink to rosy purple, 2-inch flowers. Novel flowers and foliage distinguish *O. versicolor,* which blooms in late summer or fall. Compact plants to 6 inches tall bear the typical three-lobed leaves, but each lobe is deeply cleft into two narrow segments. Flowers are about 1 inch across, white with yellow throats and a (usually) purplish margin. 'Candy Cane', with red-edged petals, is the most widely sold form; it owes its name to the diagonal red stripes on its furled buds.

The flexible, branching stems of *O. hirta* eventually trail with the weight of their small gray-green leaves. Inch-wide rose pink flowers appear in late fall and winter.

Blooming at the same time is *O. purpurea*, with yellow-throated flowers of white, lavender, or rose pink carried just above 5-inch-tall clumps of large dark green leaves. For the largest flowers (up to 2 inches across), look for forms sold as 'Grand Duchess'.

O. tetraphylla (formerly *O. deppei*) is grown primarily as a foliage plant, though it does bear clusters of red or white flowers on 6- to 20-inch stems in spring. Each 2-inch-wide leaf looks like a four-leaf clover with maroon staining on the lower third of the leaflets.

USES. Plants are attractive in rock gardens and along partly shaded walkways; all types are good container subjects.

GARDEN CULTURE. Grow *O. adenophylla* in Zones 4–9, 12–24, 30–32; *O. bowiei* in Zones 4–9, 14–24, 29–31; *O. hirta, O. purpurea*, and *O. tetraphylla* in Zones 8, 9, 12–24, 29–31; *O. versicolor* in Zones 6–9, 14–24. Plant in late summer or fall. Set bulbs 1 inch deep, 6 inches apart, in good, well-drained soil amended with plenty of organic matter. Filtered sunlight or light shade is preferable in hot-summer regions, but plants appreciate full sun where summers are cool to mild (or overcast). Water all types regularly during growth and bloom (those blooming in summer will need regular moisture then, but others can get by with little summer water). After bloom finishes, water sparingly until new growth resumes several months later. Divide infrequently, only when you need to move or increase plantings.

CONTAINER CULTURE. Follow directions "A" on page 23, spacing bulbs 2 inches apart. If you're growing plants indoors, place them in a window that receives morning sunlight. Water as outlined for in-ground plantings. Apply a liquid fertilizer monthly during growth and bloom. Leave bulbs in containers during the dormant period.

Oxalis bowiei

You'd need a botanist to explain why this plant doesn't belong to the genus *Hymenocallis*—judging by appearances, that's exactly where it ought to be. Each powerfully fragrant, 3-inch white flower is built like a daffodil: a central cuplike structure is surrounded by six narrow petal-like segments. Plants bloom for several weeks during mid- to late summer, bearing clusters of up to eight blossoms atop stems 1½ to 2 feet tall. The arching evergreen leaves are strap shaped, grayish green, and about 2 feet long.

USES. Where winter temperatures are mild and soil is very well drained, sea daffodil makes an attractive accent clump in the foreground of a mixed planting of perennials and annuals. However, it's more often grown in containers, where its needs for sharp drainage and protection from winter cold can more easily be satisfied.

GARDEN CULTURE. In early fall, plant the large, pear-shaped, long-necked bulbs in well-drained, organically enriched soil in a sunny location. Cover the tops of bulb necks by about 2 inches. In nature, bulbs grow in sand or sandy soil on Mediterranean beaches; some growers put an inch-deep layer of sand in the bottom of the planting hole to keep bulb bases from ever becoming too damp.

Plants need regular moisture from the time new growth begins in spring until flowering is finished and foliage has ceased growing. From that point until new growth resumes the next year, reduce watering, but be sure to give enough to keep foliage from wilting. In all but frost-free zones, foliage may be damaged by winter cold; if there's any danger of the soil freezing, apply a mulch around the plants.

CONTAINER CULTURE. Follow directions "C" on page 23. Several bulbs in a large pot make the best display. Set tops of bulb necks just at soil level, and allow an inch or more between bulbs and between bulbs and the edge of the container.

PANCRATIUM maritimum
SEA DAFFODIL
Amaryllidaceae
TRUE BULB

- ▲ 2 FEET
- ☼ FULL SUN
- ● NEEDS SUMMER MOISTURE
- ✄ ZONES 7–9, 12–28

Pancratium maritimum

POLIANTHES tuberosa
TUBEROSE
Agavaceae
RHIZOME WITH BULBLIKE TOP AND
TUBEROUS ROOTS

- ▲ 2½ TO 3½ FEET
- ☼ FULL SUN
- ● NEEDS SUMMER MOISTURE
- ⚘ ZONES 7–9, 14–29

Polianthes tuberosa

The intense fragrance of this Mexican native is legendary. Popular with home gardeners around the turn of the century, it is more commonly grown today for the cut flower and French perfume industries.

Each rhizome produces a fountain of narrow, grasslike leaves about 1½ feet tall. Flower spikes rise above the foliage, producing loose whorls of outward-facing white blossoms in summer or early fall. The tallest tuberose (to 3½ feet) is the form sometimes sold as 'Mexican Single', which bears trumpet-shaped single blooms about 2½ inches long. Most widely sold, however, is double-flowered, 2½-foot-tall 'The Pearl'.

USES. Though tuberoses are attractive in foliage and flower, they are primarily valued for fragrance. Locate plants where both looks and scent can be appreciated: in mixed border plantings near walkways or in containers on patio, terrace, or deck.

GARDEN CULTURE. For bloom year after year, tuberoses need a long (at least 4-month) warm season before flowering. Where this can be provided outdoors, you can plant rhizomes directly in the ground; elsewhere, grow them in containers, or start them indoors in pots and plant outside after soil warms.

Plant in spring, choosing a sunny spot and providing well-drained soil generously amended with organic matter. Check rhizomes to make sure they're healthy: they should show signs of green at the growing tips. Set rhizomes 2 inches deep and 4 to 6 inches apart, then water the planting area to moisten the soil thoroughly. As soon as leaves appear, begin regular watering; plants need plenty of moisture during growth and bloom. If soil or water is alkaline, apply an acid fertilizer when growth begins.

When foliage starts to yellow in fall, withhold water and let soil go dry. Rhizomes can be left in the ground where winter lows remain above 20°F/−7°C, but even in these areas, many gardeners store rhizomes indoors over winter—and in colder regions, of course, indoor storage is required. Dig plants after leaves have yellowed; cut off dead leaves, let rhizomes dry for 2 weeks, and store covered (see page 21).

CONTAINER CULTURE. In regions where the growing season is shorter than 4 months, start rhizomes in pots indoors, keeping them where the temperature remains above 60°F/16°C. Plant one or two rhizomes in an 8-inch container, using the soil mix described under "A" on page 23. Water thoroughly after planting, but wait until leaves emerge to begin regular watering. As soon as night temperatures reliably remain above 60°F/16°C, you can move growing plants outdoors; keep them in containers for portable display, or carefully transplant into garden beds. Give container-grown plants liquid fertilizer monthly until flowering begins.

PUSCHKINIA scilloides
Liliaceae
TRUE BULB

- ▲ 6 INCHES
- ☼ ☼ FULL SUN OR LIGHT SHADE
- ◊ WITHHOLD SUMMER MOISTURE
- ⚘ ZONES 1–11, 14, 29–43; NEEDS SOME SUBFREEZING WINTER TEMPERATURES

One herald of springtime is this stocky native of Asia Minor, a relative of glory-of-the-snow (*Chionodoxa*) and squill (*Scilla*). Each bulb produces two broad, strap-shaped, upright leaves that are a bit shorter than the 6-inch flower stem. The starlike, 1-inch blossoms—up to 15 per stem—are pale blue, with a greenish blue stripe down the center of each petal. Bulb growers usually carry *P. s. libanotica*, which conforms to the above description; a white-flowered variant is offered as *P. s.* 'Alba' or *P. s. libanotica alba*.

USES. Puschkinia is a good choice for naturalizing and for rock garden plantings. Naturalize bulbs in grassy patches or plant in drifts under deciduous trees, along pathways, or in front of shrub borders.

Puschkinia scilloides 'Alba'

GARDEN CULTURE. In late summer into fall, set bulbs 3 inches deep in well-drained soil; for a massed effect, space them about 3 inches apart. After planting, give bulbs one thorough watering to settle soil and initiate root growth. Keep soil just slightly moist until foliage appears; then water regularly until leaves start to yellow in early summer. During the summer dormant period, plants need very little water.

Established plantings seldom need dividing to relieve overcrowding. However, you can dig bulbs as needed to increase a planting or start new ones; do so in mid- to late summer and replant right away.

CONTAINER CULTURE. Follow directions "B" (subgroup 1) on page 23.

It's surprising that this native of Asia Minor has never acquired the common name "magic flower"—the production of bright, showy spring blossoms from such a small, peculiar-looking root is the equal of any conjuring trick. The 3- to 5-inch-wide, semi-double to fully double flowers have been variously (and accurately) described as resembling small peonies, camellias, and artificial crepe-paper flowers. One to four blooms are carried on each 1½- to 2-foot stem. Plants are full foliaged, with dark green, finely divided leaves; when not yet in bloom, they look much like bunches of flat-leaf parsley.

Most widely sold is the Tecolote strain, with a color range including pink, red, orange, yellow, cream, white, and multicolors; the group also offers pastel blooms edged with darker hues. The Bloomingdale strain is a dwarf equivalent just 8 to 10 inches tall. Nurseries offer tuberous roots of various sizes; both small and large roots produce equally large blossoms, but the larger ones produce a greater number of flowers.

USES. Set out plants in solid beds, use them in drifts of single or mixed colors, or spot them as accent clumps in mixed plantings of annuals and perennials. Plants are also excellent container subjects, and in mild-winter areas, they're a good alternative to tulips.

GARDEN CULTURE. The sooner you set out roots, the earlier they'll bloom. Where tuberous roots are hardy in the ground, plant in fall. In regions too cold for the roots to overwinter outdoors, plant in spring for bloom from late spring into early summer (hot weather terminates flower production). If you live in a cold-winter region, you'll get the longest possible flowering season by starting roots indoors 4 to 6 weeks before the normal last-frost date. Plant them in pots or flats, using either of the soil mixes described in "B" on page 23.

Plants need well-drained soil liberally amended with organic matter. In clay and other heavy soils, plant in raised beds to promote good drainage and set roots no deeper than 1 inch. (In lighter soils, they can be planted about 2 inches deep.) Position roots with the prongs facing down, spacing them 6 to 8 inches apart. Water thoroughly after planting, then withhold water until the leaves emerge.

Birds are very fond of ranunculus shoots, so you may need to protect sprouting plants with netting or wire. Another solution is to start plants in pots or flats (see above), then set them out in the garden when they're 4 to 6 inches tall—too mature to appeal to birds.

While plants are flowering, remove faded blossoms to encourage bloom. As the weather grows warmer, flowering will cease and foliage will begin to yellow. At this point, stop watering and let foliage die back. Where tuberous roots are hardy in the ground, you may leave them undisturbed—provided that soil can be kept dry throughout the summer. However, most gardeners in all regions dig plants when foliage yellows, cut off the tops, let the roots dry for a week or two, and then give covered storage (see page 21) until planting time.

CONTAINER CULTURE. Follow directions "B" (subgroup 2) on page 23.

RANUNCULUS asiaticus
Ranunculaceae
TUBEROUS ROOT

▲ 8 INCHES TO 2 FEET
☼ FULL SUN
◊ WITHHOLD SUMMER MOISTURE
✿ ZONES 4–9, 12–31

Ranunculus asiaticus

RHODOHYPOXIS baueri

Hypoxidaceae

RHIZOME WITH OTHER CHARACTERISTICS

- ▲ 6 INCHES
- ☼ ◑ FULL SUN; PART OR LIGHT SHADE WHERE SUMMERS ARE HOT
- ◐ NEEDS SUMMER MOISTURE
- ✄ ZONES 4–7, 14–24, 28–33

Rhodohypoxis baueri

This charming alpine plant covers itself in bloom over a long period in spring and summer, when the tufts of narrow, hairy leaves are nearly invisible beneath a profusion of inch-wide, six-petaled blossoms. The typical color range runs from pink shades to rosy red, but white-flowered varieties are available. In the wild, the plant grows in the high elevations of South Africa's Drakensberg Mountains. The bulblike structure is difficult to categorize; it is most like a rhizome, but has characteristics of a corm, tuber, and tuberous root as well.

USES. These are excellent rock garden and edge-of-border plants wherever their water requirements can be met. More often, though, they are grown as container plants, where their beauty can be appreciated at close range and their need for a dry winter period can be easily satisfied.

GARDEN CULTURE. In its native habitat, rhodohypoxis grows in organically rich soil that is moist in summer and dry in winter; the atmosphere is often cool and fog-bathed. In the garden, an ideal location is a sunny rock garden with nonalkaline, well-drained soil, where winter moisture can be kept to a minimum. In early spring, plant roots 1 inch deep and 3 to 5 inches apart. Give enough water to moisten the soil thoroughly; then, when foliage emerges, start watering regularly, keeping the soil moist (but not soggy) throughout the bloom period and until foliage yellows in fall. From that point, withhold water until new leaves emerge the following spring. Divide crowded plantings in early spring, just as growth begins.

CONTAINER CULTURE. Follow directions "B" (subgroup 2) on page 23. Move containers to a cool, dry location when foliage dies down in fall and keep them there until new growth emerges in early spring. Divide and repot when containers become crowded and performance declines.

SCADOXUS multiflorus katharinae (Haemanthus katharinae)

BLOOD LILY

Amaryllidaceae

TRUE BULB

- ▲ 1 TO 2 FEET
- ◑ LIGHT SHADE
- ◐ NEEDS SUMMER MOISTURE
- ✄ ZONES 21–27

Scadoxus multiflorus katharinae

The red stains on its large white bulbs gave this South African native its common name. In late spring or summer, ball-shaped clusters (to 9 inches across) of narrow-petaled, salmon-colored blossoms are borne atop thick flower stems; myriad threadlike, bright red stamens protrude from each bloom, giving the clusters the look of spherical bottlebrushes. Glossy, bright green, wavy-edged leaves are 12 to 15 inches long, up to 6 inches wide.

USES. Good-looking foliage and splashy flowers make this a prime accent plant for patio, terrace, or deck.

GARDEN CULTURE. In frost-free regions, you can plant blood lily in the ground—but even in such favored climates, it is usually grown in containers. To give the appearance of permanent plantings, just sink containers to their rims in soil.

Bulbs planted directly in the ground prefer a lightly shaded spot with well-drained soil enriched with organic matter. Plant in late winter or early spring, setting bulbs about 2 feet apart and keeping tips even with the soil surface. Water sparingly until leaves appear (this will occur in about 8 weeks); then water regularly throughout growth and bloom. Put out bait for slugs and snails. Leave clumps undisturbed indefinitely.

CONTAINER CULTURE. For each bulb, select a container large enough to leave 2 inches between all sides of the bulb and the container edges; use a soil mix recommended in directions "B" on page 23. Place planted containers in a fairly warm spot (no cooler than 55°F/13°C at night, around 70°F/21°C during the day) receiving plenty of bright light but no direct sun. Follow the watering regimen described above and apply a liquid fertilizer monthly.

After bloom is finished, stop fertilizing and gradually cut back on water; by midautumn, plants should not be receiving any water at all. Store the potted bulbs over winter in a dry, cool spot (50° to 55°F/10° to 13°C). Near the end of winter (or in early spring), tip plants out of containers and scrape some of the old soil mix off the root ball. Then repot in the same containers, filling in around bulbs with fresh mix. Switch to larger pots only after several years, when bulbs fill containers almost completely.

L̲ike gladiolus, this South African denizen has upright, swordlike leaves and a spike of closely set flowers—but the starlike, bright-colored, 2-inch blossoms recall those of another relative, watsonia. As the common name indicates, the basic species has crimson blooms, but specialists sell a number of named color variants, including white 'Alba', watermelon red 'Oregon Sunset', and several in pink shades: 'Mrs. Hegarty', 'Sunrise', and 'Viscountess Byng'. The plants are a standout in midautumn, a time of year when few other flowers put on a major display.

USES. Clumps of crimson flag are attractive vertical accents.

GARDEN CULTURE. In its native habitat, crimson flag grows in highly organic soil that is moist but well aerated. Plant in spring; dig generous amounts of peat moss and other organic matter into the planting area, then set rhizomes ½ to 1 inch deep and 1 foot apart. Water generously from planting time until the flowering period ends; then water sparingly until growth resumes the following spring. If clumps become crowded, dig in early spring, separate so that each division has at least five shoots, and replant.

CONTAINER CULTURE. Follow directions "B" (subgroup 2) on page 23. In climates where winter lows dip below 10°F/−12°C, bring pots of dormant bulbs indoors. Follow the watering regimen described above; apply a liquid fertilizer monthly.

G̲ardeners in cold-winter climates know squill as one of the harbingers of spring: some of the early-blooming types come into flower along with winter aconite *(Eranthis hyemalis)* and snowdrop *(Galanthus)*. The first four species described below are native to colder regions of Europe and Asia; Peruvian scilla, despite its common name, is native to the milder Mediterranean region. All squills have bell-shaped or starlike flowers, borne on leafless stems that rise from clumps of strap-shaped leaves.

Among the earliest to flower is 8-inch-tall *S. bifolia;* as the botanical name implies, each bulb usually produces just two leaves. The starlike blossoms, carried three to eight to each flowering stem, are suspended by short, threadlike stalks. A vivid, almost turquoise blue is the most common color, but you may also find forms with flowers in white, violet blue, or light pink.

Siberian squill, *S. siberica,* has several blossoms shaped like flaring bells hanging from each 3- to 6-inch stem. The typical flower color is an intense medium blue, but selected varieties bloom in white, lilac pink, and light to dark shades of violet blue, often with darker stripes. 'Spring Beauty' has brilliant violet blue blooms that are larger than those of the species.

The 6-inch-tall stems of *S. mischtschenkoana* (formerly *S. tubergeniana*) bear nodding clusters of three or four starlike blossoms in pale blue with darker blue stripes.

Unlike the previous species, *S. litardieri* (formerly *S. pratensis*) does not bloom until mid- to late spring, when it sends up 6- to 8-inch stems with dense spikes of small, bell-shaped, bright violet blossoms; there may be up to 15 blooms in each spike.

Listing continues >

SCHIZOSTYLIS coccinea
CRIMSON FLAG, KAFFIR LILY
Iridaceae
RHIZOME

- ▲ 1½ TO 2 FEET
- ☼ ◑ FULL SUN OR LIGHT SHADE
- ● NEEDS SUMMER MOISTURE
- ✎ ZONES 5–9, 14–24, 26–29, 31

Schizostylis coccinea 'Oregon Sunset'

SCILLA
SQUILL, BLUEBELL
Liliaceae
TRUE BULB

- ▲ 3 TO 12 INCHES
- ☼ ◑ FULL SUN DURING BLOOM, PART SHADE DURING REST OF YEAR
- ● NEEDS SOME SUMMER MOISTURE, EXCEPT AS NOTED
- ✎ ZONES VARY BY SPECIES (SEE "GARDEN CULTURE"); NEEDS SUBFREEZING WINTER TEMPERATURES, EXCEPT AS NOTED
- ☣ ALL PARTS ARE POISONOUS IF INGESTED

TOP: *Scilla bifolia*
BOTTOM: *Scilla peruviana*

SINNINGIA speciosa
GLOXINIA
Gesneriaceae
TUBER

- ▲ 1 FOOT
- ☼ BRIGHT INDIRECT LIGHT
- ◆ NEEDS SUMMER MOISTURE

Sinningia speciosa

Peruvian scilla, *S. peruviana,* differs from the above four species both in its appearance and its ability to thrive with little or no winter chill. Its large bulbs produce numerous rather floppy leaves; 10- to 12-inch stems rise from the foliage clumps, each topped with a dome-shaped cluster of 50 or more starlike flowers in late spring. Most forms have bluish purple blooms, but a white-flowered variety is sometimes available.

USES. Naturalizing is the best use for the four cold-hardy species; try them in small patches or larger drifts. Peruvian scilla may also be naturalized, but it's a bit coarse textured for wildflower-style plantings. Try it in clumps along pathways, at edges of mixed plantings, or in containers.

GARDEN CULTURE. Grow *S. siberica* in Zones 1–7, 10, 33–45; *S. mischtschenkoana* in Zones 1–11, 14–21, 29–43; *S. bifolia* and *S. litardieri* in Zones 2–11, 14–21, 30–41; and *S. peruviana* in Zones 14–17, 19–24, 26–29.

In fall, plant all types in well-drained soil enriched with organic matter. Set bulbs of the four cold-hardy species 2 to 3 inches deep, about 4 inches apart; plant Peruvian scilla bulbs 3 to 4 inches deep, about 6 inches apart. Water all types regularly during their growth and bloom periods; decrease water when foliage yellows. The hardy species will tolerate less moisture during their summer dormancy, though soil should not dry out completely. Peruvian scilla will accept summer moisture, but it doesn't need any.

Divide plantings only when decreased vigor and poorer blossom quality indicate that clumps are overcrowded. Peruvian scilla enters a brief dormant period after its leaves wither in late spring or early summer; if needed, dig and replant soon after foliage has died back completely. Other species may be divided in late summer or early fall.

CONTAINER CULTURE. Peruvian scilla is the best container candidate. See directions "C" on page 23.

B old-looking plants with velvety leaves and flowers, these Brazilian natives are longtime favorite pot plants. Squat and full foliaged, they have broad, oval leaves with the look of quilted green velvet, each growing to 6 inches or longer. In summer, showy blossoms cluster near the top of the plant—velvety-sheened, ruffled bells to 4 inches across. Available colors include white, red, pink, blue, and light to dark shades of purple. Many types show combinations of several hues: you'll see blooms in solid colors with light or white edges, and dots or blotches of darker color on a lighter background.

USES. Because they need 24-hour warmth, gloxinias are usually grown in greenhouses or as house plants. They can be taken outdoors during warm weather.

CONTAINER CULTURE. Tubers are available for planting in winter and spring. For each tuber, choose a container large enough to leave 2 inches between all sides of the tuber and the container edges. Fill with a soil mix of equal parts peat moss, perlite, and leaf mold or compost; then set in tubers ½ inch deep.

Place containers in a warm location (about 72°F/22°C during the day, no cooler than 65°F/18°C at night) where they will receive plenty of bright light but no direct sun. Water sparingly until the first leaves appear, then increase watering as roots and leaves grow. Apply water to the soil only, or pour it into containers' drip saucers to be absorbed through the bottom of the pot; be sure to pour off any water left unabsorbed after an hour. From the time leaves emerge until flowers fade, apply a liquid fertilizer diluted to half strength every 2 weeks.

After flowering ceases, gradually withhold water and let foliage wither. When leaves have died down entirely, plants are completely dormant; at this point, move containers to a dark place where temperatures will remain around 60°F/16°C. Mist soil just often enough to keep tubers from shriveling.

When tubers show signs of resuming growth in midwinter, repot in fresh soil mix. If you see that roots have filled a container, move the tuber to a container that's 1 to 2 inches wider; leaf and flower size decrease when plants become potbound.

O ne look at its bright late-spring blossoms explains why this South African is commonly called "harlequin flower." Each bloom has a patchwork arrangement of colors: yellow in the chalicelike center, a dark shade surrounding this, and still another color—red, pink, orange, or purple—on the rest of the spreading petals. Flowers are up to 2 inches across, borne in loose spikes on slender stems that rise from fans of swordlike leaves.

USES. The effect is best when plants are grouped as accents in borders or along pathways. For a brilliant tapestrylike effect, naturalize corms in a sunny garden spot.

GARDEN CULTURE. Well-drained soil in a sunny location suits harlequin flower. Plant corms 2 inches deep, 3 to 4 inches apart—in fall where corms are hardy in the ground, in early spring in colder regions. Water regularly during active growth. Withhold water when leaves yellow; keep soil dry during summer.

In the zones noted at right, you can leave plantings undisturbed for a number of years. In other zones, dig corms in summer after foliage dies down and store as for gladiolus (page 64).

CONTAINER CULTURE. Follow directions "B" (subgroup 2) on page 23.

SPARAXIS tricolor
HARLEQUIN FLOWER
Iridaceae
CORM

- ▲ 12 TO 15 INCHES
- ☼ FULL SUN
- ◊ WITHHOLD SUMMER MOISTURE
- ✂ ZONES 9, 12–24

Sparaxis tricolor

Sprekelia formosissima

T he linear foliage of this Mexican native is reminiscent of daffodil leaves—but wait until you see the flowers! The irregularly shaped dark red blossoms have understandably been likened to orchids. Each stem bears one 6-inch flower; the display increases if plants are left undisturbed for several years and allowed to form large clumps. Bloom comes primarily in early summer. The foliage may be evergreen in mild climates.

USES. Aztec lily is a striking accent in the summer garden. Plant it in clumps at the foreground of mixed annual and perennial beds, or grow it in containers.

GARDEN CULTURE. Plant bulbs 3 to 4 inches deep and about 8 inches apart in good, well-drained soil—in fall where bulbs are hardy in the ground, in spring in colder regions. Water regularly from the time growth begins until bloom finishes. In climates with little or no frost, plants may bloom several times a year if you can give them a dry period after blossoming, then resume regular watering to trigger a new growth cycle.

Where bulbs can overwinter in the ground, you can leave them undisturbed for many years. When vigor and bloom quality decline, dig, separate, and replant in fall. In colder regions, dig bulbs in fall before the first frost; dry them with foliage attached, then give covered storage (see page 21) until planting time.

CONTAINER CULTURE. Follow the directions outlined for amaryllis *(Hippeastrum),* but keep temperatures about five degrees lower during growth and bloom.

SPREKELIA formosissima
AZTEC LILY, JACOBEAN LILY,
ST. JAMES LILY
Amaryllidaceae
TRUE BULB

- ▲ 1 TO 1½ FEET
- ☼ FULL SUN
- ● NEEDS SUMMER MOISTURE
- ✂ ZONES 9, 12–24, 26–30

STERNBERGIA lutea

Amaryllidaceae

TRUE BULB

- ▲ 4 TO 9 INCHES
- ☼ FULL SUN
- ◊ WITHHOLD SUMMER MOISTURE
- ✂ ZONES 3, 7–10, 14–24, 26–33

An ideal choice for the impatient gardener, this plant from the western Mediterranean to central Asia offers almost instant gratification: bulbs planted in mid- to late summer burst into bloom in early fall. Each bulb produces a single flower about 1½ inches long that looks something like a bright yellow crocus—chalice shaped at first, then opening out to a wide star. Narrow, linear leaves appear at the same time as or just after the blossoms, eventually reaching about 1 foot long; they persist through winter, then die back in spring.

USES. Locate in rock gardens or pockets in paved patios, alongside pathways, or in containers.

Sternbergia lutea

GARDEN CULTURE. Plant bulbs as soon as they are available. Choose a sunny spot with well-drained soil, preferably in an area that receives little or no watering during summer. Plant bulbs 6 inches apart and 4 inches deep. To establish newly planted bulbs, water from planting time until the bloom period ends; then let winter and spring rain or snow carry plants through to the next dormant time. Once plants are established, water regularly during growth and bloom; withhold summer water.

Where winter temperatures drop to 20°F/−7°C or lower, give plantings winter protection as described on page 21. Clumps increase in beauty as bulbs multiply, so dig and separate (in August) only when vigor and flower quality decline.

CONTAINER CULTURE. Follow directions "B" (subgroup 2) on page 23.

TIGRIDIA pavonia

TIGER FLOWER, MEXICAN SHELL FLOWER

Iridaceae

TRUE BULB

- ▲ 1½ TO 2½ FEET
- ☼ ◐ FULL SUN; PART SHADE WHERE SUMMERS ARE HOT
- ● NEEDS SUMMER MOISTURE
- ✂ ZONES 4–31

This Mexican native bears flashy summertime blooms to 6 inches across. The three large outer segments of each triangular flower are red, orange, pink, yellow, or white; the cuplike center and three small inner segments are usually boldly blotched with a contrasting hue. The Immaculata strain is unspotted.

An individual flower lasts just one day, but since each stem carries a number of buds, the blooming period lasts for several weeks. Upright, branching flower stems to 2½ feet tall rise from fans of narrow, swordlike, ribbed leaves that may reach 1½ feet long.

USES. Tiger flower adds a dominant splash of color wherever you use it: in clumps, in summer flower borders, or in containers.

GARDEN CULTURE. Plant bulbs in spring after weather warms up (night temperatures should not fall below 60°F/16°C). If summer heat is not intense, choose a spot in full sun; in hot-summer regions, plants appreciate afternoon shade. Set bulbs 2 to 4 inches deep, 4 to 8 inches apart, in well-drained soil. Water regularly throughout growth and bloom, but stop watering after bloom finishes and leaves turn yellow.

Tigridia pavonia

Where bulbs are hardy in the ground, you can leave plantings undisturbed for 3 or 4 years before dividing. Then dig bulbs after foliage dies back in fall and store over winter as for gladiolus (page 64); wait until spring planting time to separate bulbs.

Spider mites (detectable by the yellowish or whitish streaks they leave on foliage) are the principal pest. Begin applying controls (see page 19) when leaves are several inches high. Gophers are another pest; they're fond of the bulbs. See "Foiling the Spoilers" (page 14) for controls.

CONTAINER CULTURE. Follow directions "B" (subgroup 2) on page 23.

Fans of swordlike leaves and branched spikes of bright, broad, funnel-shaped flowers mark this South African as a close relative of ixia, montbretia *(Crocosmia)*, freesia, and harlequin flower *(Sparaxis)*. Tritonia starts growth in early spring and blooms in late spring; after bloom, the foliage turns yellow and dies down until the next year's growth cycle begins.

The most commonly sold species is *T. crocata*, often called "flame freesia." It bears broad-petaled, reddish orange blooms to 2 inches across, arranged alternately on either side of branching spikes to 1½ feet high. *T. c. miniata* has bright red flowers, while 'Princess Beatrix' is a stunning deep orange. Occasionally, you'll find other named varieties in white, yellow, and shades of pink.

T. hyalina, the other commonly sold species, grows to about 1 foot tall; its bright orange flowers have narrower petals than those of *T. crocata*, with a transparent area near the base of each petal.

USES. Grow in clumps or drifts, as a colorful accent in the foreground of plantings that require little watering during summer.

GARDEN CULTURE. Like its close relatives, tritonia needs well-drained soil in a sunny location, regular watering during growth and bloom, and fairly dry conditions after foliage starts to yellow. Set corms 2 to 3 inches deep and 3 inches apart; plant in fall where winter temperatures remain above 20°F/−7°C, but wait until spring in colder climates. Where corms are hardy and can be protected from summer moisture, they can stay in the ground until a decline in vigor lets you know that plantings are overcrowded; at that point, dig (during the dormant period) and divide. Elsewhere, dig and store as for gladiolus (page 64) after plants die down; or grow in pots.

CONTAINER CULTURE. Follow directions "B" (subgroup 2) on page 23.

TRITELEIA. See BRODIAEA

TRITONIA
Iridaceae
CORM

▲ 1 TO 1½ FEET
☼ FULL SUN
◊ WITHHOLD SUMMER MOISTURE
▨ ZONES 9, 13–24, 26, 28, 29

Tritonia crocata 'Isabella'

TULBAGHIA
Amaryllidaceae
RHIZOME

▲ 1 TO 2 FEET
☼ FULL SUN
◆ NEEDS SUMMER MOISTURE
▨ ZONES 13–24, 26–28

One general description covers both available species (both are native to South Africa): dense clumps of straight, narrow evergreen leaves send up slim, 1- to 2-foot stems topped by clusters of small, trumpet-shaped, pinkish lavender flowers.

T. violacea has very narrow blue-green leaves and bears 8 to 20 blossoms per cluster; bloom is heaviest in spring and summer. The common name is "society garlic," and for good reason: both the leaves and the flower stems give off an oniony or garlicky odor when bruised or crushed (you can even use the leaves in cooking). Several named varieties are available. 'Silver Lace'

Tulbaghia violacea

has white-margined leaves; 'Tricolor', another white-edged type, has foliage tinted pink in early spring; leaves of 'Variegata' have a broad white stripe down the center.

The leaves of *T. fragrans* are gray green and, at 1 inch wide, broader than those of *T. violacea*. Its lightly fragrant flowers, carried in clusters of 20 to 30, bloom in winter or early spring.

USES. Grow plants in the foreground of borders; they're also attractive in containers.

GARDEN CULTURE. Plants will grow in light or heavy soil, though they do best in well-drained soil liberally amended with organic matter before planting. Plant at any time of year, from containers or divisions, in a sunny spot; give regular watering for best performance. Divide clumps whenever you want to increase plantings or when foliage and flower quality decline. (Where summers are hot, early spring and early fall are the best times to divide.)

CONTAINER CULTURE. Follow directions "C" on page 23. Where winter temperatures fall below 20°F/−7°C, move potted plants indoors at the first signs of frost; overwinter in a sunny window in a cool room (maximum temperature of 60°F/16°C).

TULIPA
TULIP
Liliaceae
TRUE BULB

▲ 3 INCHES TO OVER 3 FEET
☼ ◑ FULL SUN OR LIGHT SHADE
◐ ACCEPTS SUMMER MOISTURE BUT DOESN'T NEED ANY
✂ 1–24, 28–45; BEST AND MOST PERMANENT IN AREAS WITH SUB-FREEZING WINTER TEMPERATURES

Fringed tulip 'Blue Heron'

To many people—especially those in cold-winter regions—tulips and daffodils signify spring. But while daffodils may be strewn about with naturalistic abandon, tulips are generally thought of as orderly flowers: neatly planted in garden beds, in serried ranks of even height. In fact, many types of tulips are rather rigidly formal, but as a group, these plants vary considerably in height, form, color, and general character. Some are quite unusual (the "broken" kinds and parrot varieties); some of the short types and many of the species look like wildflowers; and the double-flowered sorts resemble peonies.

Most of the tulips in modern gardens fit into the classifications established jointly by the Royal Dutch Bulb Growers and the Royal Horticultural Society of England. These groupings are based primarily on appearance rather than on strict botanical relationship: all the varieties in each division have the same general flower shape and height range.

Tulipa hybrids

LARGE HYBRID TULIPS

The following 17 divisions encompass the familiar garden hybrid types, listed in approximate order of bloom.

SINGLE EARLY TULIPS. Tulips in this class have large red, yellow, or white single flowers on 10- to 16-inch stems. Though they are favorites for growing or forcing indoors in pots, they can also be grown outside, where they bloom from March to mid-April (depending on climate and variety). They are not adapted to mild-winter climates.

DOUBLE EARLY TULIPS. Peonylike double flowers, often measuring 4 inches across, grow on 6- to 12-inch stems. Double Early tulips have the same color range as Single Early types and are often forced for early bloom in containers. They're also effective massed in borders for spring bloom outside.

MENDEL TULIPS. Derived from Darwin tulips, Mendel tulips bear blossoms of red, pink, orange, yellow, or white on stems up to 20 inches tall. They bloom later than Single Early and Double Early tulips, but earlier than the Darwins.

TRIUMPH TULIPS. Crosses between Single Early, Darwin, and Cottage types produced the midseason Triumph class: earlier blooming than the Darwins, with heavier, shorter stems (usually not over 20 inches tall). Red, white, yellow, and bicolored varieties are available.

DARWIN HYBRIDS. Huge, shining, brilliant flowers show the influence of the *T. fosteriana* parent (see page 102), while fairly tall stems (to 2 feet) recall the Darwin parent. Colors include red and orange; bloom time comes in midseason, after the early-blooming *T. fosteriana* but before the Darwins come into flower.

Fringed tulip hybrid

DARWIN TULIPS. These popular midseason tulips are graceful, stately plants with large oval or egg-shaped blooms carried on straight stems to 3 feet tall. Blossoms are square at the base, but flower segments are typically rounded at the tips. There's a remarkably extensive range of clear, beautiful colors: white, yellow, orange, pink, red, mauve, lilac, purple, and maroon.

LILY-FLOWERED TULIPS. Formerly included in the Cottage division, these late midseason tulips have graceful, lilylike blooms with recurved, pointed segments. Flowers are longer and narrower than those of the Darwins; colors include white and shades of yellow, pink, and red. Flower stems reach 20 to 26 inches high.

FRINGED TULIPS. Variations from Single Early, Double Early, and Darwin tulips, these are late midseason bloomers with flowering stems 16 to 24 inches high. Edges of flower segments are finely fringed.

BREEDER TULIPS. These carry large oval or globular flowers on stems to 40 inches tall late in the season. Colors are quite unusual, with orange, bronze, and purple predominating.

COTTAGE TULIPS. Late-blooming descendants of varieties found in old gardens in Great Britain, Belgium, and France, the Cottage tulips are slightly shorter than the Darwins; flowers are oval or egg shaped, often with pointed segments. Colors include red, purple, yellow, pink, orange, and white.

REMBRANDT TULIPS. These late bloomers originally were exclusively "broken" Darwin tulips, so called because the background flower color is "broken"—streaked or variegated throughout—with different colors. Today, however, the division has been expanded to include the following two (Bizarre and Bybloems) as well.

BIZARRE TULIPS. "Broken" Breeder or Cottage tulips constitute this late-blooming class. Flowers have a yellow background striped or marked with bronze, brown, maroon, or purple.

BYBLOEMS (BIJBLOEMENS). Like the Bizarre division, these late bloomers are "broken" Breeder or Cottage tulips, but they have a white background with lilac, rose, or purple markings.

Lily-flowered tulip hybrids

PARROT TULIPS. This class of late tulips includes sports (mutations) of solid-colored varieties of regular form. Their large, long, deeply fringed and ruffled blooms atop 16- to 20-inch stems are striped, feathered, and flamed in various colors. Parrot tulips once had weak, floppy stems, but modern types are stouter and stand up well.

DOUBLE LATE TULIPS. As the name implies, this class of tulips—often referred to as "peony-flowered"—has double blossoms late in the season. The extremely large, heavy flowers on 14- to 20-inch stems come in orange, rose, yellow, and white.

VIRIDIFLORA TULIPS. Late blossoms are edged in green or colored in blends of green with other hues—white, yellow, rose, red, or buff. Stems grow 10 to 20 inches tall.

MULTIFLOWERED TULIPS. Members of this class bear three to six flowers on each stem late in the season; most selections grow 1½ to 2 feet tall. Colors include white, yellow, pink, and red.

For decades, nurseries have sold tulips based on the divisions just described. Recently, these 17 divisions have been reorganized and simplified, as presented below. More and more catalogs and nurseries will be offering bulbs in these groupings:

SINGLE EARLY AND DOUBLE EARLY TULIPS. The earliest-blooming, large-flowered types.

MIDSEASON TULIPS. Blooming after the early classes, this group includes Mendel, Triumph, and Darwin Hybrid tulips.

SINGLE LATE OR MAY-FLOWERING TULIPS. This group now includes the Darwin, Breeder, and Cottage classes.

DOUBLE LATE, LILY-FLOWERED, AND NOVELTY TULIPS. In this class are the Double Late and Lily-flowered tulips, as well as the novelty groups: Rembrandts (including Bizarre tulips and Bybloems) and Fringed, Parrot, Viridiflora, and Multiflowered tulips.

SPECIES AND SPECIES HYBRID TULIPS

In addition to the divisions just described, there are classes covering species and species hybrids. Three of these include varieties and hybrids of *T. kaufmanniana*, *T. fosteriana*, and *T. greigii*—all good plants for mild-winter areas.

Tulipa linifolia

KAUFMANNIANA TULIPS. A very early bloomer known by the common name "waterlily tulip," *T. kaufmanniana* features 3-inch, creamy yellow flowers (marked red on the petal backs) with dark yellow centers; the blossoms open flat in the sunshine. Stems reach 6 to 8 inches high. Hybrids encompass a variety of colors, usually with flower centers in a contrasting color; many have mottled leaves like the Greigii tulips.

FOSTERIANA TULIPS. The early-flowering *T. fosteriana* has the largest flowers—to 8 inches across—of any tulip, whether species or hybrid. These great red blossoms appear atop 8- to 20-inch stems. Hybrids include varieties with flowers of red, orange, yellow, pink, and white.

GREIGII TULIPS. Leaves heavily spotted and streaked with brown are one feature of midseason-flowering *T. greigii*. Short stems (to about 10 inches) bear 6-inch scarlet flowers. Hybrids offer flowers in white, pink, orange, and red; many feature several colors combined in a single blossom.

Tulipa fosteriana hybrids

SMALLER SPECIES TULIPS. These are sold chiefly by bulb specialists. They have a simpler, more wildflowerlike charm than their large hybrid relatives; most are native to Central Asia. Several species will persist from year to year in mild-winter regions.

Tulipa batalinii
'Yellow Jewel'

T. acuminata. This late-flowering species has 1½-foot stems bearing red and yellow flowers with long, twisted, spidery segments.

T. batalinii. Soft yellow flowers bloom on 6- to 10-inch stems in midseason. Leaves are linear.

T. clusiana, the lady or candy tulip, is a graceful plant with 9-inch stems bearing slender, medium-size midseason flowers colored rosy red on the outside, creamy white on the inside. It's a good permanent tulip for areas with little winter chill. *T. c. chrysantha* also blooms in midseason, its 6-inch-tall stems bearing blooms that are star shaped when open. Outside flower segments are pure rose carmine, turning to buff at the base; inside segments are pure butter yellow.

T. eichleri. A striking, sculptured-looking early tulip. The shining scarlet flowers have jet black centers outlined with yellow. Stems reach about 1 foot tall.

T. linifolia. A midseason bloomer, this species has 6-inch stems bearing bold scarlet flowers with black bases and yellow centers. It makes a striking companion for *T. batalinii,* which blooms at the same time.

T. praestans. Pure orange-scarlet midseason flowers, often two to four to each 10- to 12-inch stem, contrast beautifully with pale green leaves edged in dark red.

T. sylvestris. This late-flowering species is a good choice for warmer-winter zones. Its yellow, 2-inch flowers sometimes come two to each 1-foot stem.

T. tarda (T. dasystemon). An appealing little early tulip with clusters of as many as four flowers on each 3- to 5-inch stem. The star-shaped white blossoms are prominently marked with yellow in the center.

T. turkestanica. Very early in the season, each 1-foot stem offers as many as eight flowers. Slender buds open to star-shaped blooms that are gray green on the outside, off-white with yellow petal bases inside.

USES. Rows of tulips look stiff and artificial, as though plants and flowers were made of plastic. Large hybrid types really shine when planted in masses or drifts; they also make bright clumps among other spring-flowering plants, especially lower-growing annuals and perennials.

The small species tulips are good choices for rock gardens and mixed plantings, and also naturalize easily where climate permits.

GARDEN CULTURE. In their native lands, tulips are accustomed to cold winters (often long and severe), short springs, and hot summers. Except for certain species, most are short-lived in mild-winter regions, even if summers are hot: winter chill is critical for permanence. But even in cold-winter regions, there's no guarantee of a good performance after the first year. Tulip bulbs form offsets that need several years to reach blooming size, but as the offsets mature, they draw energy from the mother bulb. The result is a decline in flowering. For this reason, most tulips are best treated as short-lived perennials (some species and species hybrids excepted).

You can encourage repeat flowering by fertilizing with nitrogen before bloom and by allowing foliage to yellow and wither before removing it after bloom. In mild-winter areas, tulip bulbs should be prechilled in the refrigerator and the plants treated as annuals (in Zones 25–27, however, even prechilled bulbs usually fail to perform well).

Listing continues >

TOP: *Tulipa tarda*
BOTTOM: *Tulipa turkestanica*

Tulipa 'William and Mary' in container

In areas with warm, wet summer soil, bulbs are prone to rot and shouldn't be expected to bloom for more than a year or two.

Tulips need sunshine at least while they are in bloom; stems will lean toward the source of light if the planting area is partly shaded. It's fine to plant bulbs under deciduous trees if the trees won't leaf out until after the blooming season ends. Well-drained soil is another requirement, though the particular type is not important—both light and heavy soils are satisfactory. Be sure, though, to add plenty of organic matter prior to planting. Tulips do poorly if planted in soil where other tulips have been growing recently. Set out bulbs in new locations, or replace the existing soil with new soil to the proper planting depth.

Set bulbs three times as deep as they are wide (a little shallower in heavy soils); space them 4 to 8 inches apart, depending on the eventual size of the plant. Tulips need plenty of moisture during growth and bloom, but they can get by with less after foliage dies back. In regions where temperatures regularly dip below 32°F/0°C, plant bulbs in October or November, after soil has cooled from the heat of summer. In warmer regions, plant in December or January.

To protect tulip bulbs from gophers and other burrowing animals, plant in wire baskets; thwart pests that like to dig up bulbs by securing chicken wire over new plantings. See "Foiling the Spoilers" on page 14 and "Rodents" on page 19.

If tulips do persist in vigor from year to year, they will eventually need separating. Dig and divide clumps in late summer; replant at the best time for your area.

Species tulips, unlike most of the larger hybrid types, may be left undisturbed for many years. Dig and separate them (in late summer) whenever they become crowded, or when you need bulbs for planting elsewhere. Replant at the best time for your climate.

CONTAINER CULTURE. Follow directions "B" (subgroup 1) on page 23 for basic container culture. To force tulips for earlier bloom, see pages 26–27.

VALLOTA SPECIOSA.
See CYRTANTHUS ELATUS

VELTHEIMIA bracteata
Liliaceae
TRUE BULB

- ▲ 12 TO 15 INCHES
- ☼ FILTERED SUN, PART SHADE, OR LIGHT SHADE
- ◊ WITHHOLD SUMMER MOISTURE
- ⚡ ZONES 13, 16–25, 26 (WARMER PARTS), 27

Handsome foliage is reason enough to grow this South African native. Each bulb puts out a fountainlike rosette of wavy-edged foliage—glossy green leaves to 1 foot long and 3 inches wide in the most common (and perhaps only available) species, *V. bracteata* (formerly *V. viridiflora*). In winter or early spring, brown-mottled flower stems rise to about 1 foot, each topped by an elongated cluster of pendent, tubular flowers of pinkish purple tipped in green. At some point toward late spring, leaves yellow and die back for the summer; new growth resumes in autumn.

Veltheimia bracteata

Most plants sold as *V. capensis* are actually *V. bracteata;* the true *V. capensis* is easily distinguished by its nonglossy blue-green leaves and green-tipped pale pink blossoms.

USES. Even in the mildest climates, most gardeners prefer to treat this as a container plant for house, greenhouse, deck, or patio.

GARDEN CULTURE. In virtually frost-free regions, you can grow the large bulbs in the ground. Plant them in autumn, in organically enriched, well-drained soil; set tops of bulb necks just above the soil surface. Water regularly during growth and bloom. When foliage begins to die down in mid- to late spring, reduce watering; keep soil dry during the leafless summer dormant period. Resume regular watering when new growth appears in fall. Dig and divide (in late summer) only when growth becomes crowded. Plants can remain outdoors over the winter only where temperatures remain above 25°F/−4°C; where light frosts are possible, give them overhead protection.

CONTAINER CULTURE. Plant in August or September. For each bulb, use a container large enough to allow about 3 inches between all sides of the bulb and the container edges. Plant in soil mix described in directions "A" on page 23. Place containers in a cool location and keep the soil just barely moist until growth begins. Then provide more light and higher temperatures (around 60°F/16°C); follow the watering regimen described above and apply a liquid fertilizer every 2 weeks during the growing season. Divide bulbs when containers become crowded.

This elegant South African combines stateliness and delicacy. The fans of swordlike foliage and upright spikes of double-ranked blossoms reveal a close relationship to gladiolus, but there are clear differences as well. Watsonia's leaves are less rigid; its flower spikes are taller and slimmer, and the fragrant blossoms are smaller and more trumpetlike. Two species (and their hybrids) are commonly available. Botanists have recently changed these plants' names, but the old names persist in the nursery trade and in literature. In the descriptions below, the new names are given in parentheses.

Evergreen *W. beatricis* (*W. pillansii*) blooms in midsummer, sending up slightly branched, 3½-foot flower spikes from fans of 2½-foot leaves. The 3-inch-long blossoms are bright reddish apricot; you'll also find hybrids in colors ranging from peach to nearly red.

The late spring flowers of *W. pyramidata* (*W. borbonica*) are borne on 4- to 6-foot spikes that rise above 2½-foot-long leaves; flower color is cool pink, rosy red, or white. Hybrid forms have pink, red, or lavender blooms. Foliage dies back after flowering, then reappears with the onset of cooler weather in late summer to early autumn.

USES. These plants make handsome accent clumps in the background of mixed annual and perennial plantings, and even among shrubbery.

GARDEN CULTURE. Grow *W. beatricis* in Zones 4–9, 12–24, 26, 28–31, warmer parts of 32; grow *W. pyramidata* in Zones 4–9, 12–24, 26, 28–30.

Choose a sunny location—preferably with well-drained soil, though watsonia will perform in a great range of soils, from sandy to clay. Plant in early fall, setting corms 4 inches deep and 6 inches apart. Both species need regular water during their growth and bloom periods. Evergreen *W. beatricis* can take less moisture in summer after its flowers are finished. Deciduous *W. pyramidata* is dormant in summer; it accepts (but does not need) regular moisture at that time if the soil is well drained.

Where corms are hardy in the ground, you can leave them undisturbed for a number of years. Dig and divide only when plant and flower quality decline. In zones beyond its hardiness limits, you can grow *W. pyramidata* as you would gladiolus: plant corms in spring for late spring and early summer bloom, then dig after foliage dies down and store until planting time the following spring. Because *W. beatricis* is evergreen, it cannot be dug and stored; it grows only within its hardiness zones.

WATSONIA
Iridaceae
CORM

▲ 3½ TO 6 FEET

☼ FULL SUN

◐◑ SUMMER MOISTURE NEEDS VARY BY SPECIES (SEE "GARDEN CULTURE")

✀ ZONES VARY BY SPECIES (SEE "GARDEN CULTURE")

Watsonia beatricis

ZANTEDESCHIA

CALLA, CALLA LILY

Araceae

RHIZOME

▲ 1 TO 4 FEET

☼ ◑ EXPOSURE NEEDS VARY BY SPECIES (SEE "GARDEN CULTURE")

◖ SUMMER MOISTURE NEEDS VARY BY SPECIES (SEE "GARDEN CULTURE")

✎ ZONES 5, 6, 8, 9, 12–29

The simple, streamlined beauty of the white calla lily is familiar to many from formal bouquets. Admirers of Art Nouveau are also well acquainted with these blooms, since they were a popular motif in metal and glass pieces. The calla's "flower" is really a cornucopia-shaped bract (the spathe) surrounding a central yellow spike (the spadix); the tiny true flowers cluster around the base of the spadix. All species have glossy, arrow-shaped leaves on erect stalks, but foliage color varies—the common calla's leaves are solid green, but other species often have variegated or spotted foliage.

The largest, most familiar species is *Z. aethiopica,* the common calla. Foliage clumps reach 2 to 4 feet, with individual leaves to 10 inches wide, 1½ feet long. Beginning in spring (and sometimes continuing into summer), 8-inch spathes of pure or creamy white appear on stems just slightly taller than the foliage. 'Hercules' is larger than the species, with broad, recurving spathes that open nearly flat. 'Green Goddess', also a larger plant, has partially green spathes. Smaller varieties include 'Childsiana' (to just 1 foot) and 'Minor' (to 1½ feet, with 4-inch spathes).

Zantedeschia aethiopica

Summer-blooming *Z. elliottiana,* the golden calla, reaches 2 feet tall; its white-spotted bright green leaves reach 10 inches long and 6 inches wide. The 6-inch spathes are greenish yellow when they open, then change to a bright, rich golden yellow.

Z. albomaculata, the spotted calla, is about the same size as *Z. elliottiana* and has similar but slightly larger foliage. The spathes differ, though—they're creamy yellow or white, with a red-purple blotch at the base. The blooming season extends from spring into summer. A similar species, summer-blooming *Z. pentlandii,* features purple-throated deep yellow spathes rising above unspotted green leaves.

Shortest of the species—just 1½ to 2 feet tall—is *Z. rehmannii,* the pink (or red) calla. Its foot-long leaves, typically unspotted, are lance shaped rather than arrow shaped. The 4-inch pink to red spathes appear in midspring; 'Superba' is dark pink.

Hybrid callas flower in late spring and summer. They're usually about the size of *Z. rehmannii;* spathe colors include cream, buff, orange, pink, lavender, and purple.

USES. A clump of any calla is sure to be an accent, whether in mixed groupings of other flowering plants, amid foliage plants, or surrounded by a ground cover. For an even showier effect, plant callas in drifts among lower-growing plants.

GARDEN CULTURE. Common calla, *Z. aethiopica,* has different cultural needs from the other species. It tolerates a great range of soils but does best in an organically enriched, moisture-retentive type; it even thrives in the constantly moist soil at pond and stream margins. Where summers are hot, locate plants in light shade; in cool- or mild-summer areas, they'll grow in full sun or light shade. Plant rhizomes in autumn through early spring, setting them about 4 inches deep and 1 foot apart. Provide water all year. Clumps can remain in place for many years; dig and divide only when declining performance indicates overcrowding. Plants are evergreen to semievergreen and cannot be dug and stored over winter in cold climates. Grow them in the ground in the zones listed; in colder zones, container culture is the only option.

The other calla species and hybrids are deciduous: foliage dies down in fall, then reappears in spring. They need regular water during growth and bloom, less in the period between the end of bloom and foliage dieback. Within the listed hardiness zones,

Zantedeschia rehmannii

plant rhizomes in fall, setting them 2 inches deep and 8 to 12 inches apart, in soil that is organically enriched, well drained (good drainage is especially important during the winter rest period), and, ideally, slightly acid. Choose a sunny location, but if you live in a hot-summer region, try to select a spot receiving light shade during the heat of the day. As for common calla, dig and divide in fall when performance declines. In zones beyond their hardiness limits, plant these calla species in spring for summer bloom; when leaves die back in fall, dig and store over winter as for tuberous begonia (page 40), then replant the following spring.

CONTAINER CULTURE. All callas are good container plants. For the deciduous kinds, follow directions "B" (subgroup 2) on page 23; for common calla, follow directions "C."

ZEPHYRANTHES
FAIRY LILY, RAIN LILY, ZEPHYR FLOWER
Amaryllidaceae
TRUE BULB

▲ 1 FOOT
☼ ◑ FULL SUN OR PART SHADE
◗ NEEDS SUMMER MOISTURE
✂ ZONES VARY BY SPECIES
(SEE "GARDEN CULTURE")

Slender stems, each bearing just one blossom, rise from clumps of grassy leaves. Flowers are typically funnel shaped, resembling crocus blossoms; a few species have distinctly lilylike flowers. In their native lands—from the southern United States to Argentina—flowers often appear after rains, hence the common name "rain lily." You may be able to initiate several blooming cycles by following the procedure described in "Garden culture" (below).

The most widely available species, *Z. candida*, has foot-long, glossy leaves and 2-inch white blossoms that are sometimes stained pink in the throats; plants bloom in late summer and early fall. *Z. citrina* is similar in appearance and bloom season, but its blossoms are bright yellow.

True to its name, *Z. grandiflora* produces flowers twice as large as those of the previous two species; the rose pink petals form a lily-shaped flower in the morning, become flat by midday, then close in late afternoon. Blossoms come in late spring or early summer; foliage dies back in fall, then reappears at bloom time the next year.

With some searching, you may find named hybrids in a range of appealing colors— yellow-flushed deep rose pink 'Alamo', pink-shaded yellow 'Apricot Queen', pale yellow 'Aquarius', peach-and-yellow 'Ellen Korsakoff', pink-suffused light yellow 'Prairie Sunset', and rich cerise pink 'Ruth Page'.

From the southeastern United States comes *Z. atamasco*, appropriately known as wild Easter lily. Pink-striped white buds open to pure white, fragrant 3-inch blossoms with a distinct lilylike appearance. Unlike the other species and hybrids, this one blooms in midspring and has semievergreen leaves. Even earlier blooming (by as much as a month) is Florida native *Z. treatiae*. Its red buds open to crocuslike pure white, 4-inch flowers, carried above gray-green, nearly rushlike leaves.

USES. These trouble-free plants are attractive in the foreground of mixed perennial and annual plantings, along pathways, in rock gardens—even naturalized in grassy meadows. Grow them as container plants in zones beyond their hardiness.

GARDEN CULTURE. Grow *Z. candida* in Zones 4–9, 12–32; *Z. atamasco* in Zones 4–9, 12–31, warmer parts of 32; hybrids in Zones 6–9, 12–31; *Z. citrina* and *Z. grandiflora* in Zones 7–9, 12–29; *Z. treatiae* in Zones 12, 13, 25–29.

Choose a sunny or partly shaded site with well-drained soil; set bulbs 1 to 2 inches deep and 3 inches apart. Water regularly from the time growth begins until bloom finishes. Where the growing season is long and winter is mild, plants may bloom several times a year if you give them a short dry period after bloom, then resume watering to initiate another growth cycle. Otherwise, give little or no water after foliage dies back.

Within their hardiness zones, bulbs of the various species and hybrids can remain in the ground for many years with no need for digging and dividing.

CONTAINER CULTURE. Follow directions "C" on page 23.

Zephyranthes candida

SUNSET'S GARDEN CLIMATE ZONES

A plant's performance is governed by the total climate: length of growing season, timing and amount of rainfall, winter lows, summer highs, humidity. *Sunset*'s climate zone maps take all these factors into account—unlike the familiar hardiness zone maps devised by the U.S. Department of Agriculture, which divide the U.S. and Canada into zones based strictly on winter lows. The U.S.D.A. maps tell you only where a plant may survive the winter; our climate zone maps let you see where that plant will thrive year-round. Below are brief descriptions of the 45 zones illustrated on the map on pages 110–111. For more information, consult *Sunset*'s *National Garden Book* and *Western Garden Book*.

ZONE 1. Coldest Winters in the West and Western Prairie States

Growing season: early June through Aug., but with some variation—the longest seasons are usually found near this zone's large bodies of water. Frost can come any night of the year. Winters are snowy and intensely cold, due to latitude, elevation, and/or influence of continental air mass. There's some summer rainfall.

ZONE 2. Second-coldest Western Climate

Growing season: early May through Sept. Winters are cold (lows run from –3° to –34°F/–19° to –37°C), but less so than in Zone 1. In northern and interior areas, lower elevations fall into Zone 2, higher areas into Zone 1.

ZONE 3. West's Mildest High-elevation and Interior Regions

Growing season: early May to late Sept.—shorter than in Zone 2, but offset by milder winters (lows from 13° to –24°F/–11° to –31°C). This is fine territory for bulbs needing winter chill and dry, hot summers.

ZONE 4. Cold-winter Western Washington and British Columbia

Growing season: early May to early Oct. Summers are cool, thanks to ocean influence; chilly winters (19° to –7°F/–7° to –22°C) result from elevation, influence of continental air mass, or both. Overall temperatures, ample rain suit many bulbs.

ZONE 5. Ocean-influenced Northwest Coast and Puget Sound

Growing season: mid-April to Nov., typically with cool temperatures throughout. Less rain falls here than in Zone 4; winter lows range from 28° to 1°F/–2° to –17°C. This climate is ideal for woodland bulbs that don't need a dry summer baking.

ZONE 6. Oregon's Willamette Valley

Growing season: mid-Mar. to mid-Nov., with somewhat warmer temperatures than in Zone 5. Ocean influence keeps winter lows about the same as in Zone 5. All but tender and hot-summer bulbs relish this climate.

ZONE 7. Oregon's Rogue River Valley, California's High Foothills

Growing season: May to early Oct. Summers are hot and dry; typical winter lows run from 23° to 9°F/–5° to –13°C. The summer-winter contrast suits bulbs that need dry, hot summers and moist, only moderately cold winters.

ZONE 8. Cold-air Basins of California's Central Valley

Growing season: mid-Feb. through Nov. This is a valley floor with no maritime influence. Summers are hot; winter lows range from 29° to 13°F/–2° to –11°C. Rain comes in the cooler months, covering just the early part of the growing season.

ZONE 9. Thermal Belts of California's Central Valley

Growing season: late Feb. through Dec. Zone 9 is located in the higher elevations around Zone 8, but its summers are just as hot; its winter lows are slightly higher (temperatures range from 28° to 18°F/–2° to –8°C). Rainfall pattern is the same as in Zone 8.

ZONE 10. High Desert Areas of Arizona, New Mexico, West Texas, Oklahoma Panhandle, and Southwest Kansas

Growing season: April to early Nov. Chilly (even snow-dusted) weather rules from late Nov. through Feb., with lows from 31° to 24°F/–1° to –4°C. Rain comes in summer as well as in the cooler seasons.

ZONE 11. Medium to High Desert of California and Southern Nevada

Growing season: early April to late Oct. Summers are sizzling, with 110 days above 90°F/32°C. Balancing this is a 3½-month winter, with 85 nights below freezing and lows from 11° to 0°F/–12° to –18°C. Scant rainfall comes in winter.

ZONE 12. Arizona's Intermediate Desert

Growing season: mid-Mar. to late Nov., with scorching midsummer heat. Compared to Zone 13, this region has harder frosts; record low is 6°F/–14°C. Rains come in summer and winter.

ZONE 13. Low or Subtropical Desert

Growing season: mid-Feb. through Nov., interrupted by nearly 3 months of incandescent, growth-stopping summer heat. Most frosts are light (record lows run from 19° to 13°F/–7° to –11°C); scant rain comes in summer and winter. Summer-blooming bulbs need not apply!

ZONE 14. Inland Northern and Central California with Some Ocean Influence

Growing season: early Mar. to mid-Nov., with rain coming in the remaining months. Periodic intrusions of marine air temper summer heat and winter cold (lows run from 26° to 16°F/–3° to –9°C). Mediterranean-climate bulbs are at home here.

ZONE 15. Northern and Central California's Chilly-winter Coast-influenced Areas

Growing season: Mar. to Dec. Rain comes from fall through winter. Typical winter lows range from 28° to 21°F/–2° to –6°C. Maritime air influences the zone much of the time, giving it cooler, moister summers than Zone 14.

ZONE 16. Northern and Central California Coast Range Thermal Belts

Growing season: late Feb. to late Nov. With cold air draining to lower elevations, winter lows typically run from 32° to 19°F/0° to –7°C. Like Zone 15, this region is dominated by maritime air, but its winters are milder on average.

ZONE 17. Oceanside Northern and Central California and Southernmost Oregon

Growing season: late Feb. to early Dec. Coolness and fog are hallmarks; summer highs seldom top 75°F/24°C, while winter lows run from 36° to 23°F/2° to –5°C. Heat-loving bulbs disappoint or dwindle here.

ZONE 18. Hilltops and Valley Floors of Interior Southern California

Growing season: mid-Mar. through late Nov. Summers are hot and dry; rain comes in winter, when lows reach 28° to 10°F/–2° to –12°C. Mediterranean and Near Eastern bulbs thrive here.

ZONE 19. Thermal belts around Southern California's Interior Valleys

Growing season: early Mar. through Nov. As in Zone 18, rainy winters and hot, dry summers are the norm—but here, winter lows dip only to 27° to 22°F/–3° to –6°C, allowing tender evergreen bulbs to grow outdoors with protection.

ZONE 20. Hilltops and Valley Floors of Ocean-influenced Inland Southern California

Growing season: late Mar. to late Nov.—but fairly mild winters (lows of 28° to 23°F/–2° to –5°C) allow gardening. Through much of year, cool and moist maritime influence alternates with hot, dry interior air. Summers are warm to hot; winter is the rainy season.

ZONE 21. Thermal Belts around Southern California's Ocean-influenced Interior Valleys

Growing season: early Mar. to early Dec., with the same tradeoff of oceanic and interior influence as in Zone 20. During the winter rainy season, lows range from 36° to 23°F/2° to –5°C—warmer than in Zone 20, since the colder air drains to the valleys.

ZONE 22. Colder-winter Parts of Southern California's Coastal Region

Growing season: Mar. to early Dec. Winter lows seldom fall below 28°F/–2°C (records are around 21°F/–6°C), though colder air sinks to this zone from Zone 23. Summers are warm; rain comes in winter. Climate here is largely oceanic.

ZONE 23. Thermal Belts of Southern California's Coastal Region

Growing season: almost year-round (all but first half of Jan.). Rain comes in winter. Reliable ocean influence keeps summers mild (except when hot Santa Ana winds come from inland), frosts negligible; 23°F/–5°C is the record low. South African bulbs thrive.

ZONE 24. Marine-dominated Southern California Coast

Growing season: all year, but periodic freezes have dramatic effects (record lows are 33° to 20°F/1° to –7°C). Climate here is oceanic (but warmer than oceanic Zone 17), with cool summers, mild winters. Subtropical bulbs thrive.

ZONE 25. South Florida and the Keys

Growing season: all year. Add ample year-round rainfall (least in Dec. through Mar.), high humidity, and overall warmth, and you have a near-tropical climate. The Keys are frost-free; winter lows elsewhere run from 40° to 25°F/4° to –4°C.

ZONE 26. Central and Interior Florida

Growing season: early Feb. to late Dec., with typically humid, warm to hot weather. Rain is plentiful all year, heaviest in summer and early fall. Lows range from 15°F/–9°C in the north to 27°F/–3°C in the south; arctic air brings periodic hard freezes.

ZONE 27. Lower Rio Grande Valley

Growing season: early Mar. to mid-Dec.. Summers are hot and humid; winter lows only rarely dip below freezing. Tropical and subtropical African and South American bulbs are well adapted here.

ZONE 28. Gulf Coast, North Florida, Atlantic Coast to Charleston

Growing season: mid-Mar. to early Dec. Humidity and rainfall are year-round phenomena; summers are hot, winters virtually frostless but subject to periodic invasions by frigid arctic air. Bulbs suggested for Zone 27 (above) are best.

ZONE 29. Interior Plains of South Texas

Growing season: mid-Mar. through Nov. Moderate rainfall (to 25" annually) comes year-round. Summers are hot. Winter lows can dip to 26°F/–3°C, with occasional arctic freezes bringing much lower readings.

ZONE 30. Hill Country of Central Texas

Growing season: mid-Mar. through Nov. Zone 30 has higher annual rainfall than Zone 29 (to 35") and lower winter temperatures, normally to around 20°F/–7°C. Best bulbs for this zone are those that need or endure summer rain, winter chill.

ZONE 31. Interior Plains of Gulf Coast and Coastal Southeast

Growing season: mid-Mar. to early Nov. In this extensive east-west zone, hot and sticky summers contrast with chilly winters (record low temperatures are 7° to 0°F/–14° to –18°C). There's rain all year (an annual average of 50"), with the least falling in Oct.

ZONE 32. Interior Plains of Mid-Atlantic States; Chesapeake Bay, Southeastern Pennsylvania, Southern New Jersey

Growing season: late Mar. to early Nov. Rain falls year-round (40" to 50" annually); winter lows (moving through the zone from south to north) are 30° to 20°F/–1° to –7°C. Humidity is less oppressive here than in Zone 31.

ZONE 33. North-Central Texas and Oklahoma Eastward to the Appalachian Foothills

Growing season: mid-April through Oct. Warm Gulf Coast air and colder continental/arctic fronts both play a role; their unpredictable interplay results in a wide range in annual rainfall (22" to 52") and winter lows (20° to 0°F/–7° to –18°C). Summers are muggy and warm to hot.

ZONE 34. Lowlands and Coast from Gettysburg to North of Boston

Growing season: late April to late Oct. Ample rainfall and humid summers are the norm. Winters are variable—typically fairly mild (around 20°F/–7°C), but with lows down to –3° to –22°F/–19° to –30°C if arctic air swoops in.

ZONE 35. Ouachita Mountains, Northern Oklahoma and Arkansas, Southern Kansas to North-Central Kentucky and Southern Ohio

Growing season: late April to late Oct. Rain comes in all seasons. Summers can be truly hot and humid. Without arctic fronts, winter lows are around 18°F/–8°C; with them, the coldest weather may bring lows of –20°F/–29°C.

ZONE 36. Appalachian Mountains

Growing season: May to late Oct. Thanks to greater elevation, summers are cooler and less humid, winters colder (0° to –20°F/–18° to –29°C) than in adjacent, lower zones. Rain comes all year (heaviest in spring). Late frosts are common.

ZONE 37. Hudson Valley and Appalachian Plateau

Growing season: May to mid-Oct., with rainfall throughout. Lower in elevation than neighboring Zone 42, with warmer winters: lows are 0° to –5°F/–18° to –21°C, unless arctic air moves in. Summer is warm to hot, humid.

ZONE 38. New England Interior and Lowland Maine

Growing season: May to early Oct. Summers feature reliable rainfall and lack oppressive humidity of lower-elevation, more southerly areas. Winter lows dip to –10° to –20°F/–23° to –29°C , with periodic colder temperatures due to influxes of arctic air.

ZONE 39. Shoreline Regions of the Great Lakes

Growing season: early May to early Oct. Springs and summers are cooler here, autumns milder than in areas farther from the lakes. Southeast lakeshores get the heaviest snowfalls. Lows reach 0° to –10°F/–18° to –23°C.

ZONE 40. Inland Plains of Lake Erie and Lake Ontario

Growing season: mid-May to mid-Sept., with rainy, warm, variably humid weather. The lakes help moderate winter lows; temperatures typically range from –10° to –20°F/–23° to –29°C, with occasional colder readings when arctic fronts rush through. North Eurasian bulbs thrive.

ZONE 41. Northeast Kansas and Southeast Nebraska to Northern Illinois and Indiana, Southeast Wisconsin, Michigan, Northern Ohio

Growing season: early May to early Oct. Winter brings average lows of –11° to –20°F/–23° to –29°C. Summers in this zone are hotter and longer west of the Mississippi, cooler and shorter nearer the Great Lakes; summer rainfall increases in the same west-to-east direction.

ZONE 42. Interior Pennsylvania and New York; St. Lawrence Valley

Growing season: late May to late Sept. This zone's elevation gives it colder winters than surrounding zones: lows range from –20° to –40°F/–29° to –40°C, with the colder readings coming in the Canadian portion of the zone. Summers are humid, rainy.

ZONE 43. Upper Mississippi Valley, Upper Michigan, Southern Ontario and Quebec

Growing season: late May to mid-Sept. The climate is humid from spring through early fall; summer rains are usually dependable. Arctic air dominates in winter, with lows typically from –20° to –30°F/–29° to –34°C.

ZONE 44. Mountains of New England and Southeastern Quebec

Growing season: June to mid-Sept. Latitude and elevation give fairly cool, rainy summers, cold winters with lows of –20° to –40°F/–29° to –40°C. Spring-blooming bulbs are best, summer bloomers more of a gamble.

ZONE 45. Northern Parts of Minnesota and Wisconsin, Eastern Manitoba through Interior Quebec

Growing season: mid-June through Aug., with rain throughout; rainfall (and humidity) are least in zone's western part, greatest in eastern reaches. Winters are frigid (–30° to –40°F/–34° to –40°C), with snow cover, deeply frozen soil.

Sunset's Garden Climate Zones

| Climate Zones | / | 1 | 2 | 3 | 4 | 5 | 6 | 7 | 8 | 9 | 10 | 11 | 12 | 13 | 14 | 15 | 16 | 17 | 18 | 19 | 20 | 21 | 2 |

| 24 | 25 | 26 | 27 | 28 | 29 | 30 | 31 | 32 | 33 | 34 | 35 | 36 | 37 | 38 | 39 | 40 | 41 | 42 | 43 | 44 | 45 | Climate Zones |

INDEX